A PRACTICAL GUIDE TO UNLOCK YOUR CHILD'S UNIQUE
POTENTIAL IN THE FIRST FIVE YEARS AND SHAPE THEIR FUTURE

EARLY CHILDHOOD

WHERE THE MAGIC HAPPENS

MARGARET LARDEN

Cover Art by Lorraine Lewitzka
Foreword by Dr Darryl Cross

FIGTREE WRITINGS | ADELAIDE

EARLY CHILDHOOD
Where the Magic Happens

First Edition

Published by Figtree Writings

Figtree Writings is a registered business trading name of DML Enterprises Pty Ltd
8 Strathspey Avenue, Hazelwood Park, South Australia, 5066 AUSTRALIA

Copyright © 2025 by Margaret Larden
Email: marglarden@gmail.com
Website: marglarden.com

All Rights reserved. Reproduction and distribution in any way shape or form is forbidden. No part of this book shall be reproduced, stored in a retrieval system, or transmitted by any other means, electronic, mechanical, photocopying, recording or otherwise, without prior written permission from the author.

Passages from 'The 7 Habits of Highly Effective People' by Stephen Covey (2013) used with permission from Franklin Covey Co.

Design by Creative Mass

Cover art by Lorraine Lewitzka

Author photo by Total Capture Photography

A catalogue record for this book is available from the National Library of Australia

ISBN: 978-1-7638186-5-1 (Hardcover-Limited Edition)
ISBN: 978-1-7638186-0-6 (Hardcover-C)
ISBN: 978-1-7638186-1-3 (Paperback-C)
ISBN: 978-1-7638186-3-7 (Hardcover-B&W)
ISBN: 978-1-7638186-4-4 (Paperback-B&W)
ISBN: 978-1-7638186-2-0 (E-Book)

This publication is designed to provide accurate information regarding the subject matter at the time of publication. The author denies any liability for incidental or consequential damages resulting from the use of information in this book. This book is designed to assist with generating and exploring various child-rearing options. It does not make decisions for the individual but provides a range of options to be considered. No responsibility is accepted for any liabilities resulting from the actions of any parties involved.

The links identified in this book will be maintained and accessible via the References and Resources page on the author's website marglarden.com. If you have any issues or questions, please do not hesitate to contact the author at marglarden@gmail.com.

For my family

CONTENTS

10 FOREWORD
14 PREFACE
19 ACKNOWLEDGEMENTS

CHAPTER 1:

21 **PREPARATION IS THE KEY**
21 LEARNING FROM THE EXPERTS IS A GOOD PLACE TO START
22 HOW TO NURTURE AND GROW YOUR BABY'S INTELLIGENCE
    22 Newborn Course—Online
    23 How to Multiply Your Child's Intelligence Course—Online
    23 Introduction to Montessori Education—Online
24 FIRST AID FOR BABIES
25 NUTRITION
26 CHILDPROOFING YOUR HOME

CHAPTER 2:

29 BE THE PERSON YOU WANT YOUR CHILD TO BECOME

- 30 USING VALUES TO INFORM BEHAVIOR AND BUILD CHARACTER
- 31 TEACHING VALUES IN THE EARLY YEARS
- 32 HOW TO INSTILL VALUES
  - 32 Responsibility
  - 34 Respect
  - 37 Kindness
  - 39 Caring
  - 41 Empathy
  - 43 Gratitude
  - 45 Mindfulness
  - 48 Tolerance
  - 50 Patience
  - 54 Self-control
- 59 TEACHING VALUES IN THE PRESCHOOL YEARS

CHAPTER 3:

65 A CHILD IS BORN

- 66 ESTABLISHING THE IMPORTANCE OF:
  - 66 Bonding
  - 66 Touch—physical contact
  - 67 Crawling
- 67 CRITICAL DEVELOPMENTAL YEARS
- 68 THE FIVE SENSES
  - 69 Taste
  - 69 Sight
  - 69 Touch
  - 69 Smell
  - 69 Hearing

70 WHY READING ALOUD TO YOUR CHILD FROM BIRTH MATTERS
71 ARE BOYS' AND GIRLS' BRAINS DIFFERENT?
75 WHAT A DAY SPENT WITH YOUR BABY MIGHT LOOK LIKE
    81 Routine is reassuring

CHAPTER 4:

85 CHILD DEVELOPMENT 'PLEASE EXPLAIN'

85 THREE KEY AREAS OF CHILD DEVELOPMENT
86 HOW DOES LEARNING HAPPEN?
    88 Curiosity-driven free play
    90 Incremental building blocks
    91 Repetition
    92 'Potty/toilet' training—A practical approach
96 PRACTICAL ACTIVITIES FOR HOME-BASED LEARNING
97 YOUR BABY
    97 The first three months
    99 3 to 5 months of age
    102 5 to 7 months of age
    104 7 to 9 months of age
    105 9 to 12 months of age
    107 12 months of age
110 YOUR TODDLER
    110 Milestones for toddlers (1 to 3 years of age)
    112 Activities for your toddler
128 TIPS FOR PARENTS OF TODDLERS
    130 Positive discipline for toddlers
    132 Sharing
    133 How to respond to toddler accidents and mishaps

137   YOUR PRESCHOOLER
- 137   Milestones for preschoolers (3 to 5 years of age)
- 139   Activities for your preschooler

185   TIPS FOR PARENTS OF PRESCHOOLERS
- 185   Reinforcing values and building character
- 186   Following rules and teaching self-discipline
- 188   Promoting and encouraging sharing
- 191   Assessing the impact of screen time

CHAPTER 5:

193   PREPARING YOUR CHILD FOR SCHOOL A SIMPLE, PRACTICAL APPROACH

194   KNOWING WHAT TO EXPECT

194   START WITH THE BASICS
- 194   Personal information
- 197   Basic mathematics
- 199   Fine motor skills
- 201   School familiarization

202   MORE THAN BARE BASICS
- 202   General knowledge
- 203   Introduction to reading
- 204   Attend an interest group
- 205   Creative techniques to enhance learning
- 207   Outings—keeping track of your child

CHAPTER 6:

209 YOUR CHILD HAS STARTED SCHOOL—WHAT NOW?

209 PARENTAL INVOLVEMENT AT SCHOOL

210 DO OUR CHILDREN LEARN IN THE SAME WAY?

212 THE SEVEN INTELLIGENCES AND THEIR CAPABILITIES

- 212   1. Verbal-Linguistic Intelligence
- 214   2. Logical-Mathematical Intelligence
- 215   3. Bodily-Kinesthetic Intelligence
- 217   4. Visual-Spatial Intelligence
- 218   5. Musical-Rhythmic Intelligence
- 219   6. Interpersonal Intelligence
- 220   7. Intrapersonal Intelligence

223 LEARNING SHOULD BE A POSITIVE EXPERIENCE

223 DEVELOPING A GROWTH MINDSET AND THE KEY ROLE OF PRAISE

- 225   Practical strategies for fostering a growth mindset
- 230   How to praise your child's learning endeavors

235 ENCOURAGE YOUR CHILD'S INTERESTS AND STRENGTHS

236 WHAT IF NONE OF THIS WORKS?

237 THE BENEFITS OF CHESS

239 THE BENEFITS OF BOREDOM

- 240   My childhood days—A reflection
- 241   A parent's admission

CHAPTER 7:

- 243 **THE EXERCISE CONNECTION**
  - 244 GENERAL EXERCISE
    - 244 Physical benefits of exercise
    - 244 Intellectual and emotional benefits
    - 245 How can you promote exercise?
    - 245 When to commence exercise
    - 245 Baby—Birth to 1 year
    - 245 Toddler—1 to 3 years
    - 246 Preschooler—3 to 5 years
  - 246 THE BALANCING ACT
    - 246 Vestibular Processing System
    - 247 What are vestibular activities?
    - 248 Vestibular activities for babies or toddlers
    - 249 Vestibular activities for preschoolers
    - 250 Vestibular activities for school-aged children
  - 251 SWIMMING
    - 252 When should your baby learn to swim
    - 252 Swimming benefits for babies
    - 253 Swimming benefits for toddlers and preschoolers
  - 253 WALKING
    - 254 The benefits of walking for children
    - 255 Tips and ideas to encourage walking
  - 257 POINTS TO REMEMBER

- 259 **KEY TAKEAWAYS**
- 260 **APPENDIX 1—REFERENCES**
- 270 **APPENDIX 2—RESOURCES**
- 282 **INDEX**

FOREWORD

Very early on in my career as a psychologist, I came across a saying that has stayed with me. It goes something like this *"Give me a child until they are seven and I'll show you the person."* Clinical practice, training, and experience has shown this to be true. So very true.

That's why this book is so critical and so important. It is about laying the foundations for an effective and thriving life. Get the foundations wrong or out of alignment and the whole structure is compromised beyond. So, it is with building children into secure and contributing adults.

This book is about re-establishing basic principles. Principles that work. Principles that have stood the test of time. We really can't afford to move away from them. To do so means that we live life at our own peril. They are there to help us live life and to make the best of life for us and for our children.

Times might have changed, but there are some things that never change; they are principles. There is a call in the community now that because times are different, we need to change the way that we raise our children. Yes, part of that is true. We now have smart phones and technology that we didn't have a generation ago such that these devices intrude into our lives and distract us in ways that previously did not happen. Yes, they might be helpful, but they are also disruptive and don't really allow us to have any down time. We are constantly "on" and we often communicate more with our phones than our children.

We also now typically have two parents working and juggling their own lives and careers and trying to make ends meet with the cost of living and owning or renting a home. Previously, we usually had one parent (often the mother) staying at home to raise and nurture the children. Consequently, we now have more "stress" at home than previously. Just look at what happens when a child gets sick and can't go to the early childhood center or to school. The family system, which is running tight and intense anyhow, breaks down because everything is so finely tuned that there is no slack or give in the system so that family and individual stress mounts even more.

If you are a single parent, then life is more intense as you negotiate parenthood without a second pair of hands. There is often no back-up unless you're fortunate enough to have grandparents living nearby. The stresses, tiredness, exhaustion and fatigue are exacerbated when you're trying to do it all on your own. Not only are there constant chores to do to keep

the home running, and probably a job that means you have to show up and keep on top of (more or less), but somehow, you're also supposed to give your child (or children) time and attention. It's a big ask.

A generation ago, we were also told as parents that *"thou shalt not smack"*, but no-one told us what we could do instead as we raised our children. In a sense, we threw out the baby with the bathwater as the saying goes, and we left parents stranded. How do parents discipline now? Is reasoning with a child (like you would with an adult) going to work? I don't think so (but we still do it!).

Previously, children were allowed to go off and play by themselves and meet up with other children in the street, ride their bikes around the community, make their own fun, go to the local oval or park to play chasey or cricket or football, and sort out their own scuffles as long as they were home in time for dinner. Now we have something called "helicopter parenting" or "paranoid parenting" as Greg Lukianoff and Professor Jonathan Haidt call it in their recently published 2019 book titled, "The Coddling of the American Mind." This "coddling" might be well-intentioned, but it impacts our children negatively and does little to build resilience, confidence and courage which are invaluable character assets in a changing world.

There is little doubt that life has changed, but this book is a timely reminder that some things never change. There are basic principles which are like Stop signs or traffic lights; ignore them and you stand to not only injure or kill yourself, but others as well. They are there for a reason. This book outlines such principles in raising healthy, happy children.

Parenting is hard work. Darn hard work. Just ask any parent. However, the baby arrives with no manuals or sections on "Troubleshooting." To make things even more challenging, some hospitals discharge mothers and their newborns within just 24 hours, leaving little time for guidance on caring for a new life. While midwife nurses may visit, they're not always there when you need them most, especially in the middle of the night.

So, where do we learn to be parents and how do we prepare? Our main training ground is from the modelling we received from our own parents. Who says though that that was a demonstration of effective parenting? Who says that that was a model worth following? It gets complicated too when two parents come from different parenting models, backgrounds, or cultures and then they come together to try to formulate their own parenting style. That's certainly fertile ground for some intense conversations or arguments. It's a wonder any of us make it through! Another reason why this book is so invaluable is that it outlines key factors that help us to work out what works and what doesn't.

That's one thing about being a parent; you don't get a second crack at it, and you certainly don't want to be filled with a ton of regrets about what you "should" have done or "shouldn't" have done.

Over the last 20 years or more, there has been a cascade of work in relation to neuropsychology and research on the brain. Neuro is for "neuron", the nerve cells in our brains and nervous systems. What we know now, and we will continue to discover is literally mind-blowing. Therapist and author, Robert Cox, states that a baby is born with around 100 billion neurons and that there are trillions of connections between neurons by the time the baby is 2 years of age. Think about that for a moment.

While your child is clearly changing and growing in observable ways, the inner computer called the brain is doing all sorts of neural networking. It is the right hemisphere of the baby's brain that is active from birth, and this is where the baby is aware of body language, voice tone and volume, gestures, and touch. I vividly remember a psychiatrist giving a keynote address at a conference I attended, and he said that if we simply taught mothers to smile into their baby's face multiple times daily that we would significantly reduce mental health issues in our country.

There is a saying that *"neurons that fire together wire together."* Psychiatrist and researcher, Dr. Norman Doidge in his book "The Brain that Changes Itself" highlights the notion that it is in these early days of a child's life that these basic lessons of safety, comfort and security are laid down by the connection with the mother, father, and caregivers. This is when the neural pathways are being laid down; when habits are starting to form, when personality is starting to take shape.

Moreover, in these early years, this is where the good habits of life are laid down. Remember the foundation analogy mentioned above. Well, no matter which way you look at it, these formative years are crucial to setting up your child for success in life where they experience sound mental health, show resilience, become independent and have healthy self-esteem. Every parent wants their child to be happy.

This practical and down-to-earth book by Margaret Larden with its far-reaching insight, wisdom, research, and wealth of experience is a literal gold mine for any parent or caregiver trying to traverse the somewhat treacherous waters of parenthood. Overlook this book at your own peril because its pages contain the gold nuggets of how to achieve effective parenting for your children.

Dr. Darryl Cross (PhD)
Clinical and Organizational Psychologist

PREFACE

Parents today live their lives at a fast pace. Family, careers, and societal expectations compete for their attention, influencing their priorities and choices. Despite this, parents still strive to do what is best for their children. However, understanding what that is and how to achieve it is difficult, especially during the early years.

Children can be challenging and unpredictable. They can make you laugh and cry. Why are young children like this? The answer is simple. They are striving to understand the world around them and their place within it, a process that can often feel overwhelming.

Historically, society assumed that a child's overall development began when they started formal schooling. However, research shows that babies are born ready to learn. Their brain develops faster in the first five years than at any other time. During these early years, it is more adaptable, making it easier to embrace learning challenges.

Generally, preparation for a newborn's arrival focuses on their physical and practical needs. While this is essential, parents and caregivers must also know how to support their baby's social-emotional and intellectual development. Positive experiences provided by loving and engaged parents profoundly impact a child's early development. These experiences lay a strong foundation for future learning, well-being, and behavior. In this book, I encourage parents to create an enriched learning environment at home that supports and enhances their child's overall development.

A key feature of teaching and learning is the 'serve and return' dynamic between children and their parents or caregivers. When parents respond appropriately and consistently to their child's interactions, it fosters the child's confidence and trust. This relationship enhances their ability to learn effectively.

Under the inspired teaching of Joan Fry OBE, I discovered the importance of early learning and its lasting impact on a child's developmental journey. I became passionate about helping each child reach their unique potential. I aimed to provide them with opportunities for a fulfilling life grounded in sound values and reflective of their strengths and interests.

As an educator and mother, it was logical for me to teach my children at home during their early years. This decision was one of my life's most satisfying and rewarding experiences. Today's economic and social pressures often require parents to work outside the home.

As a result, they must find alternative full-time or part-time care and early education options for their children.

This reality has disrupted the traditional parenting role, and it is essential to acknowledge and address this shift. Grandparents, extended family, independent carers, and childcare organizations now share the responsibility of providing care and early childhood education. In this context, parents may feel disconnected from their child's developmental journey.

However, these practical arrangements do not diminish the significant role and impact that parents can play in their child's early development. Parents can monitor their child's progress by collaborating closely with caregivers or childcare providers. This collaboration helps parents reinforce new learning, address learning gaps, and improve their child's developmental outcomes.

Writing this book and documenting my teaching approach and experience was daunting. However, I was determined as I firmly believe in the central role parents can play in their child's care and early education. To support my work, I drew on various sources, including my studies, teaching experiences, personal observations, training courses, and emerging trends in early childhood education. Rather than being prescriptive, I aim to equip parents with fundamental knowledge to adapt their teaching to their child's developmental needs.

This book aims to inspire busy parents to teach their children with intent rather than by accident. It offers guidance on 'teaching in the moment' and maximizing learning opportunities. The practical tips are designed to nurture your child's curiosity and incrementally build their knowledge and skills. The approach is evidence-based and informed by methodologies used by renowned early childhood educators. This style of teaching will strengthen your relationship with your child and improve their learning outcomes and development.

Once parents understand how learning happens, they can confidently apply this approach to enrich their child's learning experiences. I highlight fundamental teaching considerations, such as using 'mechanistic' language and focusing on detail, to enhance their learning. I also describe two 'creative' techniques that I used with my children to improve their ability to learn. The content of this book is organized sequentially, allowing parents to easily access information and activities suited to their child's developmental stage.

Initially, I provide parents with an understanding of what is necessary for their child's development in the early years. I offer practical suggestions on how to achieve this development. Preparation is crucial for any new endeavor. Learning from experts through short online courses is an excellent place for parents to start. I have provided Web links for these courses. The information provided will help parents confidently nurture their baby in a safe, healthy, and developmentally appropriate home environment.

I also emphasize the vital role that parents can play in instilling sound values during their children's early years. These values shape the adults they will become, influencing how they interact, treat others, and care for the environment.

The teaching practices outlined in this book are based on well-established child development principles. These practices are discussed in terms of intellectual, social-emotional, and physical growth and the related behavioral expectations. This foundational knowledge will help parents understand how their child will develop and learn from birth. It will also provide insight into expected developmental behaviors, which will inform your teaching. I also discuss the benefits of observing your child at play. These observations will enable parents to fine-tune their child's learning experiences to meet their unique needs.

This book provides over two hundred inexpensive, easy-to-implement activities. These activities are inclusive and aligned with the critical areas of child development. They demonstrate how to use daily experiences as teaching opportunities. I have also compiled a comprehensive list of over three hundred and fifty web-based teaching resources to further assist parents. Links to the references and resources are regularly maintained and available on my website marglarden.com.

I explore potential challenges your child may face when they begin formal schooling. Parents are provided with practical advice to help their children navigate these challenges effectively. These suggestions focus on early preparation, familiarizing children with essential information and skills, and encouraging parental involvement in classroom activities. This preparation will ensure a positive and confident start to formal education. I also emphasize your child's individuality. I stress the importance of understanding that they learn best using their unique style and abilities.

Finally, I address the physical, intellectual, social-emotional, and behavioral benefits of daily exercise. These include building strong bodies, improving mood, encouraging socialization, and enhancing memory and learning. I provide easy-to-implement exercise activities that align with developmental milestones. Growing a child's confidence with positive learning experiences will empower them to develop a more determined and 'fearless' mindset, which is essential for growth and effective learning.

> *Behind every young child who believes in himself is a parent who believed first.*
>
> Matthew L Jacobson

The purpose of this book is to inspire and equip parents and caregivers with the knowledge and practical guidelines necessary for their child's early learning journey. I highlight that children learn from birth, each child learns differently, and that loving parents play a fundamental role in giving their children a strong start. Embracing these principles is essential for your child to reach their full potential.

Remember, a parent's love and time are the two greatest gifts they can give their child. I encourage you to have fun and cherish this journey with your child. It will be over before you know it.

ACKNOWLEDGEMENTS

This book would not have been possible without the invaluable contributions of several individuals who generously shared their expertise and support throughout its development.

My deepest appreciation extends to my family, whose multifaceted support—ranging from technical assistance and website development to thoughtful manuscript reviews—has been a cornerstone of this journey.

To my husband Doug, for his unwavering support, thought-provoking questions, and editorial guidance, I offer my heartfelt thanks.

My sincere thanks are also extended to Lorraine Lewitzka for her exceptional cover art which beautifully encapsulates the core themes of the book.

I am extremely grateful to Gosia Lysakowski and Susan McArthur, who reviewed the initial manuscript, and Gaynor Johnson, whose precise proofreading ensured the highest standards of clarity.

I would especially like to thank Professor Howard Gardner of Harvard University, for casting his eye over my expression and application of his pioneering and transformative work on Multiple Intelligences.

Lastly, Dr. Darryl Cross's eloquent and insightful foreword provides a compelling context that elevates the entire work. I feel privileged to have his support.

Each contributor has been essential in bringing this work to fruition, and I am profoundly thankful for their collective support.

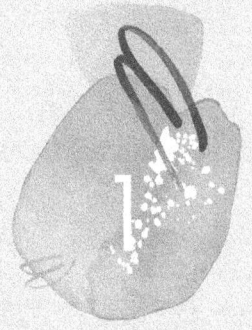

PREPARATION IS THE KEY

LEARNING FROM THE EXPERTS IS A GOOD PLACE TO START

> 'Success is where preparation and opportunity meet.'
> Bobby Unser

Every role we undertake in life requires training, and parenting is no exception. At some point, you will need to use the skills of a nurse, chef, nutritionist, teacher, and counselor to care for your child. Out of necessity and love, you must acquire knowledge and skills to prepare for what many consider the most important undertaking of your life: being a parent. I highly recommend seeking up-to-date, expert information from reputable sources. For example, https://delvy.ai is a cutting-edge, AI-powered assistant that will answer your research questions with evidence-based insights. Your endeavors will equip you to effectively address your child's educational, nutritional, and general well-being needs.

HOW TO NURTURE AND GROW YOUR BABY'S INTELLIGENCE

> *'The impact of parents may never be greater than during the earliest years of life, when a child's brain is rapidly developing and when nearly all of her or his experiences are created and shaped by parents and the family environment.'*
>
> US National Academies of Sciences, Engineering & Medicine 2016

For most parents, the initial nurturing of their baby will come naturally. However, not all parents have the specific knowledge and training to support their child's unique developmental journey. Raising your baby to become a well-balanced individual will likely require some guidance from experts in child development.

Despite studying early childhood education, I soon realized there was more to learn to support my parenting journey. To fill the gaps, I took advantage of the support and advice available to new mothers from the healthcare nurse and pediatrician. I read all I could find about raising children to extend my knowledge. In the process, I discovered a course offered in Australia by The Institutes for the Achievement of Human Potential (IAHP). IAHP is an organization founded in the United States by Dr. Glenn Doman. This course was the first of many which informed my decisions during my children's early developmental years.

Your child's future will depend, in part, on your desire to meet their needs and see them thrive. You may consider undertaking relevant courses to assist you. The following courses and resources developed by qualified experts will build your knowledge and confidence. They provide insight and establish a sound foundation for your role as a parent.

NEWBORN COURSE—ONLINE

The Institutes for the Achievement of Human Potential (2021a) have recently developed an online course for parents of newborn babies. This eight-hour course is delivered over two days. It is designed for expectant parents and parents with newborns or babies up to the age of 12 months. There are live sessions during which parents will have ample opportunity to ask questions.

As a new parent, you will undoubtedly feel a little overwhelmed. You have produced a little human, but what do you do now? The Newborn Course provides a detailed outline of the first twelve months of life, carefully guiding parents through each developmental stage. You will learn how to communicate with your baby and build a strong bond from the outset. The course also offers information on stimulating sensory pathways. It highlights opportunities to develop your baby's mobility, language, and manual skills.

As parents, you will learn how to create a home environment that promotes your baby's intellectual, physical, and social-emotional development. For further clarification or information, contact the IAHP registrar at htm_registrar@iahp.org.

HOW TO MULTIPLY YOUR CHILD'S INTELLIGENCE COURSE—ONLINE

The Institutes for the Achievement of Human Potential (2021b) have developed this course to teach you how to enhance your child's intelligence. This comprehensive course is a natural follow-on from the Newborn Course. It is delivered online over five days. It gives parents guidance on creating an enriched home environment for their children. Through this course, parents will learn how to teach 'clear facts' in a happy and stress-free manner.

The course content focuses on reading, encyclopedic knowledge, mathematics, physical mobility, nutrition, music, and foreign languages. Parents will learn how to increase their children's intellectual, physical, and social-emotional abilities before they begin formal schooling. For example, I learned how to teach my children to read using the Glenn Doman method. It was easy once I knew how. I also learned from the course that my child's reading ability would enhance their intellectual development.

Your children want to learn. This course gives you the knowledge and an effective method to teach them using various aids. In referring to this course, Glenn Doman said, *'Our children's brains grow as much as we give them the opportunity to grow. We give them the opportunity by presenting them with a huge number of clear facts. We do this when the brain is growing faster than it will ever grow again'* (The Institutes for the Achievement of Human Potential 2019).

The Gentle Revolution is the Institutes' official supplier of books and teaching materials. You can contact the IAHP registrar at htm_registrar@iahp.org for further information.

INTRODUCTION TO MONTESSORI EDUCATION—ONLINE

Maria Montessori was an Italian educator, physician, and innovator acclaimed for her educational methods. Born in Italy in 1870, she opened the first Montessori school in Rome in 1907. She wrote extensively about her approach to education and subsequently traveled the world, attracting many supporters. There are currently thousands of Montessori schools worldwide (American Montessori Society 2020).

The Montessori Method is student-led. It encourages children to explore their natural curiosities and learn in a way that suits their individual needs. This method gives children the time, space, and freedom to question and explore their environment. It is conducted in a self-paced, uninterrupted, and thorough manner. Widely practiced for over 100 years, the Montessori Method uses hands-on learning materials organized in a simple, calm, and nurturing environment. Initially, parents can guide the learning experiences in the home setting.

This method fosters a child's natural desire for knowledge, understanding, and respect for their environment and the community. It promotes rigorous, self-motivated growth for children in all areas of their development, that is, intellectual, physical, and social-emotional. As a result, students become confident, enthusiastic, and self-directed learners.

Several online Montessori training courses are available to provide parents with information on the Montessori Method. The Introduction to Montessori Education is a comprehensive foundational course. It offers practical guidance specifically designed for parents with children under the age of six years. This course consists of four modules that provide essential knowledge to facilitate learning experiences at home. The modules cover Montessori principles and theories, how to prepare the home environment, the role of the parent, and the associated teaching materials.

The Montessori Method is explained in the book How To Raise An Amazing Child The Montessori Way by Seldin (2017).

FIRST AID FOR BABIES

As a parent and primary caregiver, it is essential to know basic first aid explicitly tailored to the needs of babies and small children. Parents must have the appropriate knowledge and skills to respond quickly in an emergency. Established and accredited health organizations have developed courses for this purpose. These organizations have served us well for many years. The content of their courses is constantly evolving to address the ever-changing needs of our communities.

An example of a first aid training program tailored for infants and children in Australia is the First Aid for Babies and Children course, developed by the Australian Red Cross. This four-hour course will equip parents and caregivers with essential knowledge and skills for administering emergency first aid. It covers basic life support and a range of other emergencies (for example, infant CPR, breathing emergencies such as choking and asthma, allergic reactions, and common child-related injuries and illnesses). An online option, First Aid for Babies and Children Webinar, is offered via Zoom.

The Red Cross also offers the Adult Child and Baby First Aid Course—Red Cross (USA) in the United States and the Paediatric First Aid Course in the United Kingdom. St John Ambulance offers similar courses in Australia, for example, Caring for Babies and Kids and also in the United Kingdom, such as Paediatric First Aid. When selecting a first aid course, seek guidance from your baby's healthcare professional to ensure you choose the option that best meets your needs.

NUTRITION

We all want our children to thrive physically, mentally, and emotionally and feel good about themselves. A familiar mantra is, 'We are what we eat.' This statement is particularly true for children during their first five years when they are growing at an incredible rate. As parents, you are responsible for ensuring your child develops healthy eating habits and food preferences. These habits are essential for achieving positive health outcomes.

Parents will need to seek advice and information on the nutritional requirements of their developing child. Initially, you will feed your little one with breast milk or formula. During regular baby healthcare checkups, parents will be offered guidance on when to introduce appropriate solid foods. When your child starts eating solids, introduce and encourage healthy eating habits by providing nutritionally balanced food options. These positive habits will nourish your child's physical well-being and contribute to their intellectual development and emotional growth.

Your baby's brain is always working, even when they are sleeping. Their brain controls their thoughts, movements, breathing, heartbeat, and senses. For the brain to function well, it requires nutritious food to fuel it. For example, Selhub (2022) reports that the nutritious Mediterranean and Japanese diets have positive benefits for mental well-being. These diets endorse fresh vegetables, fruits, unprocessed grains, fish, and fermented foods. On the other hand, studies show that Western diets high in refined sugars can negatively impact cognitive functions, emotions, and physical health.

The following websites provide helpful information and suggestions on healthy eating for your developing child.

The Pregnancy, Birth & Baby website presents extensive guidance for the parenting journey. It covers various topics, including pregnancy, birth, babies, children, and parenting. The website also offers healthy nutritional advice to address the developmental needs of a baby, toddler, and preschool child. You can use the following links on this website to source this information.

- Feeding your baby covers the following topics: how to feed your baby, breastfeeding your baby, expressing and storing breast milk, a dad's guide to breastfeeding, cleaning and sterilizing baby bottles, providing your baby with formula, introducing solid food, balancing the introduction of solids with milk feeds, weaning and how to introduce 'allergy' foods.
- Healthy Eating for Kids covers the following topics: healthy eating for your child, healthy drinks for kids, five food groups, how much food my child needs, how to introduce allergy foods, junk foods, children and vitamins, food preparation and safety, understanding food labels and vegetarian feeding guide for babies and toddlers.

For reliable nutritional information in the United Kingdom, refer to the British Nutrition Foundation: Nutrition for Baby and the Nidirect: Healthy Eating for Children websites. In the United States, resources for infant and toddler nutrition are available on the

EARLY CHILDHOOD | WHERE THE MAGIC HAPPENS

USDA.gov website, while information for preschool-aged children can be found on the Stanford Children's Health website. I encourage you to consult your healthcare professional to ensure you are following the most up-to-date nutritional guidelines.

CHILDPROOFING YOUR HOME

How often have we heard the expression *'there is no place like home'*? One reason for this expression is that many families view their home as a 'safe' haven. However, this is not always the case for babies and young children, who are especially vulnerable to injuries at home. Such injuries can have a significant impact on their healthy development. Taking proactive steps and implementing preventative measures can help reduce these risks.

The following links provide expert information and practical suggestions for creating a safe and secure learning environment at home. These resources include A Parent's Guide To Kidsafe Homes and Kidsafe - Poisoning Information Sheet, Australia, Keeping Children Safe from Poisonous Substances, United Kingdom, and Childproofing Your Home and the Up and Away Initiative, United States of America.

BE THE PERSON YOU WANT YOUR CHILD TO BECOME

> 'Each day of our lives we make deposits in the memory banks of our children.'
>
> Charles R. Swindoll

Your child is likely to encounter many challenges throughout their life. Initially, these challenges will concern the ups and downs of family, school, and community life. However, as they grow older, they will become increasingly aware of broader issues that may impact their lives and the lives of others. These issues could include equity and discrimination, health and well-being, environmental concerns, and social media.

To address these challenges, your child must rely on a set of values to inform their behavior. For example, if a friend of your child sustains an injury, your child should respond with genuine care and empathy, demonstrating concern for their friend's well-being. Unfortunately, children do not inherit values, morals, or ethics. Therefore, parents should nurture these qualities to help their children become respectful and ethical individuals (see, for example, Making Caring Common Project 2022).

Initially, a child's response to life's challenges will primarily depend on their parents. A strong parent-child bond, especially in the early years, positions the parent to shape, support, and enhance their child's development. Parents are the lens through which their children see the world. The values that inform a parent's beliefs, decisions, and behavior will be 'on show' daily for their child to observe. This understanding highlights the significant role and influence a parent has in shaping their child's values and character.

As your child matures, their interactions with extended family, school, and local community will further influence their values and character. The extent to which these experiences inform their behavior will depend on the importance placed on these values by the groups involved. Ultimately, your child's temperament and choices will reflect the values they consider important.

USING VALUES TO INFORM BEHAVIOR AND BUILD CHARACTER

> *'What you do speaks so loudly that I cannot hear what you say.'*
> Ralph Waldo Emerson

People often say that values and behavior go hand in hand, but what are values? The Oxford Dictionary defines values as *'one's principles or standards; one's judgment of what is valuable or important in life.'* I encourage parents to teach and exemplify values that are time-honored and respected by society. These values include *responsibility, respect, kindness, caring, empathy, gratitude, mindfulness, tolerance, patience,* and *self-control.* They will ultimately become the foundation of your child's intellectual and social-emotional development, so start early.

Studies suggest the adoption of positive values by children in daily life will help them to:

- Make and keep friends,
- Have a positive impact on those around them,
- Develop self-esteem (see, for example, Cherry 2022), and
- Become a responsible and caring person.

Of course, a values-driven approach to living can provide not just these benefits but others as well. For example, schools are now incorporating positive values such as *tolerance, respect, kindness,* and *empathy* into their curricula. These values are essential prerequisites for a child's development (see, for example, ValuesbasedEducation.com 2021, TheKindnessCurriculum.com 2020). They can shape behaviors and underpin capabilities and skills needed for success.

The Resilience Project

Hugh Van Cuylenburg, founder of The Resilience Project, offers another perspective. He has explored the notion of 'happiness' and 'what makes us happy' (The Resilience Project 2022a). After living and volunteering in the far north of India for a few months, he was struck by the local people's happiness. He found their happiness remarkable, given their seemingly poor quality of life in the desert community.

Based on his research, Van Cuylenburg concluded that three fundamental values contributed to happiness: gratitude, empathy, and mindfulness. He determined that mental health would improve if these values were reflected in your attitude towards everyday life. As a result, you could also become more resilient and happier (The Resilience Project 2022b).

The Resilience Project offers activities and programs to help parents teach their children about gratitude, empathy, and mindfulness. These activities are designed to instill a deeper understanding of these values. The Resilience Project website has further information on future events and seminars (The Resilience Project 2022a).

TEACHING VALUES IN THE EARLY YEARS

Parents have a unique opportunity to introduce positive values during a child's early years. They also carry the responsibility to nurture behaviors that align with these values. This learning process will be incremental. Your expectations for their behavior should be informed by your child's unique stage of development. Your words and actions will kick in at some point. However, expect it to take a while.

Parents need to maintain their 'cool' while introducing value-driven behaviors. Expect that there will be times when your child is less receptive to your teachings. Their reactions will depend on their physical and emotional well-being (for example, tired, unwell, hungry). Also, consider their limited attention span at this stage of their development. Taking these considerations into account will help you put their learning outcomes into perspective.

If they act aggressively or use inappropriate language, do not overreact. Remember, they might be testing you to see your reaction, or they lack the skills to manage their strong emotions. If this occurs, it is best to sit down with them and calmly communicate your expectations. For example, *'We don't behave or speak like that in our family. If you want me to play with you, say, Mommy, can we play together, please?'* This approach teaches your child appropriate value-driven behaviors and how to communicate their needs respectfully. If parents respond with anger, this suggests that aggression is an acceptable way to handle difficult situations. This is clearly a message we do not want to pass on.

Consistency is also essential when teaching values to your child, as it helps reinforce understanding and behavior. Young children thrive on routine and repetition. Therefore, consistent messages provide clarity and stability in their learning process. Consequently, they are more likely to internalize and adopt these values as they mature.

Parents can build their child's awareness of positive values by adopting the following fundamental strategies. These strategies also help to nurture behaviors that align with those values and are central to teaching character development in early childhood:

- **Be a role model** - Parents should demonstrate value-driven behaviors when dealing with the expected and unexpected challenges of daily life. Examples could be helping a sick neighbor or transporting children to after-school activities. Your children will be watching and will mimic your habits, mannerisms, and behaviors.

- **Name, acknowledge, and encourage value-driven behavior** - There are many situations where a parent can highlight positive values in their daily routine. When your child demonstrates value-driven behavior, identify it by name, acknowledge it, and encourage their efforts. Naming the behavior will help them understand what it looks, sounds, and feels like. By explaining why their behavior is commendable, you help them understand its positive impact on others.

These fundamental strategies must be complemented by targeted teaching techniques. These techniques include reflection, books, Web resources, role-playing, practical applications, and clarification of expectations. They must be customized to address the specific nature of the value and behavior being taught.

Side note: It may seem premature for your toddler to grasp the concept of value-driven behaviors. It is, however, important to introduce them in their early years. At this stage, the objective is to lay the foundation for your child's understanding and development of these values.

HOW TO INSTILL VALUES

The following list provides examples of positive values for parents to introduce and teach their toddlers using the above guidelines. This list is not exhaustive but provides a solid foundation for your child to build on.

RESPONSIBILITY

Definition: 'something that is your job or duty to deal with' (dictionary.cambridge.org).

A toddler is not developmentally ready to grasp big-picture concepts or their place within the family or community. They have an inward focus and see themselves as the center of everything. They need time to develop their ability to undertake complex tasks and manage their time effectively. However, they crave involvement and a sense of significance, mirroring the adults around them. So, if your little one is always underfoot and eager to be involved in your activities, see it as a positive sign. This eagerness lays the foundation for behaviors that will shape them into responsible teenagers and adults.

Teaching responsibility to a toddler is a gradual process requiring patience and consistency. Children encouraged to take on responsibilities from a young age tend to develop a positive attitude towards them. This early engagement is widely recognized as beneficial for their growth and character development. They are also less likely to shy away from responsibilities as they grow older.

Here are some practical ways to begin to teach responsibility:

- **Be a role model** - The best and most challenging way for a parent to instill a sense of responsibility in their toddler is to be a good role model. Modeling is crucial at this stage. Children learn through observation, so demonstrate carrying out your responsibilities (for example, washing the car, cooking meals). Describe and demonstrate what you are doing and why it is important. For example, explain how you wash dishes to keep the kitchen clean. Encourage your toddler to join in and assist you.

- **Name, acknowledge, and encourage value-driven behavior** - Positive reinforcement and feedback from you will show your toddler that their efforts are valued and appreciated. Acknowledge and encourage the effort they put into specific value-driven behaviors. For example, *'Thank you for being responsible and pouring water into the dog's bowl. He was very thirsty after his long walk today.'* Emphasize how their efforts satisfied their dog's thirst. Another example could be, *'Now that you have packed up your toys and I didn't have to do it, I have more time to play with you.'* Help them understand that you have extra time to play together by sharing the responsibilities in this way.

- **Undertake simple tasks** - Having planted the seed of responsibility, start incorporating simple tasks into their daily routine so that, with your guidance, they will understand. Break down each new task into small steps your toddler can easily manage. The task could be as simple as packing away their toys before dinner. Explain clearly why the task is important (for example, to prevent family members from tripping). By assigning small responsibilities to your toddler, you are instilling a sense of ownership and accountability. You will be surprised by how much pride and independence they develop by doing simple chores. More complicated tasks will only overwhelm them, so keep your requests simple and easy to manage.

- **Make chores fun** - Your toddler loves spending time with you. So, dance to music while you dust together or maybe race to see who can put the most toys away.

- **First things first** - Your toddler will need to learn that work usually comes before play. For example, you might say, *'I want to take you to the beach, but first, we need to clean up the breakfast dishes.'* Discuss the situation openly in a relaxed manner and share your excitement about going to the beach. This approach will help them understand that you are not just giving orders arbitrarily. Instead, you are teaching them that specific responsibilities must be completed before they have fun at the beach.

When my boys were young, I frequently used a phrase to remind them about the appropriate order of priorities. *'When you have done what you need to do, you can do what you want to do.'* If your toddler says, *'I want to play in the garden,'* you can respond with, *'When you put your shorts on, you can go outside and play.'* Avoid bribing your toddler to carry out what should be normal behavior. An example could be, *'If you put your shorts on, I will give you a treat.'* Bribing your toddler raises the possibility that they might decide to forego the treat and avoid putting on their shorts. What then?

- **Establish a routine** - Establishing a routine early on will help your toddler develop responsible habits. Teach them to put their toys away before dinner and their dirty clothes in the hamper before their bath. They will soon realize that chores are simply a part of daily life. They are not tasks randomly assigned by Mom or Dad to upset them.

- **Increase the complexity of tasks** - As your toddler grows and develops, you should increase the complexity of their responsibilities. These responsibilities could include feeding a pet, watering a plant, or helping with household chores. Emphasize the importance of following through on their commitments. Explain how it benefits everyone when they complete their tasks and highlight the consequences if they do not.

    For instance, explain: *'Your dog, Duke, needs food to grow and stay healthy. If he is fed, he will be content; if not, he will be hungry and unhealthy. Similarly, a plant needs water to thrive; without it, the plant will die. If you do not help, Mommy will have to do the unfinished chores, leaving less time to play together.'*

- **Give your toddler time and space** - In the interest of saving time, you might feel tempted to do your toddler's chores for them. However, it is important to resist this urge. Instead, focus on acknowledging your toddler's efforts rather than solely their results. Criticizing them or taking over will dampen their willingness to help. Remind yourself that practice does lead to some level of competency.

By consistently reinforcing responsible behaviors, you are effectively laying the foundation for your child's future independence.

RESPECT

Definition: 'to feel or show admiration for someone or something that you believe has good ideas or qualities.'

Teaching respect to toddlers is a significant responsibility. However, expecting respectful behavior from them can feel as futile as squeezing blood from a stone. This challenge is partly due to their limited language skills. Therefore, it is unrealistic to presume that toddlers can express their desires. For example, they will not say, *'I'm enjoying playing with my building blocks; could we extend my playtime?'* Instead, they are more likely to ignore you, be defiant, or yell at you in frustration. However, this does not mean they are a lost cause. It means they are young. They need years of consistent teaching and repetition to understand the concept, show respect, and articulate their needs.

Here are some practical ways to begin to teach respect:

- **Be a role model** - Parents model respectful behavior by showing appreciation and concern for others. They use polite language and actively listen when their toddler speaks. It can be challenging to remain patient while your toddler expresses themselves. However, it is worth it. Get down to their level, make direct eye contact, and show genuine interest in what they say. Modeling this behavior is the best way to teach your toddler to listen to you.

- **Name, acknowledge, and encourage value-driven behavior** - Support your toddler's efforts to show respect. Name and encourage their value-driven behavior and describe it in detail. An example could be, *'Thank you for saying please when you asked for a drink. Asking me in that way showed respect.'* Being specific in this way will help your toddler identify the behavior. Simply saying, *'Good boy,' 'Good girl,'* or *'Well done,'* does not clarify the type of behavior being appreciated.

- **Communicate clearly and set limits** - Communicate your expectations for respectful behavior using language your toddler can easily understand. Acknowledge instances when your toddler demonstrates respectful behavior and gently remedy any lapses with patience and understanding.

  An effective way to show respect is to be kind yet firm in your discipline. So, if your toddler has a tantrum in the supermarket, I suggest you take them back to your car. Sit with them and offer reassurance. You could say, *'I can see you are upset. I am here to help you calm down.'* If possible, hold them close until they have settled, then gently ask what has upset them. If they cannot tell you, calmly and firmly explain, *'We need to finish our shopping, and then we are going home.'* Over time, they will learn that tantrums will not change the fact that essential tasks, such as food shopping, still need to be completed.

- **Respect your toddler's need to develop independence** - You can also show respect by empowering your toddler with choices and autonomy while providing support. Encourage them to make small decisions daily to nurture their sense of competence. Avoid doing tasks for them that they can handle by themselves. Breaking tasks into manageable steps will help your toddler practice being independent.

- **Validate your toddler's feelings** - Validating your toddler's feelings also shows respect. When you dismiss their feelings, you signal that you don't value their emotions. For example, *'It's not a big deal. There is no need to be upset because the yellow cup isn't available.'* You can demonstrate respect by recognizing their feelings. For example, *'I understand it is disappointing that the yellow cup is not available this morning. Would you prefer a red or blue cup instead? Let's place the yellow cup in the dishwasher to ensure it's clean and ready to use at snack time.'*

- **Demonstrate respect by using good manners** - You can demonstrate respect in many situations. For example, using good manners shows respect for others. Manners are socially correct behaviors that consider the feelings and comfort of others. Manners begin as learned behaviors, but with your encouragement and explanations, they will develop into authentic behaviors over time. The simple courtesies of *'please,' 'thank you,' 'excuse me,'* and *'may I be excused from the table?'* are not outdated.

For instance, when you give your toddler a gift, demonstrate the respectful response you expect from them. Your response will help them understand that you expect good manners. For instance, *'Thank you, Mommy'* or *'Thank you, Daddy'*. When your toddler requests a glass of water, repeat their request back to them with the word *'please'* inserted. For example, *'Daddy, may I have a glass of water, please?'*

Clarify why manners are important. Explain that you prefer to help your toddler when they are polite and respectful. Take every opportunity to introduce and reinforce good manners in daily interactions. Use good manners when communicating with them and others. Showing respect in action is more effective than simply talking about it. Hearing you say *'please'* and *'thank you'* will teach them that these phrases are part of everyday communication. A helpful resource book that gives tips and offers good advice is <u>Emily's Everyday Manners</u>.

- **Encourage respectful conversations** - Respecting others is essential for effective communication. You can start these conversations when your child is a baby. Respond enthusiastically to their attempts to communicate, such as, when they coo, babble, or squeal about something that catches their attention.

  As your child grows, dinnertime with family will offer a valuable opportunity to demonstrate and practice respectful conversations. Make it clear to your toddler that every family member, regardless of age, will have the chance to contribute. Each person will receive the undivided attention of those present and be listened to without interruptions. Regular, gentle reminders will help your toddler to develop these skills.

  Explaining respectful conversations to your toddler involves breaking down the concept into simple, understandable steps. Here's how you might approach it:

    o Explain the importance of looking at the person who is speaking to show your interest.
    o Encourage them to listen closely to what the other person is saying without interrupting.
    o Teach them to wait for the other person to finish speaking before they respond or ask questions.
    o Emphasize the value of asking questions to show interest in the other person's thoughts and feelings.
    o Teach your child to ask open-ended questions to encourage others to share more.

> *'Most people do not listen with the intent to understand, they listen with the intent to reply.'*
>
> Stephen Covey

- **Promote respect for the environment** - You can demonstrate respect for the environment using simple tasks, such as placing trash in bins and recycling. Explain why these actions are important. Involve your toddler in helping with these tasks at home and when you are out. An interesting book to expand your child's knowledge on this topic is The Story of Conservation by Catherine Barr.

Incorporating these strategies into your parenting approach helps your young child grasp the importance of treating others, their belongings, and the natural and built environment with care and consideration.

KINDNESS

Definition: 'being generous, helpful, and caring about other people or an act showing this quality.'

Kindness is an abstract concept that describes doing good deeds through being friendly, considerate, and generous. In its most condensed form, kindness is a way of showing love to the people around you. Many other words can describe the essence of kindness, such as caring, empathy, compassion, selflessness, generosity, and goodwill. When you use these words in conversation with your toddler, you help them understand their meaning. You can reinforce this understanding by pairing the words with actions that reflect their significance. This approach gives your child a glimpse into the essence of kindness.

Teaching kindness to toddlers can be difficult. There is no step-by-step guide for parents to follow. However, parents are in the prime position to guide their children until they recognize kindness as the norm. Children need to witness kind and charitable behavior from those around them. Between 12 and 18 months, toddlers start a process called 'social referencing.' This process prompts them to notice their parent or caregiver's tone of voice, facial expressions, body language, and actions. They rely on these cues to determine how to react in social situations. Toddlers learn social skills by observing, processing, and imitating the actions of their parents and close family members. Social skills may be challenging to teach if a child does not have a 'kind' role model in their life.

Psychologist Professor Richard Davidson suggests that kindness is inherent in children, referring to it as 'innate basic goodness.' He highlights children's natural inclination towards cooperative, generous, and warm-hearted interactions rather than selfish or aggressive behaviors (Centerhealthyminds.org 2024). When young children have the opportunity to express a preference, they usually choose behaviors like empathy and concern for others. For example, your toddler may show kindness by comforting their sibling when they are in pain or upset. However, genuine empathy, necessary to spark kindness, does not fully develop until your child is about eight years old. However, Davidson warns that cultural influences can potentially diminish this innate trait.

Understanding kindness is a work in progress for young children. It must be constantly reinforced through modeling, encouraging, and praising kind behaviors.

Here are some practical ways to begin to teach kindness:

- **Be a role model** - Initially, your toddler will learn from you by observing the 'kindness' you show towards them and others. For example, if you know of a relative, friend, or neighbor who is unwell, you could prepare a meal for them. Alternatively, you might offer to do some shopping or chores. Another way to demonstrate kindness is by participating in volunteer work as a family. Participating in this activity highlights the importance of giving back to the community and helping those in need. Providing practical assistance is a powerful example for your toddler to emulate.

- **Name, acknowledge, and encourage value-driven behavior** - The language parents and caregivers use to teach a toddler right from wrong is very powerful. Be clear in your explanation when distinguishing between kind and unkind behavior. When making this distinction, avoid negative language that could be taken to heart by your toddler. Always be on the lookout to acknowledge your toddler's kind behavior. For example, when your toddler helps their baby brother, you might say, *'You have been very kind to your brother today. Helping him sit up when he was lying on the floor was very thoughtful. As you know, he is still too young to sit up by himself; thank you.'*

    If your toddler acts unkindly, gently correct them, show them what you expect, and explain why being kind is better. For example, if your toddler pushes their little sister, you might say, *'Pushing her out of your way when you were running to the dinner table was unkind. Falling over made her upset. She is still learning to walk and cannot walk quickly. Holding her hand and walking with her to the table would be helpful. After all, we will not start to eat until everyone is seated. I hope you remember that for next time. For now, I would like you to say sorry to her.'* Reassure your toddler that their unkind action does not make them an unkind person.

- **Put kindness into practice** - There will be opportunities for your toddler to practice acts of kindness at home with your assistance. When nurturing kindness, clearly communicate your expectations for kind behavior and explain the reasons for being kind to others. For example, *'Your Nan is elderly and has difficulty walking. It's kind to hold her hand so that she feels safe when she walks. She's a little unsteady, and we do not want her to fall. Why don't you take Nan's left hand, and I'll take her right hand?'*

    Another way to explain and demonstrate kindness to your toddler could be, *'Let's bring Daddy a cup of tea because he's hurt his ankle. The doctor said he needs to rest.'* Explaining the context helps your toddler understand and appreciate why the action is kind. Actively involve your toddler by having them fetch the cup or tell Daddy that a cup of tea is coming so he is prepared. This way, your toddler will not be a passive bystander. Explain to your toddler that Daddy might feel lonely and need company. Acknowledge your toddler's kindness and discuss how their actions made Daddy feel, saying, *'Thank you for keeping Daddy company. He felt lonely, and your presence cheered him up.'* Through your detailed explanations, your toddler will understand why these behaviors reflect 'kindness.'

- **Encourage reflection** - Discuss your toddler's feelings and emotions concerning the acts of kindness they have experienced. Encourage them to recall the positive emotions they experienced when others treated them with kindness. Discuss how their acts of kindness could stir up similar feelings in others. Ask your toddler questions such as, *'How would you feel if your friend was kind and shared a treat with you?'* Conversely, *'How do you think your friend might feel if you shared your snack with them when they forgot theirs?'* These discussions will help your toddler understand how kindness can positively impact a person's feelings.

- **Use polite words** - *'Please'* and *'thank you'* are examples of polite language. When used in interactions, they show respect, consideration for others' feelings, and appreciation for their service. When your toddler hears you use polite language and you explain its importance, they will start to understand and be motivated to follow your example.

- **Read stories that encourage kindness** - Two resource books that can help teach this value are <u>Be Kind</u> by Pat Zietlow Miller and <u>Kindness Makes Us Strong</u> by Sophie Beer. Use the narrative in these books to discuss the characters' feelings and experiences. These conversations will help your toddler understand how kindness builds strong and healthy relationships.

By using these strategies, your toddler will develop a broad understanding of kindness. This understanding will help them interact well, build good relationships, and develop a caring and empathetic attitude toward others.

CARING

Definition: 'displaying kindness and concern for others.'

> *'Educating the mind without educating the heart is no education at all.'*
> Aristotle

A caring person expresses their concern through tangible acts of kindness in response to the emotions or experiences of others. Kindness is characterized by generosity, showing consideration, and helping others. Concern is showing care and understanding for the feelings and welfare of others.

Parents should teach their toddlers the importance of caring for others through acts of kindness. The most effective way to teach this is through practical examples that demonstrate how acts of kindness have directly impacted your toddler. For example, you might say *'When you fell and bumped your head, I cared for you. I hugged you, placed a wet flannel on your bump, and gave you a drink of water. These acts of kindness calmed you down and made you feel better.'*

Here are some practical ways to begin to teach caring:

- **Be a role model** - Initially, a parent can model concern by demonstrating caring behaviors toward their toddler and other family members and friends. These behaviors include showing affection, offering comfort and practical help during times of distress, or expressing genuine concern for their child's well-being.

    For instance, when your friend has a baby, involve your toddler in tasks that demonstrate your care for your friend and her baby. Ask your toddler to help gather baby clothes and toys they have outgrown. Wash these items and ask your toddler to help place them in the sun to dry. You could also bake a batch of healthy cookies together for your friend. Ask your toddler to help pick some flowers from the garden to add to your gifts.

    Explain to your toddler that sometimes people need extra support or company when they are not feeling well. Discuss how receiving these gifts and spending time together will make your friend feel supported.

- **Name, acknowledge, and encourage value-driven behavior** - Identify the value by name and acknowledge your toddler when they demonstrate caring behaviors. For example, *'Talking to your sister and showing her the crib mobile when she was upset was very caring. Look how happy you have made her.'* Your toddler will notice that you appreciate their caring actions. They will also see the positive impact these actions have on their baby sister.

    It is also vital to help your toddler understand that certain behaviors can have negative consequences. For example, family pets rely on us for loving care since they cannot care for themselves. If you own a dog, talk to your toddler about the caring behavior you expect them to display towards their pet. Demonstrate the action of gently patting while speaking softly to their dog. For example, *'Let's gently pat our dog Duke and speak softly to him, as we don't want to hurt or frighten him.'* Hold your toddler's hand and guide their patting action. Allow them to experience and understand what 'gentle' patting feels like. Hopefully, Duke will show that he enjoys the attention by wagging his tail.

    Encourage your toddler to check on Duke's water bowl to see if it needs filling. Explain that dogs get thirsty, just like people. Help your toddler refill the bowl with water while you explain that Duke cannot do this for himself. With your acknowledgment and encouragement, your toddler will gradually learn to show caring behaviors.

- **Foster the value of caring** - Parents should also look for opportunities for their toddlers to care for others through small acts of kindness and thoughtfulness. Use everyday occurrences as opportunities to demonstrate caring. Examples include giving their baby sibling a soft toy when they are fussing, helping to pick up items their mom dropped, or assisting with simple chores. These actions reinforce and foster caring behavior.

    As they mature, extend these caring acts to include friends and neighbors needing support. For example, you could encourage your toddler to make 'get-well' cards for their sick friends. You might also help them bake cookies for elderly neighbors or donate toys they no longer use to a children's charity. Explain how these actions can significantly improve the well-being of their friends, neighbors, and children in need.

- **Notice other people's behavior** - Reflect on people you and your toddler have observed demonstrating a caring attitude. For instance, you might say, *'Remember when you dropped your puzzle at playgroup? Your friend's mom helped us pick up all the pieces. She was kind to us, and her help made us feel better.'* This reflection and explanation will help your toddler understand how other people's behavior can impact their feelings.

- **Read stories that encourage caring** - Parents can explain the concept of caring by discussing how the actions of the characters in the story affect each other. A helpful book that will reinforce your teaching is <u>Ferdie Makes a Friend, a Story About Caring</u>.

By consistently reinforcing the value of caring, you lay the foundation for your toddler to become compassionate. Identifying opportunities for them to practice caring behavior will further support this development.

EMPATHY

Definition: 'to share someone else's feelings or experiences by imagining what it would be like to be in that person's situation.'

Showing empathy means being able to understand and share the feelings of others by imagining yourself in their shoes. To feel empathy for others is central to your child's development and happiness.

Humans are naturally inclined to be empathetic, at least to some extent. For example, babies who cry in response to the cries of other babies tend to grow up with more empathy. Therefore, take comfort knowing that if your baby cries when others do, it may be a sign of empathy. Keep in mind that toddlers are not yet developmentally equipped to fully grasp the concept of empathy. However, this should not discourage you from modeling and fostering this important value.

Teaching your toddler to share the feelings and perspectives of others will be a gradual process that will take time and practice. It is a complex concept to understand. However, a small percentage of children will grasp the concept between 18 and 24 months of age.

Here are some practical ways to begin to teach empathy:

- **Be a role model** - Demonstrate empathy toward your toddler and allow them to witness how you interact with others in a compassionate and understanding manner. For example, if you have a friend who is feeling lonely, invite them to share a meal with your family to provide companionship and support. By modeling empathetic behavior, you provide your toddler with a tangible example to observe, laying the foundation for their understanding and development of empathy.

- **Name, acknowledge, and encourage value-driven behavior** - When your toddler exhibits empathetic behavior towards someone, name the behavior and acknowledge their efforts. Initially, the process may involve your toddler responding to a request. For example, you may feel hot and tired after gardening and ask your toddler to bring you a wet flannel. You might then say, *'Thank you for understanding how hot and tired I felt after gardening. It was thoughtful of you to bring me a wet flannel for my face. It was just what I needed as it made me feel cooler and helped me to relax. Your understanding showed empathy.'* When your toddler begins to understand the reasons behind these actions and you acknowledge their efforts as empathetic, they are more likely to adopt and repeat these behaviors in the future.

- **Build a vocabulary** - Assist your toddler in developing their vocabulary, including the names of the emotions you and your toddler experience. Building this vocabulary will be achievable if you regularly name and discuss the feelings you both experience. Acknowledge and validate your toddler's emotions. Teach them to recognize and express their feelings in an acceptable way. You might say, *'I understand you were upset when your friend took your toy. However, pushing her did not solve the problem. It only made her sad. What could you do instead to express your feelings? Let's talk to her together and find a solution that works for both of you.'*

Assist your toddler in describing their feelings and provide support and comfort when they are upset. Use examples from your own life that your toddler has observed to demonstrate how you managed your frustration in a healthy way. You could say, *'I discussed my frustration with the person who upset me. I listened to the reason for their actions towards me. Together, we found an acceptable way to get on with each other.'*

- **Practice empathy** - Identify opportunities for your toddler to practice empathy in daily interactions. For example, when settling their youngest sibling down for an afternoon nap, talk to your toddler and clearly explain how you expect them to behave. For instance, *'We must be very quiet as your little sister is sleeping. I put her to bed because she was tired, so let's not wake her. When she is tired, she becomes frustrated and cries a lot. We all feel a little frustrated when we are tired. After your sister's nap, she will feel rested and happy again.'*

- **Encourage reflection** - Encourage your toddler to recall their reactions to past experiences, both positive and negative. Discuss how others may feel in similar circumstances. For example, if their friend falls and grazes their knee, remind your toddler of the times they have suffered similar experiences. Recall how they felt. This guided reflection will help foster empathy and compassion for their friend.

- **Recognize emotions in others** - Help your toddler look for signs (for example, facial expressions, body language, tone of voice, and words spoken). Demonstrate these signs for them so they can recognize these emotions in others.

- **Engage in role-playing** - Role-playing is another strategy parents can use to teach toddlers how to respond empathetically. Encourage them to use their toys to act out situations where someone is sad, hurt, or needs help. Discuss how they could react with empathy and kindness. Your participation in this activity, offering guidance as needed, will make it more meaningful.

- **Read stories that encourage empathy** - Discuss the characters' feelings and perspectives and look for signs. Ask your toddler questions about how the characters might be feeling. For example, *'Does the character have a happy or sad face? How do you think they feel?'* Encourage them to imagine being in someone else's shoes. You might ask, *'How did you feel when you were in a similar situation?'* or *'How would you feel if that happened to you?'* Understanding the perspectives and recognizing the emotions of others helps improve your toddler's ability to empathize with them. A storybook to complement your teaching is Dinosaur Learns Empathy by Steve Herman.

Consistently incorporating these strategies into your parenting approach will help your toddler better understand the feelings of others. It will also help them form meaningful relationships and foster positive social interactions.

What if your toddler is not empathetic?

It is typical for toddlers to be primarily focused on themselves. Their brains are still developing, and they may not fully understand the feelings of others. As children grow, they generally become more attuned to the feelings of those around them. However, if you have concerns, it is advisable to seek professional guidance for reassurance and support.

GRATITUDE

Definition: 'showing or expressing thanks, especially to another person.'

Toddlers are instinctively self-centered, which can make introducing the concept of gratitude challenging. We also live in an era of consumerism, which presents more challenges for parents. Although it may seem difficult, it is possible to introduce this concept to toddlers. Toddlers as young as 15 months can start to recognize the basic elements of gratitude.

By around 18 months, toddlers have usually developed a clear sense of their identity. They can differentiate between themselves and others, including their mothers. Your toddler can see that Mom, Dad, Nan, and Gramps are there to look after them and have fun. Even without the vocabulary to express their appreciation, they sense when people care for them and respond positively to it.

Parents can teach gratitude to toddlers by helping them recognize and appreciate the good people and things in their lives. Encourage them to be thankful for family, friends, belongings, and opportunities that enrich their lives.

Developing an understanding of gratitude is a gradual process requiring patience and consistency. Gentle reminders and praise for your toddler's efforts will help keep them on track and reinforce the desired behaviors.

Here are some practical ways to begin to teach gratitude:

- **Be a role model** - Initially, your toddler will learn from your example. So, always express gratitude for everything that makes your life easier or more enjoyable. Model the behaviors you would like your toddler to use. Parents and caregivers who take the time to show gratitude are more likely to raise children who do the same. Encourage your toddler to express appreciation for the people in their lives and the experiences, opportunities, and possessions they enjoy. You may say, *'It was lovely to see you thank Nan for the delicious cake she made for you. It was very kind of her to bake it as it took her a long time. I am sure she appreciated your thanks.'*

- **Name, acknowledge, and encourage value-driven behavior** - When your toddler shows gratitude, identify it and acknowledge their behavior. This practice will help them understand the concept of gratitude, the behaviors that define it, and the importance of fostering a positive outlook. You could say, *'I loved how you hugged Daddy for taking you to the park. Your hug made him feel very happy.'*

- **Use words of gratitude in daily conversations** - Use words such as grateful, thankful, and appreciative in everyday conversation with your toddler. For example, *'I love our cat Maxi, don't you? I feel so grateful when he snuggles up, especially when I'm unwell or tired, because it comforts me.'* Weaving the idea of what you are grateful for into everyday conversations can make this concept more understandable for a toddler. You want these words to soak in during this stage of their development. The more your toddler hears these words used in context, the better they will understand their meaning. This understanding will lay the foundation for their authentic expressions of gratitude in the future.

- **Look for teachable moments** - Something as simple as returning a cooking utensil to a neighbor can be a teachable moment for your toddler. When you return the cooking utensil with your toddler, you might say to your neighbor, *'Thank you, Aunty Mimi, for loaning me your spatula. I was in the middle of cooking for the family, and my spatula broke. I appreciated you lending me your spatula.'* Your show of appreciation highlights the importance of expressing gratitude. Witnessing this exchange will enhance your toddler's social skills and help shape their understanding of generosity and gratitude.

- **Encourage reflection** - At dinner time, encourage your toddler to reflect on the good things they have enjoyed during the day. Reflect on the people and experiences that brought them happiness. Discuss how they should respond to them in the future to show their appreciation and gratitude. This reflection could involve simply being thankful for the meals they have enjoyed. It might also include recalling a particular game they played with their sibling. Your toddler can draw their reflections in a gratitude journal. Engaging your toddler in conversation and helping them recall past experiences is an effective way to initiate their understanding of gratitude.

- **Be thankful for what you have** - Start by explaining that genuine happiness does not come from accumulating possessions. Happiness comes from appreciating what we have. Encourage your toddler to use their possessions in various ways to foster creativity and resourcefulness. This tactic may help them realize that they do not need more. Show your toddler images of people with fewer possessions who are still content and happy. This approach can help them better understand the concept of gratitude (The Resilience Project 2022b).

- **Acknowledge and be grateful for the kindness of others** - Encourage your toddler to appreciate the kindness and support they receive from others. This recognition will help cultivate a lasting sense of gratitude. Discuss acts of kindness or generosity toward them and how these acts made them feel (for example, happy, thankful). Encourage your toddler to say *'thank you'* when receiving gifts, acts of kindness, or assistance. If appropriate, help your toddler to reciprocate with suitable gestures.

- **Read stories that encourage gratitude** - There are excellent books for every developmental stage that teach children how to express appreciation (see, for example, The Thankful Book).

It will take time for your toddler to grasp the concept of gratitude. Therefore, it is important to introduce this concept in early childhood, giving it time to be fully understood. The more sincere parents are when expressing gratitude, the stronger the impact. Consistently demonstrating the value of gratitude will cultivate a strong sense of appreciation in your toddler. This attribute will benefit them and the people they encounter throughout their lives.

> *'Instead of buying your children all the things you never had, you should teach them all the things you were never taught.'*
> Quotling.com

MINDFULNESS

Definition: 'the practice of being aware of your body, mind, and feelings in the present moment, thought to create a feeling of calm.'

Mindfulness is a state of mind in which you intentionally focus on your thoughts and sensory experiences in the present moment. It involves being fully aware of the 'now' without dwelling on the past or worrying about the future. It is a process that involves being calm, alert, open-minded, aware, and accepting without judgment. When the mind is consciously focused, we actively notice new things about the familiar and become sensitive to perspective and change. Toddlers are naturally mindful. They are curious and love to explore. They like to take time to savor experiences and take notice of everything. They delight in the simple things and living in the moment.

Teaching mindfulness to your toddler is more than just teaching *per se*. It involves offering practical opportunities for them to focus their senses on their experiences entirely. Parents can encourage toddlers to use their senses during simple activities that anchor their attention to the present moment. These sensory experiences might include tasting food and listening to birds chirp. They could also include feeling the sun on their skin, smelling a flower's scent, or viewing a panoramic landscape. Parents can also teach their toddler mindfulness techniques, such as deep breathing, to help manage intense emotions like frustration and sadness. This intervention can prevent these 'big feelings' from interfering with their toddler's ability to focus on tasks.

It is important to distinguish between using the senses to enhance mindfulness and enrich learning. While both processes involve engaging the senses, the fundamental difference lies in the intention underpinning them. Using the senses to encourage mindfulness will heighten your toddler's awareness and capture the significance of the moment. However, in the learning process, children use their senses to gather information and develop an understanding of a subject or concept. They achieve this by exploring how something looks, feels, smells, sounds, or tastes, as described in Chapter 3.

Here are some practical ways to begin to teach mindfulness:

- **Be a role model** - From the moment your baby is born, they will watch you closely. As their role model, your child will learn by observing how you incorporate mindfulness into your daily life. By engaging in mindfulness techniques, you will normalize the practice for your toddler. This practice helps you manage your emotions and enables you to be more present and attentive. As a result, you will be better equipped to help your toddler experience life more fully. You will also be able to help them navigate and regulate their emotions effectively.

    Parents can use visual reminders throughout the day to help stay focused on the present moment. It could be as simple as a fridge magnet or a reminder on your phone. Each time you are reminded, take three slow, deep breaths. Then, check in with your body to notice any sensations, such as tension in your shoulders. If you notice stress and tension, sit or lie down and focus on releasing it from your body. Start by focusing on your breathing. Next, shift your attention to how your body feels and then address your thoughts. Once you have recognized and managed your stress, proceed with your day.

    Mindfulness techniques include breathing methods, guided imagery (that is, visualizing being in a calming place), and other practices intended to relax the body and mind. These methods help reduce stress and allow the participant to be fully present in the moment. Many mindfulness apps can guide you through these practices. With regular practice, mindfulness can promote emotional balance and calm, reduce stress, and improve overall well-being.

- **Name, acknowledge, and encourage value-driven behavior** - Mindfulness is difficult to describe as its application has two facets. It is informative to distinguish between the two. The first is to heighten sensory experiences, and the second is to manage emotions and feelings. When a child demonstrates mindfulness, parents should name, acknowledge, and encourage the specific behaviors they are displaying. The following two examples demonstrate how to achieve this outcome.

The first example relates to your toddler using their sense of hearing to enhance their walk in the forest. While observing your toddler, you may say, *'It is fantastic that you are tuning in, listening carefully, and being mindful of all the sounds around you.'* This kind of feedback will be encouraging and affirming.

The second example illustrates how deep breathing can help toddlers manage their emotions. When your toddler becomes upset with their brother and subsequently calms down by taking deep breaths, acknowledge and commend their efforts. You might say, *'I noticed that you were taking deep breaths and focusing on your breathing when you became upset with your brother. Taking deep breaths gave you a break from those feelings and helped you to calm down. Now that you are calmer, we can talk to your brother about sharing the truck.'*

- **Describe your feelings** - Talk to your toddler about your emotions and the accompanying thoughts and physical sensations. Your explanation will help them understand their feelings and the feelings of others. Discuss your feelings with your toddler next time you are overwhelmed or frustrated. Tell them how you plan to respond. You might say, *'I am feeling frustrated, and it is giving me a headache. I will lie down, take deep breaths, and calm myself.'* Describing your actions will help your toddler learn how to respond to situations that upset them.

- **Validate their feelings** - Parents need to convey that their toddler's feelings are valid and that others experience similar emotions. You can relay this message by responding with kindness and empathy when they express their feelings. Next time your toddler is upset, resist the urge to say, *'It's not a big deal.'* Instead, offer empathy and let them know their feelings are okay. Try saying, *'You are sad because Mommy said no to cookies. I also feel sad when I cannot have what I want.'*

Opportunities and practical techniques to enhance mindfulness:

- **Practice deep breathing** - Focusing on our breathing is an easy but effective way to practice mindfulness. You can introduce a toddler to deep breathing around two to three years of age. However, it is important to have realistic expectations. Practice will improve their technique over time. This developmental stage is about laying the foundation and appreciating that deep breathing can help manage our feelings.

  There are many ways to introduce deep breathing to toddlers. One way is blowing bubbles. Most toddlers would blow bubbles all day if you let them. It is a great way to get them to practice the correct movements with their lips and do long exhales. Breathing in through their noses can be tricky. To help them understand, you could suggest they pretend to smell a flower. Remember, they do not need to perfect the technique; you want them to understand the ideas. By the time they are closer to three years, most toddlers will be able to do this activity reasonably well.

Mindfulness for Little Ones and Finding My Calm are valuable resource books for helping your child develop healthy coping skills and behaviors. They offer developmentally appropriate activities to foster empathy, self-awareness, and joy in children aged between two to five years.

- **Engage in gentle movements** - Introduce activities such as yoga or stretching exercises. Encourage your toddler to pay attention to their breathing and be aware of how their body feels as they move. Printed yoga mats for children can be purchased from Yoga Mats for Kids.

- **Actively listen** - Provide opportunities for your toddler to practice listening and focusing on different sounds in the environment. Encourage them to listen without trying to identify or label the sounds. Listening to music and concentrating on the instruments or lyrics is a great way to focus 'in the moment' without distraction.

- **Eat slowly** - Encourage your toddler to eat slowly and savor each bite. Ask questions about the taste, texture, and aroma of their food between mouthfuls to spark their curiosity. Remind them to notice how they feel before and after eating (for example, hungry, full).

- **Go for walks** - Take walks outdoors and encourage your toddler to be aware of the sights, sounds, and sensations of nature. These sensations might include the sun on their face, the wind in their hair, the grass under their feet, and the beautiful scenery surrounding them. Avoid distractions and make time for your toddler to enjoy these experiences without being rushed.

- **Enjoy simple activities** - Help your toddler engage in simple activities that encourage mindfulness. These activities could include lying on their backs, gazing at clouds drifting across the sky, or listening to soothing music with closed eyes. Remind your toddler to think about their feelings when participating in these activities.

- **Color and draw** - Provide your toddler with coloring books or drawing paper. Urge them to notice the colors they choose and the movements of their hands as they color.

Remember to keep the activities short, simple, and fun. Be patient as your toddler gradually builds their mindfulness skills over time. With your encouragement, they will learn to focus and become aware of the sensory experiences and emotions produced by these activities.

Incorporating mindfulness into your toddler's daily routine will develop their self-awareness. This approach will help them to manage their emotions and build resilience. Cultivating mindfulness will also help them to improve concentration, enhance their well-being, and develop empathy and compassion.

TOLERANCE

Definition: 'willing to accept the beliefs, feelings, habits, or behaviors of another group, culture, as legitimate, even when they differ from one's own' (merriam-webster.com) or 'the ability to deal with something unpleasant or annoying' (dictionary.cambridge.org).

Today, we encounter diversity in many aspects of life. This diversity may include ethnicity, culture, religion, gender, and abilities. We want our children to feel relaxed and respectful of these differences and to learn from them. Diversity brings new ideas, experiences, and energy to our lives. Tolerance towards others is a significant factor in creating a peaceful atmosphere at home and in the community.

The wheels of social interactions are oiled by tolerant people. These people can accept others just as they are. They treat them with the same good humor and patience they would like to receive. Tolerance is a form of resilience that enables us to persevere and recover in the face of adversity. While showing tolerance is commendable, it is inappropriate in situations of injustice, such as bullying or exclusion. Nevertheless, tolerance is typically the appropriate response in most situations and should be actively encouraged.

Teaching tolerance to toddlers involves fostering an environment of understanding and acceptance of others' differences. Simply telling toddlers to be tolerant is not enough. They need to interact with others. These opportunities will let your toddler experience firsthand how individuals, similar or different to themselves, can contribute in diverse and meaningful ways.

When parents consistently demonstrate tolerance through their actions and words, they will inspire their toddlers to appreciate differences in others. To develop tolerance, it is also essential to cultivate respect, kindness, empathy, and patience. Encourage your toddler to embrace these values in their daily exchanges with you. Use these opportunities to foster an awareness of other people's perspectives and emotions. In addition, you can promote inclusivity, kindness, and respect regardless of differing needs, backgrounds, or cultures.

Here are some practical ways to begin to teach tolerance:

- **Be a role model** - Start with your behavior and language. Show tolerance and acceptance in your behavior towards others. Be mindful of your language and attitudes because your toddler will be listening and watching. The level of patience and understanding that parents exhibit serves as an unspoken lesson in tolerance for their toddlers. From their earliest moments, children will absorb and mimic the values and behaviors of their role models — their parents. This process begins long before they can articulate words. So, celebrate and appreciate differences in the people around you.

- **Name, acknowledge, and encourage value-driven behavior** - When introducing the concept of tolerance, use everyday situations that will make your teaching relevant. Your toddler may have to deal with a baby brother who is crying and making a lot of noise. You might ask, 'Why do you think your baby brother is acting that way?' Explain that their brother is crying because he has no other way to attract attention and have his needs met. You must help your toddler understand this reality. Encourage them to be understanding and kind, without complaint or frustration.

    When your toddler demonstrates tolerant behaviors, name the behaviors and acknowledge their efforts. Be specific so they can grasp exactly what behavior is 'appropriate.' For example, *'You showed great tolerance by sitting quietly in the car when your little brother was screaming. Thank you for recognizing how tired and hungry he was and holding his bottle to help him feed. Speaking to him quietly made it easier for him to settle down and fall asleep.'*

- **Appreciate individuality** - Begin by encouraging your child to recognize and appreciate the unique traits of their siblings and friends. These differences could include personalities, interests, and abilities. Acknowledging these individual qualities will affirm each person's uniqueness and boost their self-esteem. Children with a strong sense of self-worth are more likely to be tolerant of others.

- **Accept diversity** - Welcome people of diverse backgrounds, cultures, and beliefs into your social circle. Encourage your toddler to ask questions about the differences they notice and answer them in a simple, age-appropriate manner. It is natural to observe differences among people, and it is acceptable to discuss them respectfully. Teach your toddler to embrace these differences and treat every person fairly and kindly, regardless of background or belief. Involve your toddler in activities and environments where they can experience diversity firsthand, such as play dates, daycare, and church.

- **Engage in cultural activities** - Attend local cultural events, watch movies, and read books with your toddler. These activities will enable them to explore and gain an understanding of the diverse cultures and traditions from around the world. The World Map Floor Puzzle is a valuable resource for introducing and identifying the locations of various cultures around the globe. Encourage your child to ask questions to explore the distinctive ways different cultures celebrate special occasions and navigate daily life. Teach them about the beauty of diversity and the importance of respecting differences.

- **Read stories that encourage tolerance** - Use age-appropriate books, stories, and videos that celebrate diversity and promote tolerance. Use simple language to explain differences such as race, ethnicity, culture, abilities, and family structures. Emphasize that these differences make each person unique and special. For example, Alexandra Penfold's book All Are Welcome will provide further insight. A book that draws attention to varying levels of tolerance is Too Much Noise by Ann McGovern. This book demonstrates that everyone encounters less-than-ideal situations at some point. Learning to view problems from a broader perspective early in life is advantageous.

By incorporating these strategies, you will foster a deep understanding and respect for others in your children. Consistently emphasizing the importance of tolerance will further support this development. This approach will also help cultivate a positive and inclusive mindset in your children.

PATIENCE

Definition: 'the ability to wait, or continue doing something despite difficulties, or to suffer without complaining, or being annoyed.'

Toddlers are not known for their patience. From a developmental standpoint, they need more time to fully grasp the meaning of self-regulation, managing excess energy, and waiting for things to happen. They want 'it' now, not in five minutes! While some children find waiting easier than others, few have the patience to wait quietly and calmly for something to occur without complaint or frustration.

From a learning perspective, it is essential to acknowledge that each toddler has a unique temperament. They will develop patience in their own way. An effective strategy for one toddler might not work for another. That is perfectly fine. Your goal should be to identify effective strategies to help your toddler manage situations that require patience. When teaching patience to a toddler, it is important to set realistic expectations that align with their stage of development.

Cultivating patience early in your toddler's development equips them with a valuable life skill. It will enhance their ability to build healthy relationships, be more considerate, and excel academically. While patience is a challenging concept to grasp, it can be developed over time with consistent teaching.

Here are some practical ways to begin to teach patience:

- **Be a role model** - As always, parents need to demonstrate the behaviors they want to see in their children. When toddlers observe their parents and caregivers practicing patience, they are more likely to emulate and exhibit patience. In a world where delays and obstacles are common, remaining cool, calm, and collected can be challenging. Children learn by example. Therefore, talk to your toddler about how you manage your emotions when faced with frustrating situations.

- **Name, acknowledge, and encourage value-driven behavior** - When your toddler demonstrates patience, be sure to recognize it by naming the behavior, acknowledging it, and offering specific encouragement. You might say, *'Thank you for patiently waiting for your snack. I will prepare it for you as soon as I have finished feeding your baby brother. Your calm behavior has helped me relax and feed him more easily. Notice how sleepy he is now because you've been so quiet? Once he is asleep, we can enjoy some special time together, just the two of us. That will be fun!'* Recognizing your toddler's behavior in this way reassures them that their efforts have been noticed and appreciated. Your response will motivate them to continue practicing patience. It is equally important to emphasize how being patient positively influences the situation and benefits those involved.

- **Reflect on practical examples that illustrate patience** - Initially, outline your expectations for your toddler's patient behavior. For example, *'When you wait quietly and keep your hands to yourself, that is one way to show you are being patient.'* It is helpful to reflect on examples your toddler has observed and remembers. These examples will reinforce your teaching and their understanding of the concept. You might say, *'Remember when we were waiting in the long checkout line at the supermarket this afternoon? The girl in front of us was a little older than you. She waited quietly and calmly in line. She didn't get angry or frustrated. She wasn't pulling on her mom's arm or rolling around the floor; she just stood quietly. She was being very patient.'*

- **Be patient with your toddler** - Recognize that toddlers have limited attention spans and often find waiting or delaying gratification challenging. They need frequent reminders and encouragement to grasp the concept of patience and to understand the behaviors you expect. It is essential to set realistic behavioral expectations for your toddler based on their stage of development.

As your toddler matures, gradually increase the time they need to be patient to help them develop this skill. However, avoid teaching patience when your toddler is hungry, overtired, or needs extra affection. Recognize that patience is a skill that takes time to develop. Some days will be easier than others. Your consistent support will be vital throughout this learning process.

- **Encourage the use of coping strategies** - Toddlers struggle with waiting, but they appreciate one-on-one time with you. When they need to wait for something, always acknowledge their challenge. You could say, *'I know it is hard to wait for your turn.'* Use the delays and time spent in queues as an opportunity to engage with your toddler. You might say, *'I know waiting is not fun, but it is great to be here together!'* Ask how they would like to pass the time and suggest coping strategies. Providing choices gives your toddler a sense of control and helps distract them while they wait.

    Consider the following scenarios:

    o Your toddler is keen to go to playgroup right now! However, before attending playgroup, you need to complete some tasks at home. You must explain the reason for the delay and reinforce the need for patience. You might say, *'I understand it is difficult to wait, but you'll need to be patient. I have a few small tasks to complete before we leave for playgroup. What would you like to do in the meantime? You can quietly look at a book, help me with the tasks, or play with your toys?'*

    o We are going to visit Nan, but the drive to her home is quite long. Encourage your toddler to engage in relaxing activities to help pass the time and make the trip enjoyable. These activities could include looking at a book, coloring, singing their favorite songs, or playing a game of Eye Spy with you.

    o Your toddler is waiting by the door for his dad to come home because they plan to go swimming together. Your toddler's eagerness is making the waiting difficult. Being patient is especially hard when children have excess energy. Playing a physical game like 'Simon Says' can help them expend energy while they wait.

    o If waiting becomes too challenging and your toddler shows frustration, encourage them to join you in practicing deep breathing.

- **Activities to foster patience** - Introduce activities that help develop patience, such as puzzles, building blocks, or simple crafts. Encourage your toddler to participate in activities that require focus and perseverance. Praise their efforts and celebrate their progress along the way. Offer support and guidance when they become frustrated or impatient. Recommend simple coping strategies to help them manage their frustration. Examples could include taking deep breaths or engaging in physical exercise before returning to the activity.

- **Practice patience** - Use daily tasks to teach your toddler about patience and patient behavior. For instance, Alex and his toddler sister, Mila, have chickens that lay eggs each morning. Discuss with Mila the idea of taking turns to collect the eggs. You could say, *'Today is your brother's turn to collect the eggs. When you wake up tomorrow, it will be your turn.'* This explanation will help Mila understand that patience, in this instance, means waiting until tomorrow for her turn.

- **Refrain from resorting to bribes** - Reward-based approaches, sometimes called bribing, may cause problems. Promising your toddler a cookie for sitting still for two minutes could inadvertently teach them to expect a treat every time they wait patiently. A reward-based approach might also lead to issues with self-regulation in the future. The primary goal is to teach them that the real reward lies in the ability to move on after waiting patiently.

- **Limit screen time as a coping strategy** - When patience is required, it is tempting to give your toddler an electronic device to keep them calm and quiet. However, it is important to limit screen time. Developing patient behavior requires a conscious effort. Without opportunities to practice patience using various coping strategies, toddlers may struggle with self-regulation when screens are not available.

- **Use visual aids** - To help your toddler understand how long they need to wait patiently, consider using a sand timer as a visual aid. A sand timer is effective because it shows the passage of time. The sand stops flowing when the waiting time is up. Showing a large clock face can also be helpful. Explain where the clock hands will be positioned when the waiting period ends.

  Use practical scenarios familiar to your toddler to reinforce the concept of time. For example, you can show that the length of their favorite television show matches the time it takes for a 30-minute sand timer to run out.

- **Read stories to encourage patience** - Use stories portrayed on television and in books to discuss the values you wish to promote. There are some excellent books such as Llama Llama Red Pajama, I'll Wait, Mr. Panda, or Waiting to reinforce 'patience.' Use role-play to extend this activity and provide further opportunities for discussion. These chats will help your toddler better understand the concept and importance of patience and its practical application.

- **Expect your child to demonstrate patience** - As your child matures, it is reasonable to expect them to be patient in certain situations. For example, you might say, *'Please be patient and wait calmly and quietly while I am on the phone. I will be brief and speak to you as soon as I finish.'* There may also be situations when interruptions to your phone conversations are warranted. Expecting your toddler to be patient when an immediate response is required, for example, to accidents or with toileting assistance, is unrealistic.

Using these strategies can help your toddler develop patience. Learning to be patient will enable them to enjoy numerous benefits in life and positively impact their interactions with others.

SELF-CONTROL

Definition: 'the ability to control one's emotions and actions.'

Self-control is a cognitive process that allows children to manage and regulate themselves (for example, resist distraction, control impulses, recover from emotional experiences, delay gratification). This value is essential for a child's success at school and overall healthy development. It helps children cooperate with others, cope with frustration, resolve conflicts, and decide which of their impulses to act upon.

Babies have little to no ability to control their emotional states or behavior. They instinctively respond to their thoughts and feelings without the ability to control themselves. When they reach the toddler stage, they experience frustration and struggle with self-control. They have unique thoughts and express their strong feelings passionately to assert their independence.

The process of developing self-control begins in a baby's earliest months. It continues throughout the early years as their brain rapidly develops. Any mother will tell you that toddlers lack the self-control of their preschool counterparts. This value and its related behaviors will develop with significant changes occurring between the ages of three and seven years. Parents and caregivers can help young children learn self-control. This assistance might involve teaching them specific strategies, support mechanisms, and practical techniques. Like all of us, children have ups and downs and struggle to control their emotions and actions.

Routines are beneficial at this age to make your child feel more secure. Acknowledging children's feelings without being dismissive can help them realize they have the power to control their impulses and emotions. This positive approach encourages them to explore healthier ways to deal with them. The ability to problem-solve and substitute an acceptable action for an unacceptable action is essential for functioning well at school. Research by Dewar (2023) emphasizes the advantages for children who develop early self-regulation skills. These children are less likely to engage in risky behaviors during adolescence compared to peers who struggle with self-control.

Teachers often emphasize interacting in groups, persisting with challenging tasks, and listening to instructions as critical skills for maximizing the school experience. These skills are closely tied to self-control. Children who can regulate their emotions and actions are better able to listen attentively, focus, persevere with tasks, follow rules, and engage positively with peers. As a result, their academic performance will improve.

Here are some practical ways to begin to teach self-control:

- **Be a role model** - Once again, your toddler's best teachers are their parents. Your response as parents to challenges will be on display for your toddler to observe and mimic. For example, imagine encountering an unexpected situation, such as needing to call roadside assistance for a flat tire. This situation might arise just before you are about to drive your child to daycare. In this circumstance, you must remain calm.

A calm response will show your child that you can manage the situation without drama. Your response might include calling for roadside assistance, informing your toddler's teacher about the delay, and notifying others impacted by your late arrival.

Discuss your approach with your toddler. Emphasize that these situations occur occasionally and there is no need to be upset or angry. There will always be a solution or strategy to manage whatever the difficulty. Parents need to model the behavior they want to see in their children. This modeling will mean controlling your emotions and reacting to challenging situations with self-control.

Toddlers often have emotional outbursts. These flare-ups may be caused by their limited ability to communicate effectively, strong desire for independence, and fluctuating emotional states. Nonetheless, they are a normal part of their development but can be upsetting for parents. Responding to a toddler's meltdown calmly and constructively without escalating the situation is important. Parents should display patience and self-control, as any heightened emotional response will intensify their child's distress.

Getting down to their level, hugging them, and reassuring them of your love helps them regain composure. Try to identify and articulate their problem, especially if they are too young to communicate it themselves. Your response will demonstrate how to handle difficulties and will set clear expectations for their behavior. For example, you could say, *'I see you are upset because you want the toy your brother is playing with. Screaming and hitting him is not acceptable and won't solve the problem. Instead, let's think about what you can do while waiting for your turn. Before we do that, let's hug your brother and say sorry to him.'*

Self-control takes time to develop. Accepting this reality will help you manage your expectations.

- **Name, acknowledge, and encourage value-driven behavior** - When your toddler shows self-control, quickly acknowledge and encourage it. For example, praise them for following simple instructions and holding your hand while crossing the street. Their instinct would be to run ahead and 'do it by themselves.' If they hold your hand, take the time to point out the nature of their behavior. You might say, *'Thank you for holding my hand tightly as we crossed the busy road. I know you may have wanted to run across the road on your own, but that would have been very dangerous. Instead, you acted responsibly and kept yourself safe by demonstrating self-control.'* Recognizing and praising their efforts will reinforce their positive approach to developing self-control.

    Essential aspects of self-control include managing your emotions and being aware of and understanding the feelings of others. Parents and caregivers can encourage empathetic, prosocial behavior by emphasizing that when we help others, we feel happy—and so do they. Encouraging this mindset fosters emotional awareness and positive interactions. Likewise, naming and recognizing our feelings and emotions is essential in restoring calm and regaining self-control. Having this understanding does not mean you give in to demands. For example, you might say, *'I understand you are upset that it is bedtime. However, it is not okay to yell at me. Let's quietly read your favorite bedtime book together instead.'*

Books such as I Am Stronger Than Anger and visual aids, like picture charts such as Feelings Scale + Coping Skills, are valuable resources. They convey the benefits of self-control to your child and help them choose appropriate responses. Positive reinforcement and celebrating improvements in self-control will lift their confidence. It will also motivate them to continue practicing self-awareness and self-regulation. A strong positive correlation exists between prosocial competency and improved social-emotional and academic skills.

- **Clarify rules and behavioral expectations** - Parents must clearly define rules and provide guidance on expected behaviors. Clear and consistent explanations will give your child a framework for practicing self-control. For example, you might say, *'Reading time is quiet time,'* or *'Now is the time to listen and follow directions,'* or *'Being helpful can make you and others feel happy.'* Inevitably, your child will need timely reminders which outline your expectations. They can often be distracted and need help remembering instructions.

  Learning to listen carefully and follow directions is also vital for developing self-control at home and in the classroom. The following two examples illustrate how to nurture these skills through everyday experiences.

  The initial example outlines your expectations for your child's appropriate use of different types of footwear. For example, you could explain, *'Your slippers are designed for indoor use. They are soft and help keep your feet warm. On the other hand, your boots are meant for outdoor use because they are sturdy and waterproof. They will protect your feet and keep them dry in wet or snowy conditions.'* Having listened carefully, your child will then be in a position to follow your directions and make the appropriate choice.

  The second scenario illustrates how listening carefully and following directions are key aspects of self-control. Following directions is especially important when a toddler wants immediate attention. For instance, you might say, *'Can you calmly wait until I finish stacking the dishwasher? I will help you retrieve your ball from the neighbor's yard when I am finished.'* Engaging in collaborative activities, like playing 'Follow the Leader' or cooking using a recipe, will require your child to listen closely. These activities will help improve their ability to follow directions effectively.

- **Establish a practice that consistently rewards self-control** - Dewar (2023) highlights The Marshmallow Test, where preschoolers choose between eating one treat immediately or receiving two treats later. The suggestion is that a child who can delay gratification and wait longer for a treat or preferred activity demonstrates self-control.

  In subsequent years, the children with the greatest capacity to wait during the 'marshmallow test' achieved better academic outcomes. Even two-year-old children resisted the temptation of a cookie when the rewards for waiting were sufficiently high. However, the success of this teaching approach depends on the parents' history of following through on promised rewards. It also hinges on how reliable and trustworthy their children perceive them to be.

- **Play games to practice self-control** - A wide variety of rule-based games and activities can help your child develop self-control. These games encourage your child to manage their bodies, voices, and minds while having fun ([Dewar](#) 2023). For example, Freeze is a simple game requiring children to dance while music plays and 'freeze' when it stops.

    A more challenging game, Drumbeats, requires children to respond to drum cues with specific movements. In this game, participants might hop to a fast beat and crawl to a slow beat. After a while, the instructions are reversed, requiring them to hop to a slow beat and crawl to a fast beat. This game is designed to teach children how to respond differently from their usual reactions. It helps them learn self-regulation by neutralizing habitual impulses. A practical example could be responding calmly instead of with frustration when someone takes their toy.

    Both games require participants to focus, thereby enhancing their ability to recall information and remember subsequent actions. Research shows that children engaging in these games can enhance their self-regulation skills. Additionally, they improve their ability to switch between tasks and thought processes more efficiently.

- **Provide opportunities for choice** - Understandably, the choices you allow your child to make will depend upon their age and stage of development. Making choices will help them develop a sense of independence and responsibility and promote self-control. Encouraging toddlers to make choices demonstrates your confidence in their readiness to make decisions.

    It is essential in the early years to give your child choices that are acceptable. For example, *'Would you like to brush your teeth or put your pajamas on first?'* Likewise, rather than fetching their rain boots, help your child consider what kind of footwear they may need. You might say, *'It is raining outside today. What will you need to wear on your feet to daycare so that you can join your class on a walk in the rain? Which shoes will keep your feet dry?'* Your child will have many opportunities to make choices throughout the day, such as selecting activities, books, or snacks. However, if the decision is yours, do not offer a choice. Say, *'It is bedtime,'* not *'Are you ready to go to bed?'*

    Here is one example of how to introduce the concept of self-control to your eight-month-old baby. At this age, they can pull themselves up using a low table, grab the TV remote, and happily press the buttons. Gently remove it from their hand and put it on the bookshelf while explaining, *'The remote is not a toy, sweetheart. I cannot let you play with it. But how about this instead?'* Offer them a '[busy box](#)' with lots of buttons to push. This interaction teaches them appropriate behavior, how to cope with disappointment, and how to accept alternatives when their first choice is off limits.

    The challenges will be different as your child grows older. Consider a three-year-old who struggles with transitioning between activities because they lack the skills to manage sudden changes. This challenge might arise during changes in routine, leaving a favorite place, or shifting from playtime to bedtime. These transitions can cause a loss of self-control, leading to tantrums, frustration, and resistance. Explaining upcoming transitions and giving your toddler time to process them, will help them manage the change with composure and self-control.

Providing opportunities for choice, clear explanations, and timely reminders helps your child learn how to handle frustrations constructively. This approach also encourages them to consider the consequences of their actions. To achieve this outcome, they must learn to manage their feelings and impulses, develop techniques to calm themselves and make appropriate behavioral choices.

- **Encourage focused attention and facilitate engagement** - The ability to engage in and sustain focused attention on learning tasks is crucial for future success at school. Babies are naturally attracted to the most prominent features of their surroundings. As babies grow, they begin to focus on specific features highlighted by their parents or caregivers.

  Toddlers and preschoolers often display a remarkable focus on activities they enjoy. These could include building with blocks, creating art, or playing their favorite games. The challenge for parents is to introduce other learning activities in a way that prompts the same level of engagement. Parents will need to employ strategies such as reading with emotion and enthusiasm and creating engaging hands-on learning activities. Providing individual attention and support will also help keep children involved.

- **Coping with emotions** - When your young child becomes emotional, they are likely to respond in various ways, especially if they lack coping mechanisms. For example, some infants need a lot of physical contact, such as rocking or hugging. Others prefer swaddling when upset. In either case, they are learning to rely on a loving parent to help them regain control when they feel overwhelmed.

  As your child approaches the toddler or preschool stage, their reactions to frustration or discipline can differ significantly from those of an infant. They might respond with whining, crying, or aggressive behaviors like hitting. Teaching your child techniques such as counting to ten, deep breathing, thinking before acting, and stretching will help remind your child to pause and consider their responses. Encouraging them to use words to express their feelings is another strategy that aids in refocusing their attention. When parents consistently apply these techniques and remain calm, their child will start using them independently and feel more in control.

- **A practical tip for avoiding temptation - Out of sight, out of mind** - For a young child, this could mean putting away a toy that might lead to conflict during a play date. It might also involve avoiding the candy aisle at the grocery store to avoid temptation. Adjusting the environment is a practical method for managing potentially challenging situations. This approach will help your child maintain their self-control.

- **Create and adhere to routines** - Young children may not be able to tell the time, but they become accustomed to routines and the sequence of activities. When active children know that outdoor play follows story time, they are more likely to show self-control and sit quietly.

- **We all need breaks** - Children benefit when we allow them time to relax. Like us, they need downtime and breaks from following directions and working hard. Why? One popular thought is that self-control gets used up during the day. Both parents and children often experience a lack of energy at the end of a busy day, making it challenging to keep going.

It is also essential to accept that young children have a limited attention span. To address this limitation, parents or caregivers should alternate the learning activities. Activities that require quiet, focused attention should be followed with active play involving movement and exercise.

Self-control allows children to regulate their emotions and actions in the long term. It helps them cooperate and collaborate with others, manage frustration, and resolve conflicts effectively. It is a skill that builds upon the key values of *patience, tolerance, respect*, and *empathy*. Self-control is essential to a child's development and contributes to positive self-esteem, resilience, improved health and well-being, and future success.

By integrating these strategies into daily activities and interactions, parents and caregivers can teach toddlers the importance of self-control. This approach helps establish a strong foundation for their social-emotional development.

TEACHING VALUES IN THE PRESCHOOL YEARS

> *'Tell me, and I'll forget*
> *Teach me, and I'll remember*
> *Involve me, and I'll learn.'*
>
> Benjamin Franklin

The early childhood years, when children's minds are untainted, are crucial for developing lasting values. It is difficult to change the values learned in these years. The values you have introduced to your toddler will require continuous reinforcement by you and their teachers throughout the preschool years.

Many parents enroll their children in preschool when they are around three years of age. This decision requires parents to entrust their child's care and development to someone outside the family. Selecting a preschool with a philosophy that aligns with your parental and broader societal values can help ease concerns. This alignment will support a smooth transition for your child.

At this stage of development, your child has begun to understand and embrace the positive values you have taught at home. They are now learning to express these values through their behavior. Based on their observations of you, they have formed conclusions about the values you prioritize. These values significantly shape your child's character, personality, and future learning experiences when reinforced and expanded upon during preschool. Children exhibiting these values contribute significantly to the social fabric of the school and the broader community. Your child and their peers will thrive in this supportive environment. They will learn how to embody values that promote peace, cooperation, and harmony.

Possibly, for the first time in their life, your child will be taught as part of a group of students without you by their side. This environment will require each member to demonstrate respect, tolerance, and self-control to ensure the group's effective functioning. Additionally, values such as *honesty, fairness,* and *unselfishness* will gain increased importance in the preschool setting. There is no doubt these values will be taught to your child as part of the preschool curriculum. However, values cannot be developed through instruction alone. They must be directly experienced and internalized. Routine practice and consistent reflection of these values in behavior are essential for your child's growing self-awareness.

The preschool environment powerfully influences young minds. Preschool is a cultural setting where your child learns to interact harmoniously with peers and teachers (Lovat and Hawkes 2013). It provides real-world opportunities for your child to experience and practice the values you, society, and the community consider necessary. The values you instill at home remain relevant and integral to your child's preschool journey.

Your child will consciously and unconsciously absorb these values from aspects of the school environment. These aspects might include the school's vision statement, curriculum, classroom displays, playground interactions, classmates, and teaching staff (Johansson, 2018). This process also encompasses adhering to school rules, participating in excursions, observing diverse role models, and forming new social relationships.

The evolving environment poses potential challenges for parents due to the diverse inputs and perspectives influencing learning and values. Parents should consider how societal values may shift in response to various factors. These factors include technological advancements, socio-economic pressures, cultural integration, diversity, and environmental concerns.

Preschool educators will also become role models for your child. Just as your child observes and learns from you, they will witness their teacher's reactions and responses to various challenges. Building a relationship with your child's teacher allows you to share your values and ensures effective communication. This relationship will ultimately benefit your child. Volunteering in the classroom or on field trips can boost your child's confidence. Your involvement also provides insight into the values promoted by their teacher and school.

Schools that embrace value-driven education report numerous benefits for their students, including:

- Increased happiness and self-confidence among students,
- More motivated, responsible, and self-directed learners,
- Enhanced mental well-being,
- Improved educational outcomes,
- Greater resilience in children,
- Enhanced spontaneous collaboration among students.

If your decision is to keep your child at home during their preschool years, it will be essential to continue practicing value-based living. Persist in teaching and reinforcing old and new values as outlined in the previous section. You can expect your preschooler to have a clearer understanding of your expectations compared to their toddler years. As a consequence, they will exhibit improved self-regulation when facing challenges.

Identify opportunities for your child to interact with family and friends. Choose occasions that may present challenges and offer opportunities for your child to demonstrate and apply their values in real-life contexts. Take part in community service as a family and support your preschooler's initiatives that reflect developing values. Also, model and teach good sportsmanship and consistently reinforce your reasons for promoting value-driven behaviors.

As your child approaches school age, they will face more nuanced situations that call for your guidance informed by established values. For instance, what guidance would you provide your child in the following scenarios:

- After eagerly accepting a friend's birthday party invitation, your child may receive another invitation to a more exciting event scheduled at the same time. This situation could create a dilemma. Should your child be allowed to retract their acceptance of the initial invitation?

- Should your child invite a friend to their party who other attendees dislike?

Values may initially seem abstract. However, when children begin discussing their own experiences, it becomes clear that life is full of value-based decisions. Studies indicate that the stronger the bond between parents and their child, the more likely the values taught by parents will influence the child's worldview and decisions. Children who feel cherished and emotionally supported are inclined to respond compassionately to others, even from a young age. Parents who nurture their relationships with their children find it easier to instill values. They raise them empathetically, making their children more likely to treat others kindly.

Being 'the person' you want your child to become requires a conscious effort. It is essential to understand that the values you model and teach your children will significantly influence their relationships, behaviors, choices, and self-perception. It is well-documented that positive values lead to constructive actions. Every minute of every day, we showcase our values, so we must remain mindful of the lessons we are imparting.

Additional resources for teaching values in the preschool years are listed below:

BOOK RESOURCE	THEME
Rumpelstiltskin's Daughter	A wise and witty tale of kindness.
The Rag Coat	Affirming the message of love and friendship.
The Quiltmaker's Gift	Moral tale supporting important values.
Miss Rumphius	A celebration of nature.
The Carrot Seed	A celebration of patience, determination and self-belief.
Grody's Not So Golden Rules	Understanding reasons behind grown-ups' rules.

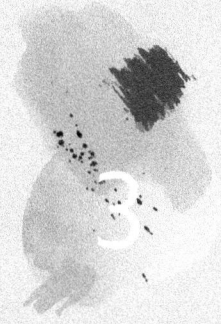

A CHILD IS BORN

In her book <u>Whispers Through Time</u>, Knost (2013) highlights that traditionally, new mothers were encouraged to focus primarily on their baby's physical needs. However, we now recognize that newborns also have intellectual, social, and emotional needs from the very beginning. Knost reminds us that babies are not solely defined by their physical needs; they also require love, attention, interaction, and stimulation. These needs are equally crucial for their development and well-being. For example, babies cry to communicate, not manipulate, and need to feel loved and heard to develop trust. Trust will not grow if they are placed alone in their cot and left to self-soothe and 'cry it out.' Babies need a prompt and loving response from a parent or caregiver.

In this chapter, I shine a light on several key considerations for a child's overall development from birth. Understanding these factors is essential for guiding your interactions with your baby, setting realistic expectations, and creating an environment that supports learning and growth. Regrettably, societal pressures can leave parents time-poor and exhausted. These constraints often make it difficult for parents to put this knowledge into practice. Despite these challenges, parents can still communicate the importance of these considerations to their child's caregiver. This guidance will ensure that the caregiver is well-informed and able to apply these principles effectively.

ESTABLISHING THE IMPORTANCE OF:

BONDING

The bond your child shares with you and loved ones is crucial for their overall development. It shapes their ability to respond to challenges and forms the foundation for relationships with others. They forge it through their interactions with you and your attentive response to their needs. Your consistent support helps create a strong sense of security. Consequently, your child will develop trust in you and feel safe.

Parents can better understand the importance of early bonding and attachment by referring to the following sources (see, for example, Winston and Chicot 2016, National Scientific Council on the Developing Child 2009, HelpGuide.Org 2019).

> *'A good mother is worth a hundred teachers.'*
> Italian Proverb

Side note: A good father is also worth a hundred teachers.

TOUCH—PHYSICAL CONTACT

Research indicates that a parent's gentle and responsive touch or hug not only alleviates pain but also positively impacts mood and the well-being of babies. Cradling a baby in your arms closely resembles the comforting sensations of the womb. When held close, babies experience a sense of security and can hear the soothing rhythm of your heartbeat. They have transitioned from a warm, dark, and muted environment to a new and unpredictable world outside the womb. For the first time they are experiencing hunger and thirst. Everything around them has changed. As parents, the least we can do to support them through this transition is to hold them close.

Babies' brains develop a connection between human interaction and feelings of pleasure through the comforting touch and warm smiles they receive. I recommend reading Born For Love: Why Empathy Is Essential—and Endangered by Perry and Szalavitz (2011), as it delves deeper into this topic.

> 'Babies regularly held and touched gain weight faster, develop stronger immune systems, crawl, walk sooner, sleep more soundly, and cry less than babies deprived of close physical contact. Children given plenty of physical affection show more task-orientated behavior, less solitary play, and less aggression at school. They also achieve higher educational qualifications in later life' (BabySensory.com.au 2020).

CRAWLING

Many parents inquire as to why crawling is important for their babies. The research leaves no room for doubt on this matter. Crawling enhances the physical strength of your baby's neck, arms, back, and legs. It also contributes to the development of gross and fine motor skills. The intricate movements in crawling stimulate various regions of the brain that play a crucial role in facilitating successful learning.

Coordination skills develop when the left and right sides of the brain are engaged. During crawling, your baby also simultaneously processes hearing, sight, and movement. If your baby tends to scoot on their bottom, creating opportunities to encourage crawling will be necessary. One way to encourage crawling is by providing a cardboard tunnel made from connected open-ended boxes. You can demonstrate its use by rolling toy cars through the tunnel or having a sibling show them how to crawl through it.

You can obtain further insight into the importance of crawling from the following sources (see, for example, Kidspot.com.au 2015, CogniKids.com 2021).

> *'Wisdom begins in wonder.'*
> Socrates

CRITICAL DEVELOPMENTAL YEARS

From a child development standpoint, your baby enters the world as a blank slate. The critical developmental years typically span the first 5 to 7 years of life. Your child will develop and learn more in these early years than at any other period in their life. The experiences your baby encounters and the feedback they receive will significantly influence the type of person they will become. It is important to remember that each child is unique and will have a distinctive learning style.

Your baby is born ready to learn and does so through their five senses: taste, smell, touch, hearing, and sight. Engaging in sensory experiences stimulates your baby's brain, forming countless connections that are the basis for future learning. When these experiences are positive, your child develops a favorable and confident attitude toward learning.

Talk, talk, talk—this is how babies learn to speak and gain an understanding of the world around them. Engage your baby by continuously talking about their surroundings, activities, thoughts, feelings, and your own experiences. Take a genuine interest in all that captures their attention and respond, treating it as a conversation. For instance, if your baby is fascinated by a flower, express your excitement through animated speech, tone of voice, facial expressions, and enthusiastic gestures. Remember, babies learn language not only by hearing words but also by observing these accompanying cues.

We all enjoy listening to a charismatic speaker passionate about their topic. The excitement is contagious. Therefore, when engaging with your child, be equally enthusiastic. The discussions could include the scents they encounter, the textures they feel, the sounds they hear, the tastes of their food, and anything they observe. Make sure you give your baby ample time to explore these experiences.

Be clear in your explanation of any new information you present to your child. Whenever feasible, support your descriptions of objects or phenomena with tangible examples. For instance, when introducing a ball, physically hand it to your child and identify it by name. Describe the ball by emphasizing its shape, color, texture, smell, and the sound produced when squeezed or bounced. Use the word *'ball'* in sentences. For example, say phrases like *'I am throwing the ball,' 'I am rolling the ball,'* and *'I am bouncing the ball'* while demonstrating each action. This approach enhances your child's comprehension of what a ball can do. It also demonstrates how to use the word 'ball' in a sentence.

Explaining phenomena not visible to your child, such as wind or sound, can pose a challenge. Utilizing objects that can help them grasp these concepts is necessary. For instance, you can use a kite to demonstrate the force of the wind. Help your child fly the kite and experience its impact firsthand. Similarly, playing a musical instrument enables them to hear the sounds produced. These tangible examples provide concrete experiences that aid your child in understanding abstract concepts, such as wind and sound.

> *'Nothing will ever replace human contact between learner and teacher.'*
> Woke Soyinka, Nobel Prize in Literature 1986

THE FIVE SENSES

Babies, like adults, possess the five traditionally recognized senses: taste, sight, touch, smell, and hearing. They rely on these senses to understand their environment, which you, as their parent, play a significant role in shaping. For instance, when introducing solid food, your baby will use their senses to explore and understand the characteristics of the food they are eating.

Take every opportunity to discuss your child's experiences. For example, you might say, *'Your yogurt tastes sweet, feels smooth, looks pink, and smells like strawberries.'* Parents can enrich this experience by demonstrating how they use each sense. For example, you can say, *'Let's smell a strawberry. It has a sweet smell.'* Similarly, *'Let's feel the strawberry. It feels bumpy.'*

TASTE

Initially, your baby will taste breast milk, formula, or water. Later, you will introduce solid foods and juice when advised by a healthcare professional. For example, when your baby has a morning snack of juice and mashed banana, you might say, *'Your juice tastes sweet,'* and *'Your mashed banana is also sweet.'*

SIGHT

When your baby is born, their sight is limited between 20 and 30 cm (8 to 12 inches) in front of their face. Initially, their visual system is not fully developed, making their world somewhat blurry. At this stage, they primarily focus on your face while being breast or bottle-fed. Newborn babies can only see black, white, and shades of grey. Therefore, providing books and mobiles in black and white is logical. Around five months, their ability to see the full spectrum of colors and their perception of depth improves. However, it is beneficial to move close to the object of their interest when describing its features.

TOUCH

Your baby will have opportunities to explore tactile sensations. Let them touch different things, such as your face, Daddy's prickly beard, bathwater, grass, rocks, dog or cat fur, blankets, or soft toys. Describe what they touch and use appropriate language to express these sensory experiences. For instance, you can say, *'Daddy's beard feels prickly and sharp.'*

Receptors responsible for sensing touch are positioned in the outer layers of the skin. These receptors enable babies to feel the pressure of the wind and the sun's temperature. Let them feel the breeze on their face or the sun's gentle warmth on their skin. However, keep the exposure brief as their skin is extremely delicate and needs protection. Make a point of using descriptive language to explain these sensory experiences.

SMELL

Your baby will encounter various smells, such as flowers, cut grass, dogs, body wash, or food. It is important to describe each new smell enthusiastically to enrich their expanding vocabulary. For example, you can say, *'My perfume smells sweet and fruity'* or *'The smell of your dinner is making me hungry. It smells yummy.'* Additionally, ensure that your facial expressions and tone of voice reflect your appreciation of these smells.

HEARING

Your child will encounter various sounds, such as your voice, music, crashing waves, barking dogs, meowing cats, or rustling leaves. During autumn (fall), a simple and enjoyable activity could involve holding your baby and strolling through fallen leaves. Draw their attention to the leaves crunching under your feet as you walk. Engage in conversation about these experiences and provide clear explanations to your baby.

To avoid confusion, begin with simple experiences that enable your baby to absorb and understand new knowledge. Start with their immediate surroundings. Take your time and draw attention to the sounds they can hear, such as Daddy talking, water running, or music playing. Bring your baby closer to the source of the sound so they can observe its origin. Exposing your baby to noisy environments is not recommended. Remember, they have spent the previous nine months in the warm and quiet environment of the womb. Therefore, carefully introduce them to our occasionally noisy world.

In summary, as your baby grows, they will naturally become more independent in exploring their environment. However, it will be important to remain attentive and aware of their activities. For instance, babies and toddlers explore flowers by seeing, touching, and smelling them. They might even attempt to taste them. It is important to understand that at this stage they cannot distinguish between edible and non-edible flowers. Therefore, it is advisable to wait until they have acquired the appropriate knowledge to identify safe-to-eat flowers.

Side note: Remember you are the adult, so keep your baby safe while they explore and learn.

WHY READING ALOUD TO YOUR CHILD FROM BIRTH MATTERS

In her book Reading Magic, Mem Fox (2012) speaks about the need to read aloud to your child every day, starting from birth. Fox notes that *'the foundations of learning to read are set down from the moment a child first hears the sounds of people talking, the tunes of songs and the rhythms and repetitions of rhymes and stories.'* Reading aloud to your child will 'spark the fire' of literacy. This shared, enjoyable experience also nurtures a strong bond, even amid the busyness of modern life.

> *'The fire of literacy is created by the emotional sparks that fly when a child, a book, and the person reading make contact.'*
>
> Mem Fox

Early exposure of your child to the elements of language, reading, and conversation will:

- Ignite a love of language.
- Create a platform for learning how to read.
- Introduce words and their meanings, which are essential in building thought connections.
- Enrich their vocabulary and language with new words and phrases not commonly used in everyday conversations.

- Sharpen their brains and develop their ability to express themselves more easily and clearly.
- Develop their speaking skills and communication skills.
- Improve their concentration and their ability to solve problems.
- Enhance their intellectual and social development, making school more manageable.
- Provide clear evidence to them of your love, care, and undivided attention.

In Reading Magic, Mem Fox shares an effective technique she used to accelerate a young boy's reading skills. She selected three picture books: Time for Bed, Hattie and the Fox, and Who Sank the Boat? to read aloud to him. These books featured consistent animal characters and shared the key elements of rhyme, rhythm, and repetition. What made the experience even more impactful was the playful, exciting, and relaxed interactions that Fox enjoyed with him. These interactions created a 'winning' environment that facilitated his reading progress and fostered his ongoing enthusiasm for learning.

When parents read aloud, it promotes meaningful conversations about the story, illustrations, words, emotions, values, and ideas conveyed in the book. These discussions contribute to a child's intellectual and social-emotional development.

ARE BOYS' AND GIRLS' BRAINS DIFFERENT?

Whether boys' and girls' brains exhibit differences has been extensively investigated for decades, resulting in many findings. Although these findings were derived from numerous smaller-scale research studies, they supported the notion of distinct 'male brains' and 'female brains.' Lise Eliot, a Professor of Neuroscience at the Chicago Medical School, emphasizes that this belief has profoundly influenced how we have historically treated boys and girls. It has shaped our perceptions of their achievements as they progress through life.

In a recent comprehensive study, Professor Eliot synthesized and analyzed three decades of research on the human brain. The study aimed to re-examine potential differences between male and female brains (Eliot et al., 2021). The conclusions emphasize that the disparities are minimal. The key finding is that the distinctions primarily arise from variations in brain size rather than from sex or gender differences. Further research found that when head size is accounted for, sex differences in the brain are tiny and inconsistent (Rosalind Franklin University of Medicine and Science 2021).

In the past, the prevailing belief was that genetics played a dominant role in driving the development of the human brain. It was thought that brain growth followed a biologically predetermined path. However, we now understand that various factors beyond genetics can influence early brain development. These factors include parental responsiveness and love, food and nutrition, daily experiences, and physical activity. Together, these factors shape the intricate wiring of the circuits of the brain.

Given these understandings, we could ask which factors shape the distinct traits and competencies we observe when comparing boys to girls. In her book, The Gendered Brain,

British neurobiologist Gina Rippon (2020) reinforces the view that there are no category-defining differences between the brains of men and women. Rippon concludes that external factors, such as gender stereotypes and everyday experiences, are likely responsible for any discernable variations in brain functioning.

Rippon unpacks the stereotypes surrounding our lives from an early stage. She shows how these messages influence our self-perceptions and even shape our brains.
The brain goes beyond being a mere genetic blueprint. The brain is adaptable and capable of change throughout our lifetime as we encounter various experiences. This adaptability is especially significant during the crucial early years of a child's development (Developingchild.harvard.edu 2018).

In this context, parents and society play a significant role in shaping the development of children's brains. This influence is evident in their behavior, skills, and personality. Hence, it is crucial to exercise caution and avoid letting our ingrained beliefs and biases dictate how we shape our children's lives. Unintentionally, we might direct them toward a predetermined path that does not align with their unique interests and talents. A consequence of this stereotyping is the current underrepresentation of women in science, technology, engineering, and mathematics (STEM) professions.

So where does that leave you as parents, the first educators of your children? How should these research conclusions inform your thoughts, decisions, and behavior? First and foremost, it is crucial to acknowledge that boys and girls are born with brains that exhibit minor differences in size. When provided with equal learning experiences, they will have an equal opportunity to develop comparable knowledge and skills.

The following Table provides several practical examples of how parents can foster and implement a balanced approach to educating their children at home. These tweaks will help you avoid limiting your child to learning and skill development paths based on outdated stereotypes.

FACILITATING A BALANCED APPROACH TO INTERACTIONS WITH YOUR CHILD

APPROACH	PRACTICAL EXAMPLES
Provide experiences for your children that are not limited or influenced by previously held gender stereotypes.	Engage in a wide range of experiences with your children regardless of gender. For example, this could include cooking, woodwork projects, gardening, science experiments, and camping. The toys and experiences we offer can influence learning. Rather than offering dolls to girls and construction toys to boys, a more balanced approach would be to provide both types of toys to all children. This method will allow your child to decide where their interests lie.
Adjust and expand long-established experiences to avoid a narrow gender-biased approach.	Dramatic play is a well-established activity that allows your child to unleash their imagination. Typically, the props used in this activity are dress-up clothing, shoes, and jewelry. Additional materials can be introduced to encourage your child's imaginative play and creativity. These materials might include blocks, sheets, pegs, cardboard boxes and rolls, string, glue, and sticky tape. The addition of these resources will also help develop their problem-solving skills as they construct complementary props. These props could include computers, hairdressing equipment, petrol pumps, cars, grocery stores, hospitals, restaurants, offices, and houses. Consider providing additional props to expand your child's imaginative experience. These props could include a <u>wooden tool set</u>, <u>hard hat</u>, <u>workbench</u>, <u>toolbox</u>, <u>medical kit</u>, <u>kitchen tools</u>, <u>cleaning tools</u>, and <u>briefcase</u>. These additions allow your child to engage in imaginative play beyond gender stereotypes.
Have equal behavioral expectations for your children.	Teach and expect adherence to age-appropriate rules and good manners.

APPROACH	PRACTICAL EXAMPLES
Have realistic academic expectations for your children.	Academic expectations should be tailored to each child's unique interests and talents, regardless of gender.
Expose your children to experiences beyond your interests.	If you cannot provide specific experiences, such as musical or scientific ones, seek out someone who can. The more opportunities you provide, the greater their chances of discovering their interests and talents.
Give your children equal attention regardless of their gender.	Allocate equal time to each child for experiences they value and enjoy. Spending quality time with your child helps build their self-worth. Letting them lead the activities enhances this development. This shared time makes them feel valued by you, leading to increased positivity and self-esteem.

Some interesting books that provide additional insight on this subject are Pink Brain, Blue Brain by Eliot (2012), and What's Going on in There? by Eliot (2000).

A Funny Story

My youngest son enjoyed playing Lego, climbing trees, riding bikes, and playing musical instruments. One day, I decided to do something different and offered him a toy doll to play with. He became determined to find out how long it would take to fill the doll with water after submerging its head in a bucket of water. I didn't expect that reaction!

WHAT A DAY SPENT WITH YOUR BABY MIGHT LOOK LIKE

In the early stages following your baby's birth, you may find that your days primarily involve feeding, changing, and soothing your baby. Hang in there. You will soon observe signs of growth and development. The primary role of a parent is to love their baby and be responsive to their needs. Additionally, it is important to introduce and clearly communicate the features of their new environment. Through these interactions, the bond you share with your baby will grow. Carefully follow the guidance healthcare professionals provide regarding your baby's care at each stage of their development.

This section presents a potential daily routine and provides simple suggestions for activities and interactions suitable for a 9-month-old baby. Note that this routine is not intended to be prescriptive. More detailed activities and interactions tailored to specific age groups, are provided in Chapter 4.

Let's begin … The activities in the following Table will be interspersed with periods of sleep, feeding, and diaper changes.

ESTABLISHING A DAILY ROUTINE FOR A 9-MONTH-OLD BABY

TIME OF DAY	SUGGESTED ACTIVITIES
Sun's up	Cuddle and hold your baby until they are fully awake. You can then choose to breastfeed, offer formula, or provide solid food for their breakfast. The food you provide will depend on their stage of development and your informed nutritional choices. When your baby is ready to eat solids, chat with them about the steps involved in preparing their food. For example, you can say, *'I'm preparing your porridge. I am stirring it with a wooden spoon and adding the milk.'* While feeding your baby, they will enjoy hearing you speak softly to them. Take the opportunity to count the mouthfuls of porridge as your baby eats. Describe their sensory experience while eating, such as *'the porridge is warm, smooth, or lumpy.'* Maintain the conversation to help them associate appropriate words with your observations and actions. You might say, *'I am rinsing your porridge bowl and spoon and placing them in the dishwasher.'*

TIME OF DAY	SUGGESTED ACTIVITIES
Getting ready for the day	Take every opportunity to talk to your baby. Use descriptive language that explains their experiences. For example, you might say, *'Let's count your fingers and toes,' 'Let's wash the porridge off your fingers,' 'Let's put your socks on your feet. I have two socks, one for each foot. Your socks are red.'* Allow your baby's curiosity to guide your interactions. Research shows that babies learn more from our words when we speak about something they are interested in (zerotothree.org 2010). Respond enthusiastically to their 'baby talk' to ensure the conversation continues. If your baby becomes fixated on something, explore it together until they are ready to move on. Demonstrate your emotions and reactions to whatever you are discussing. For instance, show excitement or happiness or even express mild sadness. This type of interaction makes the conversation more meaningful.
Morning walk	Take your baby for a morning walk. Talk to them about the sights, smells, sounds, and textures you encounter. If it is safe, encourage your baby to touch or smell anything that captures their interest. When pointing something out to your baby, ensure they can clearly see what you are discussing. If you have a family dog, bring it along for the walk, but only if you feel confident that you can manage both the dog and the stroller.
Home again	When you return home, continue describing your actions, such as taking off your baby's jacket and hanging it in the wardrobe. Also, describe preparing a bottle for your baby and pouring yourself a glass of water. Express how refreshing the water is after a long walk. Discuss your actions as you provide a bowl of water for the dog. Explain that the dog is also thirsty. Always explain your actions in detail so your baby can learn and understand.

TIME OF DAY	SUGGESTED ACTIVITIES
A time to explore and play	• It might be snack time for your baby. Discuss the color, taste, texture, and smell of their food. Ensure both your hands and your baby's hands are washed before and after meals. Before eating, clean your baby's hands to remove any dirt or germs, as they may have touched the dog or crawled on the floor. After eating, wash their hands again to remove any food residue or stickiness. Give the reasons for your actions. • Place your child on the floor to allow them to crawl and explore the safe environment you have prepared. Explore the surroundings together. You could give them a toy, such as a ball, and identify it as a 'ball.' Discuss its color, shape, size, texture, and the sound it makes when bounced. Let them play with it. Show your baby how to roll and bounce the ball and encourage them to try. Use appropriate language for each action. • Babies of this age enjoy interactive toys with buttons, doors, music, and lights. Encourage your baby to play with these toys until they lose interest. • Play some music, such as orchestral or vocal music. Talk about it, saying, *'I am going to play you some music.'* Use your facial expressions to show how the music makes you feel. Indicate whether the music makes you feel happy, sad, or sleepy. • You may feel like dancing. So, pick up your baby and dance around the room to the music. • Demonstrate how to play a maraca and rattle. Allow your baby to choose one of the instruments while you select the other. Play along to the music and encourage them to 'shake' their instrument too. • Play peek-a-boo with your baby using your hands or a scarf to hide your face. You don't need elaborate props for this activity, as babies generally find it amusing.

TIME OF DAY	SUGGESTED ACTIVITIES
A time to explore and play *Continued*	• Snuggle up with your baby and read colorful books to them. Identify the people, animals, and objects in the pictures. Enhance each story with emotive expressions and gestures that support how the images and stories make you feel. Choose books with realistic pictures of people, animals, the environment, and household items like cars, bikes, lawnmowers, and garbage bins. Avoid cartoon illustrations for now, as babies will better understand realistic images. • Draw attention to the color of their toys. Group their toys by color and play with a different color group each day. Let your baby know you will play with all the red toys today, such as a red truck, red ball, and red blocks. Take your baby around the house, pointing out red items like a red apple, red leaf, or red coat. Show enthusiasm for each discovery. • Hold your baby and replicate the movements they experienced in the womb, such as rocking, rolling, and gentle upside-down motions. Keep these movements brief and perform them slowly, allowing their brain time to recognize and respond. These vestibular activities will help their balance (refer to Chapter 7—Vestibular Activities).
Lunch and dinner	Lunch and dinner are times when your baby will discover the taste, smell, and texture of food. Discuss the characteristics of the food your baby eats and their drink at mealtime. Count the number of mouthfuls they take. For example, you may say, 'One mouthful of banana, one mouthful of avocado, and one tiny piece of fish.' Express your enjoyment while eating your meal. While your baby is comfortably seated in their highchair, you can show them a few flashcards. A highchair is ideal for this teaching activity as they cannot crawl away. Showing flashcards to your baby is another form of stimulation and will only take a minute or two to complete. You can refer to the book How to Teach Your Baby to Read: The Gentle Revolution by Doman and Doman (2006) for guidance on this simple teaching exercise. Ensure that the words on the flashcards are meaningful, such as 'Mommy, Daddy, dog, cot, bath, banana.'

TIME OF DAY	SUGGESTED ACTIVITIES
Afternoon activities	Babies benefit from playing in various settings, as they can become restless if they stay in the same spot for extended periods. To address this issue, you can create safe 'play stations' around your home. These settings could include the family room, the baby's bedroom, or an outdoor area. Take every opportunity to converse with your baby about whatever has caught their attention. For example, a discussion around playing with blocks could involve the following steps: • Identify the object: *'This is a block.'* • Name the block's color: *'This block is yellow.'* • Let them hold it: *'It is heavy.'* • Let them feel the surfaces: *'The surfaces feel smooth.'* • Demonstrate how to build a tower: *'We can build a tower out of blocks.'* • Count the blocks as you stack them: *'One, two, three, four, and five.'* • Knock the tower down and show your excitement: *'Down it falls.'* • Count the blocks again as you rebuild the tower: *'One, two, three, four, and five.'* • Hold your baby's hand and help them knock the tower over again. You might say, *'Down it falls.'* Clap your hands excitedly and continue the game until they tire of it. • Sing the nursery rhyme: 1,2,3,4,5 Once I caught a fish alive. Another example demonstrating a discussion around touch, smell, and taste might be as follows: • Identify the source: *'This is an orange.'* • Let them hold it: *'It feels bumpy.'* • Cut an orange in half and allow them to smell it: *'It smells yummy.'* • Let them lick it: *'It tastes sweet.'*

TIME OF DAY	SUGGESTED ACTIVITIES

Afternoon activities *Continued*	• Stroll in the garden and let your baby smell the scent of different flowers. Describe and discuss the scent of each flower, such as:
	  o Roses: *'These roses smell fruity, sweet, and musky,'*
	  o Daphne: *'Daphne flowers smell sweet and spicy,'*
	  o Freesias: *'These Freesias smell sweet and a bit like honey and mint,'*
	  o Mexican Orange Blossom: *'These Mexican Orange Blossom flowers smell like oranges and pepper.'*
	• During meal preparation, let your baby smell the various ingredients. Describe and discuss the aroma of each ingredient, such as:
	  o Cinnamon: *'Cinnamon smells sweet and spicy,'*
	  o Nutmeg: *'Nutmeg smells warm and sweet.'*
	• At bathtime, draw attention to the fragrance of the bath gel. Identify the scent and let them smell it, too.
	
	These conversations aim to inform your baby about their experiences. Therefore, using informative language to describe these experiences accurately is important.
	
	Additional activities might include:
	
	• Hide a toy behind the lounge while your baby watches. Then, let your baby crawl over and find it. Show excitement when they locate the toy. Repeat the game with different toys until they lose interest.
	
	• Lie your baby on their back. Hold their hands and wrists securely and gently pull them up into a sitting position as you say, *'Up you come.'* As you gently lay them down, say, *'Down you go.'* Encourage their efforts and verbalize their movement. Your baby will take their cues from you. So, smile at them during the activity to make it more enjoyable.
	
	• Allow your baby to play with an age-appropriate Unbreakable Mirror. Show them their reflection and point to their nose, eyes, ears, mouth, and hair while naming each part.

TIME OF DAY	SUGGESTED ACTIVITIES
Continued	• Show different facial expressions for your baby to observe like happy, sad, or surprised. Tell your baby the emotion your face is portraying, such as *'This is my happy face.'* Encourage them to mimic you. • Read a 'touch and feel' book to your baby like Baby Touch and Feel Animals. Let them explore the different textures on the pages. Identify other items in the house with similar textures and let them feel them. For example, say, *'The benchtop is smooth, the teddy bear is soft, and the pathway is rough.'*
After dinner	If your baby is still awake after sunset when it is dark, securely hold them and carry them outside. Use a rechargeable torch/flashlight to shine a beam of light into the darkness. Slowly move the light around, allowing your baby to follow the beam with their eyes.
Bathtime	Bathtime presents the perfect opportunity to blow bubbles and play quietly with bath toys. It serves as a calming routine to prepare your baby for bedtime. While dressing your baby for bed, consider playing soothing lullabies in the background.

ROUTINE IS REASSURING

Establish a consistent routine to help your baby anticipate the next activity. Following a routine gives your baby a sense of calm and security, as it lets them know what to expect.

Take every opportunity to show your baby how much you love them. Hold them close, smile at them, talk to them, listen to them, and promptly respond to their needs. Demonstrating your love creates a safe and nurturing environment where your baby can thrive.

> *'Children need at least one person in their life who thinks the sun rises and sets on them, who delights in their existence and loves them unconditionally.'*
>
> Pamela Leo

A Reflection from My Childhood

I remember sitting with my blind grandmother in the warm afternoon sun. I rested my head on her lap as she gently stroked my hair and asked about my school day. I can't recall a single gift she gave me. However, what remains vivid in my memory is the overwhelming sense of unconditional love I felt during those precious afternoon chats.

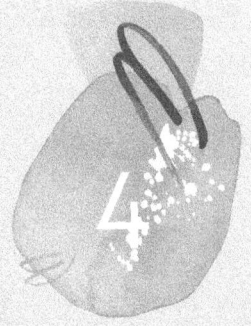

CHILD DEVELOPMENT 'PLEASE EXPLAIN'

> 'Child development refers to the natural growth and learning that occurs in all children from birth to adulthood, including intellectual, physical, and social-emotional growth.'
> Famlii.com 2020

THREE KEY AREAS OF CHILD DEVELOPMENT

- Intellectual (Cognitive) development - refers to how several mental processes continuously develop and change throughout a child's life, beginning at birth. These processes include learning, remembering, problem-solving, and thinking. Honing these processes allows your child to live a fulfilling life.

- Physical development - refers to how a child's body matures and develops fine and gross motor skills. This development allows children to explore the world around them.

- Social-Emotional development - refers to the acquisition of skills that help your child manage their emotions and interact with others. These skills are needed to make friends, share, understand right and wrong, and care about others.

EARLY CHILDHOOD | WHERE THE MAGIC HAPPENS

Your child's development in these three areas is influenced by various factors, including their interests and your awareness of their developmental stage. Providing opportunities for repetition is also essential in supporting their growth. Other factors include your enthusiasm, encouragement, focused attention, and your child's environment and their readiness to learn. All these factors work together to shape their overall growth and progress.

The three areas of child development are rarely taught or learned in isolation. For example, when you play with your child at the local playground, you might assume that this activity supports physical development. You would be correct in this assumption. However, playing on the slide will require the acquisition of social-emotional skills, such as patience when waiting for their turn. It also promotes intellectual development as your child experiences the effects of gravity. Similarly, listening to a story at the library can contribute to intellectual development. While this is true, sitting quietly and listening in a group also fosters the development of your child's social-emotional skills.

HOW DOES LEARNING HAPPEN?

> *'Children may forget what you say but they'll never forget how you made them feel.'*
> Carl W Buehner

In Chapter 2, I highlight the profound impact values have on shaping children's behavior and, more importantly, their self-perception. Values also influence parents' attitudes, emotions, and actions, which in turn shape how they teach and communicate with their children. By instilling and modeling these values, parents play a pivotal role in shaping their children's self-esteem and overall learning experiences.

Parents must maintain a supportive, open-minded, and flexible attitude to enhance their child's learning experiences and outcomes. Spending quality time, offering focused attention, and engaging in their child's learning journey demonstrate a parent's love and respect.

> *'The most desired gift of love is not diamonds, or roses, or chocolate. It is focused attention.'*
> Rick Warren

The fundamental learning process involves three key elements: *curiosity, incremental building blocks,* and *repetition.* Your child is born curious. Your attitude toward your child's curiosity will determine how they respond to learning opportunities. Be a role model. Openly and curiously explore the world and actively seek answers to your questions. Your example will inspire and motivate your child to expand and deepen their knowledge. Encourage their curiosity by responding enthusiastically to whatever has captured their attention. Parents can nurture this interest by gradually adding building blocks of knowledge and providing opportunities for repetition. Over time, your child will develop a wealth of knowledge and build essential competencies.

> *The future belongs to the curious. The ones who are not afraid to try it, explore it, poke it, question it, and turn it inside out.'*
> Anonymous

It is important to praise your child's efforts to learn, not just their achievements. This approach will reassure them, build their confidence, and help them understand that learning is an ongoing journey of improvement. Interacting with your child in this way will bring to life the principles that support the development of a growth mindset. With this positive support, your child will be free to discover their passions and strengths, paving the way for a lifetime of learning.

Of course, learning will take place in all circumstances experienced by your child. However, each child will learn differently and have different strengths. Accept and celebrate your child as a unique human being. People attribute the saying, *'comparison is the thief of joy,'* to President Theodore Roosevelt. I encourage parents to value their children for who they are and avoid comparing them to others. Let them develop at their own pace and in their unique way to become the person they are meant to be. Your acceptance and love will empower them.

To teach specific skills, such as a second language, math tables, music, poetry, or the national anthem, adopt a daily routine incorporating the new learning. Choose a regular time and place and integrate the teaching into your routine. Always express your enthusiasm when introducing new information.

Regular times and places to present this information could be:

- **Bathtime** - Introduce your child to a new language through music. For example, the resource Teach Me French by Judy Mahoney and Mary Cronan features 19 songs, including classics like *'Frère Jacques'* and *'The More We Get Together.'* Each song alternates between English and French verses, making it an engaging way to build language skills.

- **Car journeys** - Introduce your child to various music genres. For example, you could say, *'Would you like to listen to* Dance of the Sugar-Plum Fairy? *This classical piece is composed by the Russian composer Tchaikovsky. Or would you prefer to sing* The Wheels on the Bus, *an American folk song written by Verna Hills and sung by The Wiggles?*

> One example that illustrates this point occurred when I was a small child. Each Saturday morning, my dad enjoyed listening to his 'vinyl records.' One record featured Mario Lanza, a well-known singer and Hollywood film star. My dad never asked me to come and listen with him. The record played in the background as we spent our Saturdays together as a family. I guarantee that if I could play that record today, I would be able to sing most of the words.

CURIOSITY-DRIVEN FREE PLAY

> *'Children must be taught how to think, not what to think.'*
> Margaret Mead

Curiosity is a powerful driver of learning, and children need ample time to explore and nurture their curiosity. They develop their imagination and make discoveries while exploring their environment through free play. Free play is an unstructured, voluntary, and spontaneous play that stems from a child's natural curiosity, love of discovery, and enthusiasm.

The *five senses* are tools your child will use to discover all they can about their environment. Allow time for free play and explore the details and nature of their discoveries. As you add your informative commentary to the focus of their attention, you will witness their knowledge grow. Be enthusiastic and curious with them.

Encourage your child's *observational skills,* as this will improve the quality of their learning. Initially, you will make the discoveries on their behalf as they are new to this world. You will discuss your shared experiences with them, for example, *'This leaf is smooth and shiny.'* Be sure to let them see and feel it so they can understand your description of this 'discovery.' As your child matures and begins to speak, ask them inquisitive questions. These questions will encourage them to reflect on their new knowledge, skills, or experiences in more detail.

Parents and caregivers should always encourage their children to evaluate new learnings using the familiar multi-sensory approach. Instead of providing your child with all the answers up front, ask questions and encourage them to assess the knowledge. For example, you might ask, *'What does it smell like? How does it feel? Is it rough or smooth? Does the leaf have a straight edge or a curved edge?'* Remember, you are not testing your child but merely drawing their attention to the detail. You are trying to establish a habit of discovery, which will give them answers to fuel and satisfy their curiosity.

> I recall teaching my eldest child how to identify the footprints of various animals. Years later, as an adult, he joked with me about still waiting for an opportunity to use this knowledge. I laughed and replied that I hoped he could use it one day, but that had not been my goal. My goal was to teach him to notice the distinctive details of each animal's footprint to differentiate between them. Learning to look for and appreciate detail will enhance your child's knowledge on any topic.

Initially, your young child may lack the vocabulary to describe their observations in detail. In such cases, provide them with the appropriate descriptive language. For example, if you and your child have identified that their plastic baseball bat is smooth, search for other items with the same characteristic. You may say, *'Your plastic baseball bat is smooth, the bench top is smooth, the tabletop is smooth.'* By determining that all these items are smooth, your child will gain confidence in recognizing and evaluating smooth objects. The more they question new knowledge, the more accurate, memorable, and useful it will be.

Side note: Always encourage your child's curiosity by welcoming their questions and exploring their 'why' inquiries. For example: *'Why do birds have differently shaped beaks?'* or *'Why do camels have humps?'*

When your children ask questions, give them an age-appropriate answer that considers their current knowledge on the topic. Don't brush them off. If you don't know the answer, find out. How you respond to your child will impact their performance in the future.

Research has determined that a particular type of language, known as 'mechanistic' language, promotes child development. The results suggest that mechanistic language leads to well-informed and high-achieving children. Mechanistic language provides detailed and thorough explanations using precise terminology. These explanations will empower your child with accurate knowledge about their interests (Juntti 2019). The following three examples help to illustrate this point:

- A mechanistic answer to *'Why do I have to eat dinner?'* is *'You need food to support your body and brain and keep you healthy and strong. Food also provides the energy you need to run and play.'* A non-mechanistic answer would be, *'It is dinner time.'* This response does not contribute to building understanding.

- If your child asks, *'Where has Daddy gone?'* you can provide a detailed answer to help them understand. You might include the location, the reason for the trip, and how Daddy traveled there. You can also mention the time he is expected to return.

    One possible response is, *'We didn't have anything to cook for dinner, so Daddy has driven to the store to buy food. He is purchasing fish, probably salmon, and lettuce, tomatoes, and cucumbers for a salad. He should be home in about 30 minutes, around 5 p.m.'* Alternatively, you could give a limited response such as, *'He has gone to the store,'* which may leave your child wondering. This answer only tells part of the story and will not build your child's understanding.

- Using correct terminology also empowers and provides your child with accurate information to build their knowledge. For example, you might say, *'Look at the vapor trail the airplane is producing,'* rather than *'Look at the smoke coming out of the airplane.'*

The language used in these three examples gives your child detailed and accurate information. Importantly, these responses may prompt more questions from your child. This back-and-forth conversation encourages the kind of interaction that supports brain development.

INCREMENTAL BUILDING BLOCKS

Combining incremental 'building blocks' develops skills and bodies of knowledge. With each building block added, the learner gains a more comprehensive understanding of the skill or subject. This process will be unique for each child. It will depend on their stage of development and knowledge level in a specific area. Two examples that demonstrate this process are:

- When teaching your child to read, start by introducing single words on flashcards. Once they are familiar with each word, string a couple of words together, for example, cold day, hot food. Over time, increase the number of words to form short sentences.
- When your baby begins water familiarization classes, you will observe the use of the incremental building block approach. Guided by the instructor, the process might involve:
    o Familiarizing your baby with the sensation of being in a large body of water,
    o Wetting their face,
    o Blowing bubbles,
    o Kicking,
    o Pulling with their arms,
    o Total immersion in the water,
    o Floating, and
    o Treading water.

After consistent practice and repetition, your child will gain confidence in performing each building block. Around four years of age, they will be ready to participate in formal swimming lessons. Their level of swimming competency will rely on their enthusiasm for swimming and their commitment to disciplined practice.

A story highlighting the need to break down skills into building blocks features me as the central character. It began when my husband and I joined the neighborhood tennis club after moving to Adelaide. I had never played tennis before and made this clear to the club members when we first met. Throughout my school years, I played competitive netball and volleyball—both 'big ball' sports.

To achieve a basic standard and understand the rules of tennis, I needed some private coaching. I suggested joining in when I had reached a reasonable level of competency. I had to learn the fundamental building blocks of the game: serving, forehand, backhand, and volleying. The members encouraged me to start straight away. They reassured me that it was only a game and that they didn't mind if I learnt 'on the job.'

Due to my lack of preparation and skill, I began dreading Saturday afternoon tennis and felt embarrassed on the court. Had I received coaching before starting to play, I may have developed a love for the game. As it turned out, the only thing I developed was tennis elbow—ouch!

To master tennis or any sport, a player must break down each skill into building blocks. Competency in each of these building blocks is preferable before they can be successfully combined to create a new skill.

REPETITION

> *'Repetition is the secret of perfection.'*
> Dr. Maria Montessori

Children require repetition to develop skills to a competent level. Dr. Maria Montessori, a renowned authority on child development, emphasizes the importance of this approach.

You may ask, why is repetition necessary? There are many reasons for this, and here are some for you to reflect on:

- Repetition strengthens the brain's capacity to remember. It enables your child to recall memories of 'how they did it' or 'how it worked.'
- Repetition teaches children that through practice, they can improve or master a new skill.
- Repetition builds confidence. It helps children internalize their learning and use their knowledge in new situations.

Repetition can involve doing the same thing repeatedly or using new knowledge or skills in various situations. Children can also experience other forms of repetition. These could include watching someone demonstrate a skill or being taught how to perform a skill.

Repetition can happen as part of the regular daily routine, such as getting dressed, cleaning teeth, or eating with a spoon.

Repetition does not guarantee success for everyone. However, it will show your child the level of competency they can achieve independently. It is unrealistic to expect to excel at everything. However, going through this process will give your child an understanding of their strengths and passions at a particular point in time. Skills that your child may find challenging to master can be revisited later. There may be several reasons for their initial lack of success.

The Montessori method refers to supporting repetition at home in terms of the following:

- Give your child opportunities without time constraints to repeat activities that interest them.

- Suggest ways to reinforce these activities, such as drawing a picture of them or acting them out.

- You can also extend an activity to create a more challenging version based on the initial one. For example, start by teaching your child how to catch a small bean bag. Then, progress to teaching them how to catch a ball.

- Encourage your child to consider activities in terms of their senses. For example, *'How does it feel, look, smell, taste, or sound?'* These questions will cause them to evaluate and sharpen their observational skills, thereby enhancing their knowledge.

- The following day, ask questions to prompt your child to reflect on the previous day's activities. Reflecting in this way will help reinforce their newly acquired knowledge.

I encourage you to visit the Montessori Academy website (Montessori Academy 2017) to better understand the importance of repetition in child development.

'POTTY/TOILET' TRAINING—A PRACTICAL APPROACH

I was living in the United States when my eldest son turned 18 months old and required potty training. I sought advice from my friends who had already successfully trained their children. They described the practical approach below, which was easy to implement and achieved the desired outcome. This technique relies on the three key elements of the learning process: curiosity, building blocks, and repetition.

For this exercise, we will name your child *Sophie*. When you decide it is time to potty/toilet train *Sophie*, you will need the following teaching aids:

- Nappy, pants, potty, and bottle for *Sophie*—Teaching aids that you will need for *Sophie* can be sourced at the following links: BabyBjorn Smart Potty and Sippy Cups.

- A doll with 'weeing' and drinking capabilities—We will name the doll *Emma* for this exercise. Teaching aids that you will need for *Emma* should include a nappy, pants, potty, and bottle. You can find these aids at the following links: Dream Doll and Accessories—girl doll and Corolle Doll and Accessories—boy doll.

- Small treats that you know *Sophie* enjoys (for example, sultanas, small toys). Whatever you choose as a treat should be something *Sophie* likes and rarely has access to.

POTTY TRAINING USING THE ORGANIC LEARNING PROCESS

PRACTICAL APPROACH	COMMENTS AND TIPS
The preparation	In the week before starting potty training, let Sophie play with Emma. Avoid filling Emma with water until the day you plan to begin potty training. Also, encourage Sophie to sit on the potty and become familiar with it. Explain to Sophie that 'big' girls use the potty, just like Mommy uses the toilet because she is a 'big' girl. Sophie has probably watched you using the toilet, which may have sparked her curiosity.
Let's get started	It is ideal for one parent to take on this training to avoid confusion. Keep your approach simple, as this will allow your child to maintain their focus. You will need two full days clear of interruptions as Sophie will require your undivided attention. Give your phone to your partner so they can take your calls and messages.
The process - Day 1	After breakfast, find a comfortable place to sit with *Sophie* on the floor. Arrange your teaching aids nearby: *Sophie's* bottle of water, *Sophie's* potty, her doll *Emma*, and *Emma's* bottle and potty. Ensure you have treats in your pocket and *Emma's* tummy is full of water. Demonstrate the incremental building block approach for *Sophie*, detailed in the process below, using *Emma* as the role model.

PRACTICAL APPROACH	COMMENTS AND TIPS
The process - Day 1 *Continued*	**Setting the scene** • Chat about how big girls and boys don't wear nappies. They use the potty for 'wees' and 'poos' just like Mommy and Daddy use the toilet. • Explain that *Emma* wants to be a big girl and no longer wants to wear a nappy. • Remove *Emma's* nappy and put her pants on. • Explain to *Sophie* that after *Emma* has had a lot to drink and eat, she will need to use the potty. **Practical demonstration** • Feed *Emma* with her bottle. • Pretend *Emma* is talking to you and repeat back to *Sophie* what *Emma* supposedly said to you, that is, *'I need to do a wee now.'* You say, *'It would be best to pull down Emma's pants so she can wee in the potty.'* • Before placing *Emma* on the potty, check it and comment that nothing is in it. Also, have *Sophie* check that the potty is empty. • Pick *Emma* up and say, *'Emma is a big girl. She will try to wee in the potty as she does not want to wear a nappy anymore.'* • Then, place *Emma* on the potty and squeeze her gently so that the water comes out. **Praising the effort** • Exclaim excitedly, *'Look, Sophie, Emma has done a wee in the potty.'* • Make a big fuss of *Emma*. Clap your hands and kiss her. You may say to Sophie, *'I am giving Emma a treat because she did a wee in the potty.'* • Show *Sophie* the sultanas, or whatever you decide will be the treat, and pretend to give it to *Emma*. Without *Sophie* seeing, pop the treat back in your pocket. • Tell *Sophie* she will also get a treat when she wees in the potty. • Reinforce that *Emma* only got the treat because she did a wee in the potty.

PRACTICAL APPROACH	COMMENTS AND TIPS
The process - Day 1 *Continued*	**Tidying up** • Pull *Emma's* pants back up and sit her somewhere comfortable with a book to read. • Make sure that *Sophie* sees you emptying the contents of *Emma's* potty into the toilet. • Remember to make sure that *Sophie* has plenty of water to drink. Give *Emma* a drink each time *Sophie* has a drink. • Avoid stimulating activities between each training demonstration to keep *Sophie* engaged in potty training.
Repetition, repetition, repetition	You will need to repeat the above process many times throughout the day. Remind *Sophie* to let you know if she wants to wee in her potty. If you think Sophie needs to use the potty, ask her, '*Do you need to use the potty?*' If she does, explain that you will need to remove her pants. Provide positive encouragement to *Sophie* when she wees in the potty. Make a big fuss of her (for example, cheer, clap) and give her a treat. Reinforce that she is receiving the treat because she has done a wee or poo in the potty. Watch for the cues to get *Sophie* to the potty in time. At the end of the day, praise *Sophie* and *Emma* for their efforts to wee in the potty.
Day 2	On Day 2, repeat the entire process from Day 1.
Day 3 and beyond	• After breakfast, lunch, and dinner each day, briefly demonstrate the potty-training process to *Sophie* using *Emma*, the doll. This repetition reinforces the learning necessary for *Sophie* to succeed in her potty training. • Following all meals and snacks, give *Sophie* the opportunity to use the potty. • Only give *Sophie* the special treat when she uses the potty.

Wrapping Up

After the two days of intense training, the other parent or caregiver can become involved. They should also show enthusiasm for *Emma* and *Sophie's* successes and continue reinforcing the potty-training process. It is important not to look upset or react negatively if *Sophie* doesn't make it to the potty in time. However, when she does succeed, show your excitement and produce a treat. She will soon be telling you she needs to use the potty. Your child will likely still need a nappy at night, as staying dry while asleep presents its own challenges. You can address these challenges when your child is a little older.

PRACTICAL ACTIVITIES FOR HOME-BASED LEARNING

> *'Learning is experience. Everything else is just information.'*
> Albert Einstein

The following activities are designed to promote, target, develop, and reinforce the key areas of early childhood development: intellectual, physical, and social-emotional. I have grouped suitable activities into three categories: *baby*, *toddler*, and *preschooler*. These activities provide a good starting point for parents who are keen to enhance their child's development while in their care.

All three areas of child development are encountered, to some degree, in each activity. The activities listed below are coded in sequence. The sequence indicates the emphasis placed on each area of development addressed: Intellectual (I), Physical (P), and Social-Emotional (SE). The first code indicates the greatest emphasis, and so on. Importantly, these activities are inexpensive and easy to implement. They will act as building blocks in the organic learning process and grow knowledge. You can expect your child's social-emotional development to improve as they interact with you.

The knowledge your child gains from each activity will depend on their starting point and how the learning process is implemented. Remember, this process depends on three key elements. These elements are the extent of their curiosity, their uptake of incremental building blocks, and the repetition engaged in consolidating this information. When a parent or caregiver provides positive and proactive support, their child will have the opportunity to achieve successful learning outcomes.

Toy Safety

Parents need to be aware that not all toys are safe. These days, the law requires toy manufacturers to provide strict guidelines on age-appropriate recommendations for toys. The appropriateness of a toy is determined by safety factors, not the intelligence or maturity of a child. Following these recommendations as a primary preventative measure is essential for minimizing the risk of choking and other potential hazards.

Manufacturers follow strict guidelines and label toys for specific ages. The following websites (see, for example, The Royal Children's Hospital Melbourne, Australia, American Academy of Pediatrics, USA, and Royal Society for the Prevention of Accidents, UK) provide useful information that addresses the suitability and safety of toys.

If you are considering purchasing construction blocks, remember to opt for larger and lighter ones for toddlers. For instance, Lego Duplo is generally suitable for toddlers from 18 months onwards. However, it is crucial to supervise them, as they are likely to try and put the pieces in their mouths. Smaller construction blocks, such as Lego Junior, are suitable for preschoolers from around four years of age. Lego Junior requires more refined dexterity, which children develop through opportunities and maturation.

YOUR BABY

All children grow, learn, and will reach specific milestones on their developmental journey. How they play, learn, speak, act, and move will provide vital clues to parents on how their child is progressing.

Some general milestones for a baby's development up to 12 months of age are summarized below. However, parents should note that each child will demonstrate their unique trajectory and timeframe for milestone achievement. To ensure your baby is progressing satisfactorily, consult the healthcare nurse or pediatrician during regular check-ups.

THE FIRST THREE MONTHS

During this period, your newborn baby can suck, is easily startled, and has jerky leg and arm movements, which they cannot control. They learn through their senses how things feel, sound, look, smell, and taste. Their repeated movements are strengthening their brain growth and memory. Meeting your baby's primary needs for food, sleep, and personal hygiene will consume most of your time.

The activities for this age group are basic and will be scheduled around their primary needs. A natural bond will develop between you and your baby as you speak gently to them, respond to them, and hold them. Showing love by promptly responding to your baby's needs is crucial for their growth and development. Cuddling your baby will have a calming effect on both of you.

> *'Brain architecture provides the foundation for all future learning, behavior, and health. It develops through the interaction of a child's genes and early experiences, relationships, and environment.'*
>
> National Scientific Council for the Developing Child (2007)

ACTIVITIES FOR YOUR 0 TO 3-MONTH-OLD

CODE	DESCRIPTION OF ACTIVITIES
(I, SE, P)	Talk to your baby about what you are doing. Speak gently and quietly as you engage with them. They have come from a warm, dark place where noises from the world outside the womb are muffled. The most significant sound that your baby could hear in the womb was your voice.
(I, SE, P)	Play gentle music while you hold your baby, such as Baby Lullaby Academy - Calm Music for Babies.
(SE, I, P)	Take your baby for walks, either in a stroller or in your arms, when the weather is mild. Walking allows them to enjoy the fresh air and sunlight on their face. A baby's skin is delicate. So, seek advice from your pediatrician or healthcare nurse on how best to protect your baby's skin.
(I, SE, P)	Read aloud to your baby. Your newborn's vision is very blurry, so it is necessary to show them simple books. Research suggests that your newborn can more easily see bold images in black and white. Hold the book close to their faces as they can only see between 20 and 30 cm (~8 to 12 inches) from their face. Your baby will enjoy the tone of your voice and snuggling close to you. An excellent example of a black and white picture book for young babies is Baby Animals Black and White by Phyllis Limbacher Tildes.

CODE	DESCRIPTION OF ACTIVITIES
(I, P, SE)	Sing to your baby, whether using familiar songs written by others or creating your own about everyday activities, such as getting dressed.
(I, P, SE)	Wrap your baby in a soft blanket. Run their hands over it so they can feel it. Comment on how it feels. You could say, *'Your blanket feels soft.'* Give your baby a soft animal toy to hold. Rub the toy against their skin and identify the texture of its coat. You could say, *'This toy also feels soft.'*
(P, SE, I)	Give your baby 'tummy time.' This activity strengthens your newborn's neck and shoulder muscles. It will also help prevent flat spots from developing on the back of their head. Be guided by your baby's healthcare nurse on the length of time your newborn should devote to this activity. Never leave your newborn unsupervised.
(I, P, SE)	Hang a Black and White Baby Mobile above their cot. The mobile gives them something to focus on and reach for, which will help with their spatial awareness.

Note: (I) = Intellectual, (P) = Physical and (SE) = Social-Emotional

Additional home-based activities to stimulate your baby's brain development are available online at Montessori at Home: Newborn Babies and thrivebyfive.org.au. These two sites are valuable resources. Parents can use these activities to supplement the activities listed in the previous Table.

It is well-known that the first three months are often challenging. It will be busy as you attend to your *'new baby'* responsibilities. You should accept help from trusted caregivers and take some time for yourself. Feeling relaxed will benefit both you and your baby.

3 TO 5 MONTHS OF AGE

Your baby can now prop themselves up on their arms and hold their head up momentarily when lying on their tummy. They can follow objects with their eyes from side to side. They are starting to recognize faces up close and at a distance. They can now coordinate their eyes and hands to reach for, grasp, and pick up toys. A prolonged activity may cause them to be fussy. They pay attention to the faces of those close to them and are sometimes able to imitate expressions. They smile, coo, and babble, enjoying the company of those they have grown to love and trust. They respond to love and affection and can show both happiness and sadness.

Consistently engage your baby in daily activities to build their knowledge. As you move through the following stages of development, continue to revisit activities from previous stages. Extend these activities by adding incremental building blocks of knowledge, which include more detail and variety. For example, let's consider how you can introduce the concept of a bird to your child starting from when they are a baby. The process could consist of the following steps:

- Identify the birds in your garden as birds.
- Next, identify the different species of birds, for example, *'That bird is a … parrot, magpie, dove, hawk, robin, eagle.'*
- Identify the common features of a bird. For example, you might point out that birds have beaks, wings, and feathers, and most birds can fly.
- Identify the differences between bird species. Little Kids First Big Book of Birds is a helpful resource for this purpose. Encourage your child to notice the unique features of each bird species. Emphasize the differences in size, eggs, beak shape, leg length, feet structure, feather types, preferred diet, bird calls and whether the bird can fly or is flightless.

Keep in mind that building knowledge on any given topic takes time. For instance, the first three steps in the example above could be accomplished within the first 18 months. The final step might be achieved during your child's preschool years. Your child's uptake of this knowledge will depend on their developmental stage, level of curiosity, and your enthusiastic approach. The frequency of repetition you provide will also be crucial for their successful learning.

Continue providing the activities from the newborn list. However, extend these activities with additional detail and variety.

NEW ACTIVITIES FOR YOUR 3 TO 5-MONTH-OLD

CODE	DESCRIPTION OF ACTIVITIES
(SE, I, P)	Talk to your baby. Engage in conversation with them as you perform activities. For example, you might say, *'I am putting your socks on,' 'I am opening the door,'* and *'I am preparing your bottle.'* By listening to your commentary, they will begin to understand the world around them. Be enthusiastic in your response to whatever they show an interest in. Your baby's curiosity and your enthusiastic response is a way of engaging in a conversation with them.

CODE	DESCRIPTION OF ACTIVITIES
(P, SE, I)	Continue to give your 3-month-old <u>tummy time</u>. This activity will continue to strengthen your baby's neck and shoulder muscles. It will also help prevent flat spots forming on the back of their head. Be guided by the healthcare nurse on the length of time your 3-month-old should devote to this activity. Never leave your baby unsupervised.
(I, P, SE)	Show your baby a <u>ball</u> and say, 'This is a ball.' Roll the ball for your baby to observe its movement. Speak about what your baby is watching. You might say, 'Look at the ball rolling on the carpet.' Offer the ball to your baby and allow them to hold it.
(I, P, SE)	Lay your baby on their back either in their cot or on the floor with a mobile above them (see, for example, <u>Baby Crib Mobile</u>, <u>Multi-Purpose Floor Mobile</u>). Move the mobile parts to allow your baby to follow the movement with their eyes.
(I, SE, P)	During autumn (fall), take your baby outside into the garden and let them hear the leaves crackling under your feet. Talk about what you are doing and hearing. You could pick up a leaf and show it to your baby. Crush it in your hand close enough so they can listen to the sound it makes. Finally, show your baby what happened to the leaf when you crushed it in your hand.
(I, P, SE)	Introduce <u>rattle 'n rock maracas</u> to your baby. Play the maracas softly while you sing or play music to them.
(P, I, SE)	Rock your baby gently back and forth while sitting in a <u>rocking chair</u>. For a comprehensive understanding of the benefits of this simple activity, please refer to the section on Vestibular Activities in Chapter 7.
(P, I, SE)	If your baby is awake after dark, shine a torch or flashlight into the darkness. Slowly move the beam of light, allowing your baby to track it with their eyes.
(I, P, SE)	If you, or someone you know, enjoys sewing, consider making a patchwork rug with brightly colored fabrics. Each patch should be made from a different type of fabric, such as silk, wool, linen, cotton, or faux fur. The combination of fabrics will provide a variety of textures for your baby to feel.

Note: (I) = Intellectual, (P) = Physical and (SE) = Social-Emotional

CODE	DESCRIPTION OF ACTIVITIES
Continued	You could also use patchwork squares of different colors and textures to make a colorful touch-and-feel book. These activities offer additional opportunities to provide appropriate language to describe your baby's sensations and experiences.
(I, P, SE)	Provide opportunities for your baby to smell their world, for example, spices (cinnamon, nutmeg) and flowers (rose, gardenia, or daphne). These examples have pleasant fragrances. Use descriptive language and facial expressions to support this experience.
(I, SE, P)	Introduce counting to 10 by gently touching and counting each of your baby's fingers one by one. Repeat the activity by doing the same with their toes.
(P, I, SE)	Offer your baby a soft rattle for their curious exploration and amusement.
(I, SE)	Point out and identify whatever is in your baby's line of vision. Always use correct terminology, for example, a bird, a dog, a car, or grass.
(SE, I)	Smile at your baby often. Ensure you are close to them, as their vision is still developing.

Additional activities that address the specific interests and achievement of developmental milestones for 3 to 6-month-old babies are available online at Montessori at Home: Activities for Babies 3-6 Months. Parents can use these activities to supplement the activities listed in the previous Table.

5 TO 7 MONTHS OF AGE

By the age of five months, your baby can reach for objects and grab them easily. They can pass items from one hand to the other hand and bear weight on their legs when standing on flat ground. They can rock on their stomach and, occasionally, roll from their stomach to their back.

Around this age, your baby will have good color vision and be able to perceive depth. Their curiosity extends to everything they can see. They explore and try to understand their environment by putting items in their mouth. When you speak to your baby, they will respond with various sounds. They will start to recognize and respond to their name. Your baby will use various methods to engage you in play, which you will soon recognize. These may include patting a toy, sticking out their tongue, pointing at something, or making noises. They may also start to react to unfamiliar faces with some anxiety.

Continue providing the activities from the newborn and 3 to 5-month lists. However, extend these activities with additional detail and variety.

NEW ACTIVITIES FOR YOUR 5 TO 7-MONTH-OLD

CODE	DESCRIPTION OF ACTIVITIES
(SE, I, P)	Direct your attention and commentary to whatever captures your baby's interest. Follow their line of vision and explore whatever has caught their eye. Engage with them enthusiastically and talk through their discoveries for as long as they remain interested.
(I, SE, P)	Read colorful books to your child that depict accurate images of the world around them. These images might include a picture of a dog, a person, or a piece of fruit. They are trying to learn a language and understand how the words relate to all they observe. Refrain from using cartoon illustrations to depict real life, as this could lead to confusion. Read with emotions that support the storyline to make the story more enjoyable and understandable.
(I, SE, P)	Start using flashcards to teach your baby how to read. Using flashcards may sound extraordinary, but it is simply another activity to provide stimulation and only takes a minute or two. Reading the book How to Teach Your Baby to Read: The Gentle Revolution by Doman and Doman (2006) will build your confidence and provide a clear and straightforward approach to follow. The approach highlights the importance of the font size, letter case, and the color of the words on the flashcards. The Flashcards are available on the Glenn Doman product site, 'The Gentle Revolution.' When your baby is very young, show them the flashcards while they are sitting in their highchair. This tactic will prevent them from crawling away.
(I, P, SE)	Your baby may have started eating solids by now. Identify the food you give them, for example, mashed avocado or mashed banana. Count each spoonful of food out loud as you feed them.
(P, SE, I)	Continue to give your baby tummy time. This activity will strengthen your baby's neck and shoulder muscles and help prevent the formation of flat spots on the back of their head. Be guided by your baby's healthcare nurse on the length of time that your 5-month-old should devote to this activity. Never leave your baby unsupervised.

Note: (I) = Intellectual, (P) = Physical and (SE) = Social-Emotional

7 TO 9 MONTHS OF AGE

Your 7-month-old baby is becoming more mobile and can now roll from their tummy to their back. They can also sit unsupported and push up with their arms when lying on their stomach. They will show signs of wanting to move forward. Their conversational skills are developing, and they are starting to engage in two-way conversations with their parents or caregivers. They use sounds like *eh*, *ah*, and *oh* in their chatter and attempt more difficult sounds, such as '*b*' and '*m*.'

They are also curious about cause and effect. They observe what happens when they shake a toy, knock over a tower of blocks, or hit the bath water. They find it interesting to look at their reflection in a mirror. They can also verbally express their emotions of happiness, sadness, and frustration.

Continue providing the activities from the newborn, 3 to 5 months, and 5 to 7 months lists. However, extend these activities with additional detail and variety.

NEW ACTIVITIES FOR YOUR 7 TO 9-MONTH-OLD

CODE	DESCRIPTION OF ACTIVITIES
(I, SE)	Engage in continuous and meaningful communication with your baby. Use the correct terminology to identify everything you show them, for example, bird, dog, banana. Also, talk to your baby about what you and they are doing, and discuss anything else that captures their attention.
(I, SE, P)	Allow your baby to play with an <u>unbreakable mirror</u>. Let them look at themselves while you gently touch their nose and say the word 'nose.' Repeat the process with their eyes, ears, mouth, and hair.
(I, SE, P)	Introduce classical music to your baby, for example, Brahms, Mozart, and Tchaikovsky. While the music is playing, hold your baby and gently move in time with the rhythm.
(I, P, SE)	Introduce new and different foods to their menu. Ensure you describe the food they are eating and its characteristics in detail with enthusiasm. For example, 'warm, lumpy porridge.'
(P, I, SE)	When your baby is learning to crawl, place them on stable surfaces, such as fixed carpets or wooden floors. Crawling is challenging on a rug that shifts or moves. Place toys just out of your baby's reach to encourage them to crawl.

CODE	DESCRIPTION OF ACTIVITIES
(I, P, SE)	Blow bubbles so they can see them fall to the ground and burst. Also, blow bubbles within their reach so they can touch and watch them burst.
(P, I, SE)	Provide soft, age-appropriate bath toys for your baby to feel, push, grab, throw, and chew as they bathe.
(P, I, SE)	Build plastic block towers for your baby to knock over. Demonstrate the process using descriptive language to describe the actions and outcomes of what you are doing.

Note: (I) = Intellectual, (P) = Physical and (SE) = Social-Emotional

Additional activities that address the specific interests and achievement of developmental milestones for 6 to 9-month-old babies are available online at Montessori at Home: Activities for Babies 6-9 Months. Parents can use these activities to supplement the activities listed in the previous Table.

9 TO 12 MONTHS OF AGE

Around nine months, your baby will reach milestones such as sitting unsupported and engaging in crawling, creeping, or scooting movements. They can also stand with your support and use their index finger and thumb to pick up various objects, including food. Your baby can now track moving objects, mainly when the objects are falling. They will also enjoy looking for and retrieving objects they have seen you hide.

Your baby is starting to understand the meaning of the word 'no.' When teaching your baby this new concept, shake your head while saying 'no.' Gently remove them from the object or activity you want them to avoid. By consistently doing this, they will begin to associate the word 'no' with the action and eventually understand its meaning.

Your baby will enjoy conversing with you by saying *'dada,' 'mama,'* or *'baba.'* They will mimic your facial expressions and gestures and will recognize and respond to their name. Your baby will become upset when separated from you or their caregiver and anxious around strangers. Usually, they will have a favorite toy by now that will provide some comfort in these situations.

Continue providing activities from the newborn, 3 to 5 months, 5 to 7 months, and 7 to 9-month-old lists. However, extend these activities with additional detail and variety.

NEW ACTIVITIES FOR YOUR 9 TO 12-MONTH-OLD

CODE	DESCRIPTION OF ACTIVITIES
(SE, I, P)	Continue to engage in conversations with your baby. Offer more detail about everything that captures their interest so they will begin to understand the world around them. They will want to talk with you, so chat about your shared activities and experiences. Look expectantly at your baby and speak with animation, as this will encourage their response.
(P, SE, I)	Play 'peek a boo' enthusiastically with your baby, as this activity is enjoyable for them.
(I, P, SE)	Provide your baby with opportunities to practice self-feeding by offering them small pieces of food. Discuss their food; identify it, how it feels, what it smells like, the color, and what it tastes like. Be excited when they successfully feed themselves a mouthful of food. Clap your hands with enthusiasm to celebrate this achievement.
(I, P, SE)	Hide toys under a pillow or behind the lounge while your baby watches you. Encourage them to retrieve the toys and show your excitement when they find them.
(I, SE, P)	Encourage your baby to identify familiar people, animals, or objects by asking them to point to Mommy, Daddy, the dog, or a tree. If they seem unsure, enthusiastically demonstrate for them and praise their efforts to engage and learn.
(P, I, SE)	Create a safe area within your home for your baby to explore (see, for example, A Parent's Guide To Kidsafe Homes and Kidsafe-Poisoning Information Sheet, Australia, Keeping Children Safe from Poisonous Substances, United Kingdom, and Childproofing Your Home and the Up and Away Initiative, United States of America).
(P, SE, I)	Roll a ball towards your baby and encourage them to roll the ball back to you. Demonstrate this activity with another adult or older child so that your expectation is understood.

CODE	DESCRIPTION OF ACTIVITIES
(P, I, SE)	With their increased dexterity, your baby will enjoy playing with interactive toys. Some age-appropriate examples are the Pop-Up Activity Toy and the Early Education Activity Board. These examples offer a variety of features that promote learning.
(SE, I, P)	Demonstrate different facial expressions (for example, happy face, sad face, surprised face) for your baby to observe and mimic. Say the word that describes the emotion your face is portraying.

Note: (I) = Intellectual, (P) = Physical and (SE) = Social-Emotional

Additional activities that address the specific interests and achievement of developmental milestones for 9 to 12-month-old babies are available online at Montessori at Home: Activities for Babies 9-12 Months. Parents can use these activities to supplement those listed in the previous Table.

12 MONTHS OF AGE

By 12 months, most babies are becoming more mobile. They should be able to move around independently while holding onto furniture. They may even be able to stand alone, take a few steps, point their finger, wave their hand, and shake their head to indicate 'no.' They can pick up, release, shake, bang, and throw objects. They can also search for and recognize specific images in storybook pictures. They explore and examine everything you offer them, using all their senses to understand the properties of any new item. They can follow 'one-step' directions, such as clap hands, come here, and wave goodbye.

As your baby develops, their language skills will improve, and they will start imitating words you say. Initially, they will use simple words such as *'dada'* and *'mama.'* When they speak 'their language,' they will use inflections and pauses to mimic the sound and tempo of conversations they have already heard. Your baby will make it clear who they want to spend time with and use sounds and gestures to get your attention. Around this age, they fear new situations and display anxiety towards strangers.

Continue with the activities from the newborn, 3 to 5 months, 5 to 7 months, 7 to 9 months, and 9 to 12-month-old lists. However, extend these activities with additional detail and variety.

NEW ACTIVITIES FOR YOUR 12-MONTH-OLD

CODE	DESCRIPTION OF ACTIVITIES
(I, P, SE)	Maintain an ongoing dialogue with your baby, describing their surroundings and engaging with topics that capture their interest. This approach will build their knowledge and provide opportunities for 'conversation.' Your baby will want to engage in conversation with you. They may exhibit this in several ways. For example, mimicking words, talking in their unique language, and showing emotion. So, look expectantly at them and speak with animation, as this will encourage their response.
(I, P, SE)	Introduce basic musical instruments appropriate for their age, for example, a shaker or trumpet. After your child has engaged in free play with the instrument, encourage them to play along to their favorite music.
(I, P, SE)	Continue using flashcards to teach your baby familiar and meaningful words. Verbalize each word and show your baby what it represents (for example, mama, dada, bath, food, and car). Some words will have more meaning when demonstrated (for example, walk, sleep, dance, or sing).
(I, P, SE)	Buy a plastic shape sorter. The design of each shape allows it to fit through the corresponding hole in the container. This activity can be challenging, so demonstrate what is required and encourage your child's efforts. Follow up with a book that illustrates various shapes.
(I, SE, P)	Reading out loud to your baby is an important daily activity. To avoid confusion, read books that accurately and vividly portray real people, animals, the environment, infrastructure, and household items.
(P, SE, I)	Buy toys your baby can enjoy pulling around your home, such as a baby bird pull-along toy.
(P, I, SE)	Roll different-sized balls to your baby. Encourage them to roll the balls back to you. This activity may require a demonstration with an older child or adult. Use large textured plastic balls, soft foam balls, dense rubber balls, and furry tennis balls. Identify the balls using descriptive language. For example, you might say, 'Let's roll the large plastic ball to each other. It feels rough.' Run your baby's hands over the surface of the ball as you describe the rough texture.

CODE	DESCRIPTION OF ACTIVITIES
(P, I, SE)	Buy soft stacking blocks or stacking cups, such as The First Years Stack Up Cup Toys. Demonstrate how to build towers with blocks or cups until your baby can build them independently. Show them how to knock the tower over and encourage them to do the same. Be enthusiastic, as this will contribute to their enjoyment.
(P, SE, I)	Source some large cardboard boxes from a 'white goods' store. Make a tunnel from the boxes and encourage your baby to crawl through the tunnel. Additional activities could involve rolling balls and pushing toy cars through the tunnel.
(I, P, SE)	Play 'Hide and Seek.' Let your baby see where you hide, such as behind a couch or bed, so they can easily find you. Keep it simple, and make sure your baby is always in sight. Once more, bring enthusiasm to the activity to enhance the fun.
(I, P, SE)	Crush a clove of garlic and pass it under your baby's nose. Use detailed and accurate explanations to describe the smell and your baby's reaction to it. Other interesting smells you may like to introduce could be coriander, a crushed eucalyptus leaf, bread fresh from the oven, mango, and lavender oil.

Note: (I) = Intellectual, (P) = Physical and (SE) = Social-Emotional

Some activities might only be feasible if your baby has reached a certain level of mobility. However, you can modify most activities to accommodate their physical abilities.

Additional activities that address the specific interests and achievement of developmental milestones for 12 to 15-month-old babies are available online at Montessori at Home: Activities for Babies 12-15 Months. Parents can use these activities to supplement the activities listed in the previous Table.

Consult your healthcare provider if you have concerns about your baby's development during their first year and need reassurance or support.

YOUR TODDLER

When your baby reaches 12 months, they enter the 'toddler' stage of development. Around this time, they will begin to walk or 'toddle.' This stage covers the period from 12 to 36 months of age. You will witness their rapid and significant intellectual, physical, and social-emotional growth during this period. They will progress from crawling and babbling as an infant to running, jumping, and excitedly telling stories as a preschool child.

MILESTONES FOR TODDLERS (1 TO 3 YEARS OF AGE)

> *'Play is often talked about as if it were a relief from serious learning. But for children play is serious learning. Play is really the work of childhood.'*
>
> Mr. Rogers

Here are some milestones you may observe during the toddler stage. It is important to remember that each toddler will continue to follow their unique pathway and timeframe for milestone achievement.

Your toddler's fine motor and cognitive skills will continue to develop from one to two years of age. They can demonstrate these skills through construction activities such as building towers using blocks and placing pegs in a pegboard. They may be able to turn several pages of a book at once and scribble with a crayon held in their fist. When attempting to paint, they often use their whole arm. They paint this way because their dexterity and fine motor skills are still developing. Self-feeding and drinking from their cup independently are becoming more achievable.

At around 18 months, your toddler will generally show a strong attachment to you or their primary caregiver. As a result, they may be distressed when you leave them and clingy when you return. They can usually show their emotions, such as happiness, sadness, or anger. They enjoy being held by those they love and trust. At this stage of their social-emotional development, your toddler may still be afraid of strangers. They may recognize and respond to the emotions of others and start to empathize with those in need of comfort. Their gross motor skills are developing rapidly. This development is evident in their ability to walk alone, throw a ball, sit on toddler chairs, and climb onto furniture.

Around two years of age, a toddler's intellectual development will become more apparent. They will begin to say their name and phonetically pronounce new letters of the alphabet (for example, b, d, h, m, n, p). At this time, a parent should also be able to understand about 50% of their toddler's conversation. They will have a vocabulary of about 50 words and will be able to combine them into two to four-word sentences.

Their perception of the world they observe will blend reality with imagination. Your toddler will also become curious about their physical characteristics and the diversity of others. They will play alongside other children but not with them and may have started to play simple, imaginative games. However, they are still in the process of learning how to share and take turns. Remember, they are not misbehaving. Their behavior simply reflects their current stage of intellectual and social-emotional development.

Between the ages of two and three, toddlers undergo significant intellectual, physical, and social-emotional development. This rapid growth can make it challenging for them to manage their emotions. As they become more independent, toddlers may resist your instructions and boundaries. This growth can lead to tantrums, defiant behavior, and frequent use of the word 'no.' During this period, commonly known as the 'terrible twos,' toddlers often comprehend more language than they are able to express. This disparity can also lead to 'meltdowns,' which can be challenging for parents to handle and interpret. To navigate this stage, parents should provide positive guidance and empathy to help their children cope with frustration.

As their stability and strength increase with gross motor development, they will learn to go up and down stairs and kick a ball. They will also learn to jump off a step and stand on their toes. Their fine motor skills will continue to improve as their fingers and hands strengthen. As a result, they will learn to undress independently and put on some clothes with your help. They will also learn to thread large wooden beads onto a cord, turn single pages in a book, and snip paper with scissors. They will learn to hold a crayon with their thumb and fingers while drawing circles and straight lines. In addition, they will learn to play with playdough and eat without assistance.

By three years of age, the 'terrible twos' will hopefully be over. Your toddler will show increased physical independence. They will learn to climb, run, ride a tricycle, and walk up and down stairs one foot at a time. They will also begin to feed, dress, and toilet themselves. They will undergo considerable growth in their social-emotional development. For example, you will notice behaviors emerging as they mature and interact more often with family and friends. They will exhibit many emotions, including affection for their friends and remorse when they misbehave. They can also cope more easily with separation from their parents. However, they may get upset if you change their daily routine.

Your toddler is beginning to learn how to make new friends, join in activities, and cooperate with other children. However, they may still struggle to see situations from someone else's perspective. It is essential to continue modeling 'taking turns and sharing' within your family. This repetition will give your toddler a clear example to follow and reinforce behavioral expectations.

You will notice improvements in your toddler's intellectual development through a longer attention span and a better understanding of stories. They will show an increased ability to grasp the relationship between numbers and objects. Your toddler will develop the ability to identify themselves by name, age, and sex. In addition, they will understand the concepts of 'mine,' 'his,' and 'hers.' Their dexterity and problem-solving skills are improving, allowing them to do up and undo buttons, screw and unscrew lids, and complete puzzles.

Your toddler is now able to engage in conversations with family and friends, using two to three sentences at a time. At this stage, they should be able to phonetically pronounce several new letters of the alphabet (for example, f, g, k, t, w). They can follow two to three-step instructions, such as *'Please wash your hands and then come to the table for dinner.'* Of course, predicting when children can pronounce certain letters of the alphabet is almost impossible. It is not an exact science and will vary from toddler to toddler. If you are concerned that your child's speech is affecting their quality of life, consulting a speech pathologist can offer reassurance.

More detailed lists of milestones for the 1 to 3-year-old toddler age group can be found online (see, for example, CDC Developmental Milestones, FFY Developmental Milestones 1-2 Years, FFY Developmental Milestones 2-3 Years). Parents with concerns about their child's developmental progress should consult and seek advice from healthcare professionals.

ACTIVITIES FOR YOUR TODDLER

The toddler activities are designed to align with and support your child's new and developing milestone capabilities. These activities will satisfy and stimulate their curiosity while incrementally increasing their knowledge and skills using the building block approach. To enhance their learning experience, parents need to recognize the significance and value of the following practical considerations.

Helping your toddler to speak is pivotal to their overall development and well-being. Their ability to speak enables them to be heard and understood, express interests, communicate needs, convey emotions, and develop relationships. Increasing their vocabulary should be a priority in every interaction with your child. This outcome is achievable by simply encouraging your child to say the word that describes what they are pointing to or looking at. For example, if they are pointing at their bottle, say the word *'bottle.'* Repeat the word multiple times and encourage them to say it with you as you hand the bottle to them. As their confidence grows and vocabulary increases, you can prompt them to say the whole sentence, *'I want my bottle, please.'*

Background research is fundamental to your preparation for each planned activity. Being 'knowledge ready' ensures you can offer your toddler manageable, age-appropriate information. It also allows you to provide specific answers to their curiosity-driven questions about the activity. If you don't know the answer to a question, say so. Look it up and pass the new knowledge on to your toddler as quickly as possible. Try to revisit the activity that sparked their question to achieve the best learning outcomes.

For example, a zoo visit provides an opportunity for you to apply your background research and focus on specific details. You could explain that although all birds have feet, the shape and structure of their feet can vary. This variation is due to the different functions their feet need to perform. Some birds, like crows, have three toes pointing forward and one pointing backwards. This structure helps them grip branches while perching. On the other hand, ducks use their feet to swim. They have webbed feet uniquely designed like paddles to help them move through the water.

It is important to remember that repetition plays a crucial role in learning. This fact holds true for any activity you engage in with your toddler. What may seem like a one-dimensional learning experience may reinforce other newly acquired concepts and skills. Take, for example, learning how to throw and catch a small beanbag. Beanbags are usually colored. To reinforce your toddler's knowledge of colors, ask them to choose which color beanbag they would like to throw. For example, you might say, *'Milly, would you like to throw the red or the blue beanbag?'*

When it comes to throwing and catching the beanbag, you can expand your toddler's learning by introducing the concept of distance. For example, position yourself one long stride away from your toddler. Take this opportunity to measure the length of your stride. Use a tape measure and count out loud the number of units, for example, centimeters or inches. As their throwing and catching skills improve and their confidence grows, gradually increase the distance. Each time you increase the distance, measure it with your toddler. Take time to discuss the total number of units in the new distance. Note how many units they are throwing now compared to when they first started. Use markers on the ground to identify the lengths of the two distances.

To reinforce your child's ability to count, count out loud the number of times they catch the beanbag. Have them count with you. When the beanbag is not caught and falls to the ground, mention that gravity caused it to fall. At this stage of their development, simply mentioning this fact without providing a detailed explanation is sufficient. As your toddler grows, you will have numerous opportunities to elaborate on this concept, especially because most objects tend to fall to the ground. However, there are reasons why helium balloons, airplanes, and birds, to name a few, don't immediately fall to the ground. Explain these reasons when your child shows a deeper interest in this topic.

Once your toddler tires of the beanbag game, write down all relevant words from the activity on flashcards. Flashcards enable you to teach these words while they are still fresh in their minds. The words might include the colors of the beanbags and numerals corresponding to the number of catches (that is, 1, 2, 3, …). Also include terms like tape, measure, gravity, throw, and catch. Each activity will introduce new vocabulary specific to their learning experience.

As you can see, there is more going on than simply learning to throw and catch a beanbag. Parents or caregivers can apply this multi-faceted approach to any teaching activity. Your child's knowledge and confidence will grow with the constant references and reminders of all they are learning.

During the toddler stage, your child will become more aware of their physical characteristics and those of others. This new awareness will provide opportunities to engage in broader discussions about diversity. You can embrace different aspects and promote acceptance and respect. I have incorporated examples of how to achieve this awareness in a selection of activities below.

CODE	DESCRIPTION OF ACTIVITIES FOR TODDLERS
(I, SE, P)	If you want to teach your child to read, reading books to them should be an essential part of their daily routine. Using flashcards to introduce and reinforce new words will further support their learning. Teach them words that appear regularly in their storybooks and words related to their experiences, interests, and important people in their lives. Also, include words for places they frequently visit. These words will be easy to teach as they will have relevance.
(I, P, SE)	Visit the local zoo. Identify and discuss each animal with your toddler as determined by their curiosity. Point out the unique features of each animal, such as the number of legs, wings, and body color. Also, mention their coat type, whether fur, feathers, or tough skin. Discuss the sounds made by each animal. Record these sounds on your mobile phone so your child can listen to them later and recall the animals that made them. Children enjoy playing with language. They love rhyme and rhythm because it helps them hear the sounds and syllables in words. This experience enhances their reading development. Your children will chuckle over the Collective Nouns for Groups of Animals, for example, a 'Cackle of Hyenas,' a 'Shrewdness of Apes,' or a 'Scurry of Squirrels.' Look for the specific food the animals prefer to eat and discuss why they may like it. For example, lions and tigers are carnivorous and like eating meat with their big, sharp teeth. All birds have beaks of varying shapes and sizes for eating. However, birds like eagles and owls are carnivorous and prefer meat. Others, like parrots and budgerigars, are granivorous and like to eat seeds and grains. Your detailed commentary will give your child the necessary vocabulary to describe what they see, hear, and smell at the zoo. They will also begin to understand the distinct characteristics of various animal groups, including birds, mammals, fish, amphibians, and reptiles. Capture photographs of the animals that attract their interest. Your child can use these photos to reflect on their experiences and observations from the zoo when they return home. Use craft ideas to reinforce and build on these experiences, such as, Paper Plate Animal Masks. Another valuable resource is Learning About Animals with the Wiggles. Examples of possible 'flashcard' words are *fur, lion, feathers, bird, cackle, hyena, scurry,* and *squirrel*.

CODE	DESCRIPTION OF ACTIVITIES FOR TODDLERS
(I, P, SE)	As an introductory exercise, teach your child the names of the plants in your garden. Identify each plant by its correct name. PlantAI from the App Store will help you with this activity. You may have plants growing in your garden that are native to other countries. Point these out if you can. For example, the Bird of Paradise plant is native to South Africa. There are many sophisticated plant identification apps available from the Apple Store. For example, PlantSnap, iNaturalist, PlantNet, and PlantAI are just a few. Providing your child with accurate information is essential. This information will be a foundational building block in their understanding of this topic. To build on this knowledge, visit your local botanical garden or nature reserve. Identify the flowers and discuss their color and perfume. Count their petals, then point out and discuss the parts that form the flower's structure. Research this information before leaving home so that you can confidently share relevant knowledge with your child during the visit. Bring a magnifying glass to closely examine the petals, stamen, stem, and other interesting details of the flowers your child discovers. One resource that may be helpful for you is <u>Flowers Leaves and Other Plant Parts</u>. Smell the flowers, talk about the bees buzzing around, and any other insects you may observe. Provide your child with crayons, paper, and a plastic clipboard. Suggest they draw their favorite flower while you highlight the basic components, such as the petals, stamen, and stem. Also, take photos to provide a visual record for your child to reflect on and discuss later. You can also extend and apply this activity to include trees and shrubs. Encourage your child to pick a small posy of flowers from your garden for their grandmother. Explain that this gesture will bring her joy. Examples of possible 'flashcard' words are *flower*, *plant*, *posy*, *Nan*, and *perfume*. > *'Let's raise children who can name plants and animals, not celebrities and brands!'* > Dr. Joel Gator

Note: (I) = Intellectual, (P) = Physical and (SE) = Social-Emotional

CODE	DESCRIPTION OF ACTIVITIES FOR TODDLERS
(P, I, SE)	Visit the beach with your child. Bring their bucket, spade, and perhaps a small boat and engage in activities that teach them about sand and water. Dig holes in the sand, build sandcastles, and create tunnels. Let your child pat the sand when it is dry. Then, pour water on the dry sand and let them pat it again when it is wet. Draw your child's attention to the temperature, texture, and smell of dry and wet sand. After completing the activity, wash the sand off their hands to prevent them from eating it or rubbing it in their eyes. Tie a long piece of string to their boat and place the boat in the water. Get your child to hold the string securely while standing at the water's edge. Describe what is happening to the boat as the water tosses it around. Your commentary will give your child the language that accurately describes their observations. Remember to hold your child's hand when they are near the water to keep them safe. Examples of possible 'flashcard' words are *bucket, spade, boat, sandcastle, sand, sea, wet,* and *dry.*
(I, P, SE)	Visit the countryside and observe the surroundings. Discuss the landscape with your child. For example, you might say, *'It is hilly here but over there, it looks flat.'* Sit on the grass under a tree. Discuss the difference in color between the grass where you are sitting and the grass in the open spaces. Chat about the types of trees that grow and animals that inhabit the countryside. Stand out in the sun for a few minutes and feel the heat. Then, move under a tree and ask your child if they feel cooler. Collect twigs and leaves to use for a collage activity at home. The Nature Craft Projects for Kids book is a helpful resource that can support these activities. If you are near a dam or pond, look out for dragonflies, as this is where they like to live. Keep hold of your child's hand when you are near water. An interesting fact about dragonflies is that one dragonfly can eat hundreds of mosquitoes in a day. While in the countryside, you may also experience the annoyance of the Australian Bush Fly. It tends to buzz around and land on your face and body. These small grey flies with big brown eyes are native to Australia. In Australia, we have the Australian Cork Hat to help deter these flies from bothering us. Examples of possible 'flashcard' words are *hill, grass, sun, hot, dry, twig, leaf, mosquito, dragonfly,* and *fly.*

CODE	DESCRIPTION OF ACTIVITIES FOR TODDLERS
(I, P, SE)	Read the book <u>The Lifecycle of the Butterfly</u> by Bobbie Kalman to your child before you visit a butterfly farm. This book provides useful background knowledge on butterflies.
	Visit a butterfly farm, discuss the colors and sizes of different butterflies with your child. Having read about the life cycle of a butterfly, spend some time searching for butterfly eggs, caterpillars, or chrysalises. If you find butterfly eggs on the underside of a leaf, encourage your child to inspect them closely using a magnifying glass. Take a photo of a butterfly so your child can study it at home. They can use finger paint to recreate the image of the butterfly. Another activity you could try with your child is creating an origami butterfly using an <u>Origami Butterflies Kit</u>. An excellent bedtime story to reinforce this newly acquired knowledge is <u>The Very Hungry Caterpillar</u> by Eric Carle.
	To bring the butterfly experience closer to home, search the Internet for 'food and habitat' plants that attract butterflies to your garden. Check on the availability of these plants at your local nursery. Before planting, consider the specific requirements of the plants, such as full sun, shade, or well-drained soil. These requirements will help you determine the best locations to plant them. Share this information with your child and involve them in the ongoing care of the plant, such as regular watering.
	Buy butterfly charts for your local area. Place a checkmark on the chart next to the pictures of butterflies your child observes in your garden or the local nature reserve. Always call each butterfly by its correct name. For example, you might say, *'There is an orange and black Wanderer butterfly.'* There may be many types of butterflies in your country, but not all of them will be found in your local area. You might look up some country-specific reference books to broaden your child's knowledge and understanding (see, for example, <u>A Naturalist's Guide to the Butterflies of Australia</u>, <u>Familiar Butterflies of North America</u>).
	Examples of possible 'flashcard' words are *butterflies*, *orange*, *eggs*, *caterpillar*, and *chrysalis*.

Note: (I) = Intellectual, (P) = Physical and (SE) = Social-Emotional

CODE	DESCRIPTION OF ACTIVITIES FOR TODDLERS
(I, P, SE)	Look for ladybirds, also referred to as ladybugs, in your garden as these insects are an all-time favorite with children. Do background reading on <u>ladybirds</u> before engaging in this activity with your child. Planting herbs like dill, fennel, and coriander will help attract ladybirds to your garden. Low groundcover herbs like thyme and oregano will also provide the ladybirds with a protective hide-out from predators, such as birds and toads. Ladybirds must live in a well-watered garden as they like to drink frequently. Ladybirds are natural predators. As such, they are an environmentally friendly solution for controlling the damage aphids cause in the garden, mainly to roses. Photograph a ladybird and display the enlarged image on your computer screen. Ask your child questions about the ladybird that will draw their attention to its unique features. For example, you might ask, 'How many spots does it have? Let's count them together. What color is it? How many legs does it have? Let's count them.' This approach will encourage your child to focus on the details. Your main purpose here is to fine-tune their observational skills. As a follow-up activity, help your child draw their version of the ladybird on a sheet of paper. Use the knowledge gained from the discussion and the observation of its features from the image. This interaction may require some targeted prompting to complete the activity. There are around 6,000 species of ladybirds around the world. See if you can find charts documenting at least some of the many species to show your child. Note their differences in size, color, number of spots, and country of origin (see, for example, <u>Guide to Ladybirds of the British Isles</u>). Examples of possible 'flashcard' words are *ladybird*, *bird*, *toad*, *spots*, and *herbs*.
(I, P, SE)	Create three bird charts—one for a suburban garden, another for the beach, and the last for the countryside. In the first instance, take a digital photograph on your mobile phone of at least one bird that your child has seen at each of these locations. Assist your child in pasting the printed photographs onto the corresponding chart representing the area where the birds were observed. Identify and discuss the different species that live in each of these areas. For example, seagulls live by the sea, and crows live in the suburbs and the countryside. Sulphur-crested cockatoos mainly live in the countryside but sometimes in the suburbs. A useful resource to further enhance your child's knowledge on birds is the memory game <u>Match a Pair of Birds</u> published by Laurence King.

CODE	DESCRIPTION OF ACTIVITIES FOR TODDLERS
Continued	Use the photographs to draw your child's attention to the unique features of each bird species. Discuss the comparative size of each species and their unique bird calls. Consider the size and shape of their beaks, the length of their legs, and the shape of their feet. Also, discuss the shape, colors, and texture of their feathers. Encourage your child to ask questions as a mechanism for discovery and to build their knowledge. An example might be, *'Why do some birds have webbed feet?'* Provide your child with a variety of craft materials. Help them create a collage of a bird to consolidate and enhance their knowledge. Prompt your child and help them include a bird's basic features in their collage (for example, beak, wings, and feet). *Interesting fact:* 'Lots of animals, including chimpanzees and orangutans, create useful implements which help them survive in the wild. The New Caledonian crow is one of only two species on the planet that can craft its own hooks in the wild' (Mancini 2020). Examples of possible 'flashcard' words are *crow, seagull, cockatoo, beak, wings,* and *feet*.
(P, I, SE)	Photograph your child while they engage in a variety of activities. For example, these activities may include swimming, hiking, music class, story time at the library, playgroup, beach visits, kite flying, birthday parties, dinner with their grandparents, zoo visits, eating ice cream, cooking with Daddy, washing the car, and taking the dog for a walk. Create a scrapbook with these photos to recall and reflect on each of these experiences. Use the photos to discuss how each experience made your child feel. Examples of possible 'flashcard' words are *swim, hike, music, story,* and *beach*.

Note: (I) = Intellectual, (P) = Physical and (SE) = Social-Emotional

CODE	DESCRIPTION OF ACTIVITIES FOR TODDLERS
(I, SE, P)	Regularly walk and explore your local area with your child to familiarize them with some of the nearby landmarks. These landmarks could include the homes of trusted neighbors, parks, street signs, bus stops, and local shops. If the opportunity arises, chat with these neighbors. These interactions will enable your child to grow their social skills as they model your behavior. Take a bag with you to carry the items your child will collect along the way, like twigs, leaves, feathers, and bark. When you return home, make a collage with their 'finds.' Discuss the detail of the items they have collected. For example, you might highlight shape, texture, weight, smell, and the sound the items make when tapped. Examples of possible 'flashcard' words are *park*, *street*, *sign*, *bus*, and *stop*.
(I, P, SE)	Before undertaking this activity, read your child a beginner's resource book, such as <u>Learning About Insects</u> or <u>The Big Book of Bugs</u>. These books provide basic knowledge about common insects to prepare your child for an insect-finding adventure in your garden or the local nature reserve. Allow your child to wander around the garden or reserve with you close by their side. Encourage them to look for insects like those in the resource book. Try to identify each insect using a magnifying glass and discuss their unique features. Photograph each insect so that you can research and confirm its identity and name when you return home. Print the photos of the insects and write their names in large red letters on the back of each photo. Then, add the printouts to your flashcard collection. Using information from the resource book or other sources, discuss the role played by each insect in its natural environment. For example, spiders and dragonflies eat mosquitos, ladybirds eat aphids, and bees pollinate and make honey. *Interesting fact:* Bees are the only insect that produce food that humans eat. To help consolidate this new knowledge, encourage and guide your child to recreate individual insects using playdough or clay. Examples of possible 'flashcard' words are *insect*, *magnifying*, *glass*, *bee*, *clay*, and *reserve*.

CODE	DESCRIPTION OF ACTIVITIES FOR TODDLERS
(I, P, SE)	Your toddler will now be aware of the different colors in their world. This awareness makes it an ideal time to explore the concept of color further. Young children are attracted to color. The ability to recognize specific colors will be helpful in many everyday situations your child encounters. For example, red is often used as a code for danger, and different colors on traffic lights have specific meanings. Additionally, red and blue are commonly used to indicate hot and cold water taps in bathrooms. Knowledge of colors can also help your child when they describe things to you. Let's begin this activity by introducing the three primary colors: red, yellow, and blue. It is best to introduce these colors to your child one at a time to avoid confusion. Spend the first week focusing on the color red. For example, let them finger paint with red paint, draw with red crayons, play with red playdough, pick and eat red strawberries, pick a red flower, and wear a red piece of clothing. During the second and third weeks, use this same approach to introduce yellow and blue, respectively. During this process, refer to the colors you introduced in previous weeks. For example, during the second week, when the focus is on the color yellow, you may visit the fruit shop to buy yellow bananas. Once your child has found the yellow bananas, you might say, *'Those bananas are yellow. Can you find any other fruit or vegetable that is yellow?'* You can also revisit last week's new learning by saying, *'Oh, look over there. I can see some red strawberries. We learnt about the color red last week, didn't we?'* A valuable resource to support your teaching is <u>Curious George's First Day of School</u>. Examples of possible 'flashcard' words are *red, yellow, blue, traffic, light, danger, stop, hot, go, wait, cold* and *tap*.

Note: (I) = Intellectual, (P) = Physical and (SE) = Social-Emotional

CODE	DESCRIPTION OF ACTIVITIES FOR TODDLERS
(I, P, SE)	Having taught the three primary colors in the previous activity, continue to build on this new knowledge using colored cellophane. Buy red, yellow, and blue cellophane paper and let your child look at their environment through the individual colors. Ask questions about what they can see. How does the cellophane make their environment look? Does it change the color of their environment? What happens if they place blue and yellow cellophane together and look through that? Explore the different combinations and discuss the resulting colors with your child. Give your toddler separate tubs of red, yellow, and blue finger paint to reinforce this new knowledge. Finger painting is always popular with this age group. It is an easy and fun way to experiment with colors. Encourage your toddler to mix colors. Express your curiosity by asking questions like, *'What color do you get when you combine blue and yellow paint?'* Confirm the process and results by saying, *'When you mixed blue and yellow, you created the color green.'* Suggest trying other combinations, such as mixing red and blue, and confirm that the resulting color is purple. Examples of possible 'flashcard' words are *green, tub, mix,* and *purple*.
(I, P, SE)	Purchase some age-appropriate percussion instruments for your child to play, such as castanets, bells, drums, a xylophone, or shakers. These instruments can be sourced online (see, for example, Percussion Instruments for Toddlers (1-3), Musical Instruments for Toddlers, and Xylophones). Ask your child which instrument they would like to play and choose one for yourself. Play some of their favorite music and show them how you play to the beat of the music. Encourage your child to join in. Instructional videos on how to play the individual instruments are available online, for example, How to Play Baby Shark on the Xylophone. Allow your child to enjoy watching shows like the 'Wiggles' for short periods. Encourage them to sing and play along with their instruments (for example, beating the drum and shaking the bell to the beat of the music). To promote some cultural awareness, watch a didgeridoo performance with your child (see, for example, Traditional Didgeridoo Rhythms). Examples of possible 'flashcard' words are *musical, instrument,* and *play*.

CODE	DESCRIPTION OF ACTIVITIES FOR TODDLERS
(I, SE, P)	Take every opportunity to sing your child's favorite songs with them. This approach is particularly effective when they are a captive audience, such as during car rides or bath time. Having a recording of a professional artist performing the song can help ensure that both you and your child stay in tune and on beat. *Interesting fact:* 'All types of singing produce positive psychological effects. The act of singing releases endorphins, the brain's *feel-good* chemicals' (Layton 2009). Examples of possible 'flashcard' words are *sing, beat,* and *melody.*
(P, I, SE)	Dance with your child to recorded music. Provide popular and classical music for your child to listen to, dance to, and enjoy. Talk about how the music makes you feel. For example, you might say, *'Some music makes me happy, and some makes me sad.'* Demonstrate these emotions through facial expressions and movement. Then, ask your child how a specific piece of music makes them feel. You might say, *'Does this music make you happy or sad?'* You can also discuss the music's tempo, pitch, and volume. For example, *'Some music is fast, some is slow, some is high, some is low, some is loud, and some is quiet.'* Give your child a scarf to accentuate their movement while they dance. Since dance styles are closely linked to their origins, make time to watch dances from various cultures with your toddler (see, for example, The Harvey Sisters Irish Dance Performance, Australian Aboriginal Crane Dance). Examples of possible 'flashcard' words are *dance, classical, listen, happy, sad,* and *volume.*
(I, P, SE)	Buy your child some Magnetic Boats for the bath. Allow them to experience the push and pull of the magnets through 'free play' with the boats. *Interesting fact:* A freely suspended magnet will always point in a North–South direction, which may be helpful when hiking or camping with your child. Examples of possible 'flashcard' words are *magnet, boat, hike, camp, north,* and *south.*

Note: (I) = Intellectual, (P) = Physical and (SE) = Social-Emotional

CODE	DESCRIPTION OF ACTIVITIES FOR TODDLERS
(P, I, SE)	Buy a hammering toy, such as a <u>Pounding Bench</u> with colored wooden pegs and a wooden hammer. Encourage your child to experiment with hammering. Point out the color of the pegs they are hammering. For example, you might say, *'Oh, you are hammering the red peg and now the blue peg.'* Take every opportunity to remind them of the colors they have recently learned. Examples of possible 'flashcard' words are *hammer, peg,* and *wooden*.
(P, I, SE)	Once your child is steady on their feet, encourage them to play with a <u>push-toy</u>. These toys often produce different sounds, so take the opportunity to discuss the sounds together. You can also count the number of wheels on the toy. Ask your child to find something else with wheels in the house or garage. Discuss the texture and color of these wheels. Count out loud the number of wheels on each of their discoveries. For example, *'The bike has two wheels, and the tricycle has three wheels. The car has four wheels, and the lawnmower has four wheels.'* Examples of possible 'flashcard' words are *wheels, round, black, roll, two, three, four, lawnmower, bike, tricycle,* and *car*.
(P, I, SE)	Set up an obstacle course for your child inside or outside your home. Encourage them to climb over obstacles like logs or poufs and crawl through <u>tunnels</u>. Guide them to walk around trees or furniture and climb up and down hills or stairs. Always use descriptive language for their actions to inform and enrich their vocabulary. Examples of possible 'flashcard' words are *obstacle, log, crawl, tunnel,* and *climb*.
(P, SE, I)	Buy reusable silicone <u>water balloons</u> and fill them with water. Demonstrate throwing and catching the ballons with another adult in the yard while your toddler observes. Miss some of the catches and allow the balloons to hit the ground. Show your enjoyment when the water splashes everywhere. Now, have your toddler throw a water balloon towards you. Catch it, if possible, and throw it back to them. They will love this activity, particularly on a hot day. If you are teaching your child a specific color (for example, red), use only red balloons to reinforce their learning. Examples of possible 'flashcard' words are *balloon, water, toss,* and *catch*.

CODE	DESCRIPTION OF ACTIVITIES FOR TODDLERS
(P, I, SE)	Buy a Bubble Blowing Toy. Blow bubbles with your child in the bath or outside in the garden. If there is a breeze, discuss what is happening to the bubbles as they float on the breeze. Talk about what the sunlight does to the surface of each bubble. For example, you could draw their attention to the rainbow colors on the surface of the bubbles. Discuss what happens when the bubble lands on an object or the ground. Talk about the sizes of the bubbles they blow. You might say, *'Are all the bubbles the same size?'* Examples of possible 'flashcard' words are *bubble, blow, breeze,* and *float*.
(P, I, SE)	Make a simple Garbage Bag Kite with your child. Outline the steps involved in making the kite and assist them in following the instructions. Take your kite to the beach on a windy day to test it. Explain that the beach is usually windy and perfect for kite flying. It is unrealistic to expect your toddler to launch the kite themselves due to their small stature. However, you can demonstrate the process by running into the wind to generate enough updraft for launching. Afterward, allow them to try it themselves. If they are unsuccessful, explain why it may not be possible at their age. After launching, let your child enjoy holding the string and controlling the kite while it flies high in the sky. As a follow-up activity, your child may enjoy the Kite Coloring Book for Kids, a fun and creative coloring book for two to eight-year-olds. Examples of possible 'flashcard' words are *kite, wind, string, sky,* and *high*.
(I, P, SE)	Demonstrate how to play games with balls and encourage your toddler's efforts. Initially, use a variety of textured balls of different sizes that are easy to handle and light in weight. Sit on the floor or ground and roll these balls to each other. Discuss the size, color, and texture of all the balls you use. Allow your child to hold the balls while you point out and discuss these characteristics. As their eye–hand coordination and dexterity improve, reduce the size of the ball and increase the difficulty of the game. For example, consider using soft foam balls and plastic bats for cricket and baseball. Small Velcro balls can be used for throwing at a felt dartboard, or plastic balls and pins used for ten-pin bowling. Use these games to reinforce your child's counting skills. For example, have them count the number of balls that stick to the dartboard. Also, have them count the number of bowling pins they knock over, as well as those still standing after their turn.

Note: (I) = Intellectual, (P) = Physical and (SE) = Social-Emotional

CODE	DESCRIPTION OF ACTIVITIES FOR TODDLERS
Continued	Discuss the distance your child can throw each ball. Some balls will be easier to throw than others. Discuss why that could be. For example, larger balls are more cumbersome and challenging to throw. They require two hands to hold and throw them. Smaller balls with some weight, such as tennis balls, can be thrown longer distances. Remind your child that gravity causes the balls to fall to the ground. Reinforce this observation without going into the science. Families enjoy popular games like these because they involve and entertain everyone. These games offer opportunities for your toddler to observe sharing in action. Examples of possible 'flashcard' words are *ball, bumpy, furry, rough, big, small, heavy, light, throw, catch, pin, bowl, dart, board,* and *Velcro*.
(P, I, SE)	If your local park has a creek running through it, take the opportunity to enjoy some 'twig' races with your child. You will hopefully find a variety of twigs of different sizes scattered on the ground to select from. Choose a starting point for the race. Hold your child's hand securely while tossing your twigs into the flowing water. Watch and follow the twigs as they float downstream. Some twigs will get caught on rocks or tree roots, while others will flow more freely and travel longer distances. When the twigs finally come to rest, measure the distance traveled by each twig. Count, out loud, the number of paces your child takes from where they launched their twig to where it ended up. Then, ask them to count the number of paces your twig traveled. Compare the number of paces traveled by each of the twigs. Continue providing commentary to ensure that, once again, your child hears descriptive language that explains their experience and observations. Bark also makes an excellent 'boat.' During their visit to the park, your child will observe the surrounding environment. They will notice the abundance of green and brown flora, including grass, leaves, twigs, and trees. A follow-up activity at home could involve experimenting with different combinations of red, yellow, or blue finger paint. This activity will help your child create the colors of green and brown. They could then use these colors in a painting that reflects their observations in the park. Examples of possible 'flashcard' words are *park, creek, twig, leaf, brown, green, float, sink, snag, rock, root,* and *water*.

CODE	DESCRIPTION OF ACTIVITIES FOR TODDLERS
(P, I, SE)	Activity boards, such as the Busy Book for Toddlers and the Montessori Wooden Busy Board, offer your child opportunities to be challenged. Boards like these enhance your child's fine motor skills and teach basic life skills through playful activities. They provide various challenges, ranging from easy to difficult, to keep your child engaged and continuously learning. Encourage your child to persevere even when the tasks are challenging. Examples of possible 'flashcard' words are *buckle, zipper, elastic,* and *shoelace*.
(I, SE, P)	Most of us find a cold popsicle refreshing on a hot day. Creating delicious homemade popsicles is a quick and easy activity. This activity allows your child to make decisions and participate in the preparation process. They can then enjoy the satisfaction of experiencing the results of their efforts. Cold popsicles also soothe sore gums when your child is teething. To prepare for this activity, collect Popsicle Molds and the ingredients for popsicles, like freshly squeezed juice, soft fruits, and yogurt. You can create a variety of combinations using these ingredients. For instance, you could mix fresh fruit juice with diced fruit or combine yogurt with mashed fruit. Alternatively, you can use pureed or mashed fruit or fresh fruit juice. Involve your child in the decision-making. These decisions could involve the preparation of ingredients and their selection of the ingredients to combine. My children's favorite was Greek yogurt mixed with mashed mango and banana. Encourage your child to pour or spoon their choice of ingredients into the popsicle molds. Position the popsicle sticks in the molds and place the popsicles in the freezer until frozen. To remove the popsicle from the mold, dip the mold in warm water and gently remove the popsicle. Examples of possible 'flashcard' words are *popsicle, freeze, juice, fruit, yogurt, mash,* and *puree*.

Note: (I) = Intellectual, (P) = Physical and (SE) = Social-Emotional

EARLY CHILDHOOD | WHERE THE MAGIC HAPPENS

CODE	DESCRIPTION OF ACTIVITIES FOR TODDLERS
(SE, I, P)	Cooking is an excellent way to introduce your child to the unique cuisines of various cultures from around the world. As a simple example, you could prepare a pizza, which is a popular Italian meal. Encourage your toddler to actively participate in preparing the pizza by selecting and arranging their favorite toppings. You could also play Italian music while you cook to create a more immersive experience (see, for example, Italian Music—Background Chill Out). Examples of possible 'flashcard' words are *pizza*, *salami*, *cheese*, and *olives*.
(SE, I, P)	Read books to your toddler that discuss and promote cultural diversity as an effective way to highlight the value of diversity and inclusion. Examples of books are What If We Were All The Same! and This Is How We Do It. Examples of possible 'flashcard' words are *same* and *different*.
(P, SE, I)	Your toddler will enjoy helping you with everyday household chores, such as sweeping and filling the dog's water bowl. They can also carry placemats to the dinner table and help water the garden. Build your toddler's skills by gradually involving them in simple tasks. These might include flushing the toilet after they have used it or turning the pages of a book while you read to them. Regular involvement in chores and tasks will build skills and eventually lead to greater independence. Examples of possible 'flashcard' words are *sweeping*, *water*, *bowl*, *placemats*, *dinner*, *table*, and *garden*.

TIPS FOR PARENTS OF TODDLERS

We are all aware of the emotional struggles that toddlers experience as part of their developmental growth. These struggles can often be overwhelming and leave your toddler upset and frustrated. From a development perspective, their focus is on themselves rather than the needs of others. This natural preoccupation can create tension in their daily routines and requires careful handling. As parents, navigating this period will be challenging and require patience and understanding.

In this section, I will outline three common challenges that parents of toddlers may encounter, along with strategies for effectively addressing them. Many parents find it difficult to manage these issues due to a limited understanding of their toddler's developmental abilities. This gap in knowledge can result in setting unrealistic expectations.

Society often expects toddlers to be 'well-behaved,' but child development experts view this as unrealistic. Toddlers generally achieve such outcomes only when they reach the appropriate developmental stage and are receptive to their parents' expectations. However, parents must appreciate their toddler's ability to meet their expectations. They must also be realistic in their attempts to nurture acceptable behaviors. A toddler will primarily learn these behaviors by observing and imitating their parents.

The first issue focuses on how parents can use positive discipline to achieve 'acceptable behaviors.' To discipline means to teach. As a parent, your responsibility is to guide your child in learning the fundamental behaviors valued by your family and society. These behaviors are crucial for both safety and social acceptance.

Parents can achieve success by ensuring their communication with their toddlers is measured. For example, threatening or yelling at your child is damaging and not helpful. It will cause your child to comply through fear and negatively impact their ability to develop healthy self-discipline.

Suggestions for acceptable behaviors need to be encouraged and integrated into your toddler's daily life. Sometimes, you must suggest age-appropriate consequences if your toddler misbehaves. This approach should provide additional motivation for them to behave in an acceptable manner. For example, if your toddler hits the family dog, immediately stop them. Explain that this behavior is unacceptable because it hurts and frightens the dog. To ensure the dog's safety and comfort, supervise your toddler closely. Let them know that you will hold their hand while they pat the dog and learn how to interact gently.

Furthermore, parents should take every opportunity to reinforce good manners as an essential part of their toddler's daily routine. Good manners are a core feature of acceptable behavior. They reflect polite societal conduct and foster positive relationships and enjoyable interactions. With your guidance and encouragement, good manners will develop over time and evolve into genuine behaviors that reflect gratitude and respect.

In the section, 'Positive Discipline for Toddlers,' I have provided simple strategies and suggestions to help shape your child's behavior. However, it will take time to establish the desired behaviors. The process requires your patience and frequent gentle reminders. Your approach to discipline is just as important as your decision to discipline. If you show frustration in response to your toddler's inappropriate behavior, it is important to take a step back. Give yourself a moment to calm down before addressing the situation. The key to positive discipline is to remain unruffled. Communicate calmly with your toddler about what is acceptable behavior and what is not.

The second issue concerns sharing and how parents introduce this concept to their toddlers. Toddlers need help comprehending this concept. While an ability to share is fundamental to healthy social-emotional development, a toddler's focus is primarily on their feelings, wants, and needs. They are not ready to consider the social-emotional dynamics of sharing, like cooperation, patience, and empathy. With this in mind, I have outlined strategies to assist parents in managing situations where the expectation for toddlers to share may not be realistic.

POSITIVE DISCIPLINE FOR TODDLERS

> *'Too often we forget that discipline really means to teach not to punish. A disciple is a student, not a recipient of behavioral consequences.'*
>
> Daniel J. Siegel

The third issue addresses the minor accidents and injuries that can occur every day in the life of a toddler. How a parent responds to these mishaps will have a lasting impact on their toddler. It will also affect how their toddler interacts with others. I will explain why actively acknowledging and addressing your toddler's mishaps will benefit their overall development. As a parent, you need to understand your toddler's behavioral capabilities at each stage of their development. This insight will help you establish realistic expectations and give you the confidence to guide them effectively.

Why do we need to discipline? The goal is to help your toddler learn and understand the rules for acceptable behavior and how to manage their frustration. This understanding will reduce the likelihood of tantrums and potential meltdowns. Positive discipline is necessary and beneficial for your toddler's happiness and well-being and is fundamental for healthy child development. With consistent discipline, your toddler will learn about acceptable behavior, self-control, and the consequences of, and responsibility for, their actions.

Given that discipline means to teach, I have outlined simple strategies to support your teaching efforts. These strategies are:

- Model acceptable behaviors as young children will usually do as you do, not as you say.

- Be consistent in your approach to discipline. 'Let your yes be yes and your no be no. Children need to know the boundaries and to know that these are set—it makes them feel safe' (Colab.thekids.org.au 2024).

- A well-structured routine goes a long way towards avoiding toddler frustrations. A routine gives them certainty about what to expect next. Children find a predictable structure to their day comforting and relaxing.

- Gentle reminders are helpful when your toddler is unsure or maybe testing the boundaries and exhibiting unacceptable behaviors. For example, if your toddler is screaming in the house, a gentle reminder of … *'Let's use our inside voices while indoors'* may suffice. Similarly, when you see them throwing balls inside the home, you could comment, *'I can see you are keen to throw your ball. Let's go outside. Outside is where Mommy and Daddy prefer you to play ball games.'*

- Providing choices is also an effective strategy. Toddlers like to dress themselves; however, their choice of clothing is often inappropriate for the weather conditions or occasion.

To avoid upset, provide your toddler with appropriate options. For example, *'Would you like to wear your red or blue jacket?'* This approach will allow your toddler to feel in control even though you are guiding their decision.

- If your toddler is having a meltdown and lying on the floor screaming, get down to their level and hug them. Show them that you care and are there to support them. When they have settled, determine what has caused the upset. Talk through how it made them feel and discuss a practical solution that deals with the issue. Everything is new and sometimes overwhelming for your toddler, particularly if they are tired, hungry, or anxious. When you provide them with support and assistance, the issue will be resolved more quickly. Remember, your toddler constantly learns new problem-solving skills with your guidance.

- As your toddler's development progresses, modify their behavior gradually. Offer more detailed explanations of what constitutes acceptable and unacceptable behavior. Emphasize the behaviors you and society value. Give them opportunities to behave appropriately in various settings. These settings might include outdoors, indoors, parties, restaurants, libraries, music classes, kinder-gym, and playgroups.

   To prepare your toddler for these occasions and outings remind them of the expected social behaviors. For example, they should speak softly in a library or church, use a louder voice when singing at playgroup, and cheer at a sporting event. Praise your toddler for following these instructions. Praise the desired behavior, as this will build their self-esteem and reinforce their understanding of what is acceptable. Remember, your toddler wants to please you. Gently guide them and tailor your suggestions to accommodate their stage of development and the circumstances at hand.

An interesting book on discipline is <u>Positive Discipline: The First Three Years</u> by Nelsen, Erwin, and Duffy (2015). This book provides guidance on setting effective boundaries, forging strong foundations for healthy communication, and laying the groundwork for a happy, respectful relationship with your toddler. Another helpful book is <u>Peaceful Parent, Happy Kids: How to Stop Yelling and Start Connecting</u> by Laura Markham (2012). Her aim is to help parents understand their emotions and how to keep them under control to raise a happy, self-disciplined child.

Side note: There will be times when parents may feel disappointed in themselves for responding to their toddler's demanding behavior with impatience or frustration. When this happens (and it will happen), sit close to them and apologize. Your toddler will then understand that even Mommy and Daddy make mistakes. They will also observe how you address those mistakes by apologizing and committing to do better in the future.

SHARING

When my children were toddlers, I kept duplicates of several inexpensive toys for their friends to play with when they visited. For example, I had extra buckets and spades for the sandpit, boats for floating down the creek, and balls for throwing and kicking. The toys were identical in every way, which led to happier play dates. I learned many years later that psychologists agree with this strategy, as toddlers are rarely capable of sharing.

It is generally accepted that children begin to understand the concept of sharing around four years of age. Psychologist Tracy Bentin (firstfiveyears.org.au 2019) explains that children under three years of age typically engage in parallel play. They play alongside each other rather than interacting, as sharing is not yet a concept they understand. Having extra toys available reduces conflicts as it allows each child to play with a toy of their choice. This approach helps to create a more enjoyable and harmonious play experience.

Sharing for a toddler is often an ambiguous concept. Bentin gives a classic example of the confusion we can create when discussing the concept of sharing. She explains, *'If you tell your toddler to share his chips, he may not get them back because someone else may eat them! Therefore, the concept of sharing can be confusing.'* Presenting the concept of 'sharing' as 'taking turns' can help clarify its meaning for your toddler. Toddlers struggle with understanding others' perspectives and grasping the concept of time, which makes sharing more challenging and difficult to navigate.

Before toddlers learn to share, parents must model sharing or taking turns as part of everyday family activities (raisingchildren.net.au 2020a). This modeling reinforces the expectations that you have set for them. Remember, they will watch you closely and eventually model your behavior. Always explain, in a positive way, what you are doing and use the correct terminology to describe your actions. Demonstrate how to take turns with a family member while your toddler observes. Thank the family member for their cooperation.

While playing with your toddler, lead them through the process of taking turns. For example, you might say, *'Let's build a tower. You go first, and then I will have my turn.'* Show your enjoyment and thank your toddler for their willingness to share and 'take turns.' This approach will set the scene and familiarize them with the concept of sharing.

Preparation for situations where sharing is the unspoken expectation

You may find yourself and your toddler in situations where sharing is an unspoken expectation. Adults who may not fully understand child development milestones often set this expectation. This can be awkward and upsetting for you. Child development experts agree that toddlers are rarely capable of sharing. Recognizing this can reassure you and boost your confidence as you continue to teach and nurture the concept of sharing. I have provided examples of strategies to help you. Be sure to explain the concept of 'sharing' as 'taking turns.' This terminology will make your expectations clearer for your toddler to grasp.

Attending the local playgroup

Imagine your two to three-year-old toddler, Alex, is happily playing with a toy at playgroup, spending time exploring it. Then, another toddler, Milly, comes along and wants *that toy*! So, what should you do? You could suggest to Milly that she can have her turn once Alex has finished. Encourage Milly to politely let Alex know she would like a turn when he is done. In the meantime, suggest that Milly plays with a different toy while she waits.

After a reasonable time, encourage Alex to pass the toy to Milly so she can have her turn. Explain to them that the toy will be at the playgroup for a long time. Therefore, they will have plenty of chances to play with it in the future. Approaching the problem in this way will be the first step in teaching the toddlers how to 'take turns' in a group setting.

Remember, you are attempting to guide and familiarize your toddler with this process. If you cannot achieve the desired outcome, you can create a more harmonious solution by distracting your toddler with another toy. In the future, your child will understand the integral role that patience plays in sharing. For now, emphasize that moms and dads also need to practice patience. Provide specific examples from your experience, such as waiting to use the home computer, the shower, or the family car.

Having a friend over for a play date

If your toddler has a friend over to visit, explain that their friend will want to play with their toys. Now that you understand your toddler's difficulty with sharing and taking turns, you will need to adjust your expectations accordingly. Be realistic about how the play date will unfold. For example, plan activities where your toddler and their friends can play side by side without having to take turns. Activities like finger painting, water play, or ball games are great options. A supply of duplicate toys will also help avoid conflict and add to the fun of the occasion.

HOW TO RESPOND TO TODDLER ACCIDENTS AND MISHAPS

I have often wondered why some parents respond to their toddlers with little acknowledgment or empathy when they hurt themselves. They may have assessed the situation and concluded that minimal intervention is needed. Some parents also believe a minimal response will foster a resilient outlook in their toddler.

However, let's take a closer look at what your toddler needs when they experience these mishaps. They can benefit greatly if your response is calm and appropriate. While building resilience is commendable for the longer term, parents must consider other factors. Two primary considerations come to mind:

- The need for your toddler to feel comforted and supported after the shock of a fall, and
- The extent to which your response may enhance their social-emotional development.

During the toddler stage, your child will experience rapid physical growth and may still be unsteady on their feet. Their curiosity will have the energy of a roaring lion and will drive them to explore their world. However, this eagerness is likely to result in numerous spills and mishaps. These accidents will be unavoidable and require your intervention and empathetic support.

When your toddler falls or gets injured, they will naturally be upset. They may also be unsure of how to handle it, as it is a new experience for them. Although their mishaps may cause you to feel anxious, it is important to remain calm. Next, assess the level of support and comfort they need at that moment. For example, ask yourself, *'Does my toddler need help getting up and reassurance that I am here?'* or *'Do they need extra comfort before they can move on?'* Failure to respond in a supportive manner may have detrimental consequences. For example, if they are uncertain of your support after hurting themselves, they may struggle to muster the courage to 'try again.' This attitude will hinder their curiosity and natural inclination to explore and learn.

So, how can a parent safeguard their child's learning experiences in these circumstances? In her book How Toddlers Thrive, Tovah Klein (2020) explains why a parent's response to their toddler's behavior is important. How parents speak to, speak about, and interact with their child holds the key to a happier today and a successful tomorrow. She offers sound advice on how parents should respond promptly in a calm, comforting, and practical manner. This approach helps ensure that their toddler feels secure and well-supported. When parents adopt this approach consistently, it should lead to the following understandings and behavioral outcomes for their toddler:

TODDLER UNDERSTANDINGS	TODDLER BEHAVIORAL OUTCOMES
That their parents will always be there to support them, and they will not be alone.	Your toddler will have the confidence to be curious as they explore their world. As a result, their fear of falling or injuring themselves will not impact their curiosity and learning. They feel secure knowing they are not alone and confident they will be cared for. In their mind, they might think, *'I am okay. My parent is here to take care of me.'*
That their parents will always respond to them with care and understanding.	Empathy is the ability to understand or feel what another person is experiencing. It fosters security and strong relationships while promoting happiness and social harmony. A parent's caring, empathetic response will comfort their toddler and sow the seed of empathy in them.

TODDLER UNDERSTANDINGS	TODDLER BEHAVIORAL OUTCOMES
Continued	As a recipient of your care and kindness, your toddler will unconsciously internalize how your empathetic behavior made them feel supported when they needed comfort. As a result, your toddler will understand the value you place on showing empathy. With your guidance, they will ideally learn to demonstrate empathy toward others. One of the best ways to develop a sense of empathy is by modeling it, just as you have done during this exercise. Reading appropriate books with your toddler is another way to develop a deeper understanding of empathy. Discussing the feelings and actions of their favorite characters can help reinforce these concepts.
That their parents will calmly provide support, which will be proportionate to the injury they have sustained.	Your toddler will take cues from you on how to respond emotionally. They will observe your facial expression and reactions with curiosity, which will influence their emotional response. If your reaction demonstrates anxiety, your toddler's brain will automatically register anxiety and negative emotions rather than comfort and care. So, help them to regulate their emotions by remaining calm. Most accidents will likely elicit a low-key exchange with your toddler, such as: *'Oh, you fell over. Did you hurt your knee? Let me give it a rub. How does that feel now?'* or *'Let's wash the dirt off your knee with soap and put a band-aid on it.'* Sometimes, their injury may be more serious, and you may need to seek appropriate medical assistance. Ultimately, your toddler will observe and model the calm way you respond to their mishaps. Over time, they will be able to gauge the severity of their injury, and the treatment required. It is from these insights and experiences that resilience will grow.

TODDLER UNDERSTANDINGS	TODDLER BEHAVIORAL OUTCOMES
That their parents will guide and teach them how to manage future experiences safely.	Discuss with your toddler the sequence of events that led to their fall so they can appreciate the cause of their injury. Help them understand why they fell and offer practical tips to enable them to manage the activity better in the future. You might say, *'Sometimes it will be necessary for you to walk rather than run, wear appropriate shoes, or have someone hold your hand.'* If the activity is too challenging and outside your toddler's developmental capabilities, explain this to them and give your reasons. At this point, suggest alternative activities that present achievable challenges. With your guidance, your toddler will begin to understand the practicalities involved in physical activities. They will learn how to manage these activities properly in the future. As a result, their strength and agility will develop as they safely engage in these new experiences.

Although a toddler's fall can be distressing, it does present parents with a valuable teaching opportunity to encourage the development of:

- Confidence,
- Empathy,
- Resilience, and
- Practical life skills.

Nurturing these attributes ensures your toddler can self-regulate emotions, demonstrate empathy, and adapt to an ever-changing world. These traits are critical elements for healthy social-emotional and personal development. Parents are best positioned to tailor a response that will reinforce these outcomes. When a parent shows empathy and adopts a calm and practical response, their toddler will pursue future adventures and approach learning with confidence and resilience. Confidence and resilience are critical to a child's overall development.

YOUR PRESCHOOLER

From a developmental perspective, when your child reaches three years of age, they enter the preschool stage. This stage covers the period from ages three to five. During this time, they will mature dramatically and exhibit significant intellectual, social-emotional, and physical growth.

Throughout these early childhood years their world expands, and they become more independent. Their interactions with family and those around them will provide opportunities to shape their character, social behavior, and way of thinking. Your preschooler will constantly want to explore and talk, asking more 'who,' 'what,' 'where' and 'why' questions. This curiosity reflects their fascination with and effort to understand the world around them. I encourage you to take the time to show genuine interest, tune in, and listen carefully. By doing so, you will foster their curiosity and support their learning.

> Years ago, my four-year-old son asked me, 'Where does sound go when it leaves my mouth?' I could not answer him immediately as I didn't know. After delving into the topic that day, we discovered that sound waves do not persist indefinitely, as I had first thought. Instead, we learned that the energy of the sound diminishes as it spreads to more air molecules, causing its effect to fade away. My interest and timely response to his question inspired my son's curiosity. We both gained new knowledge from this experience.

MILESTONES FOR PRESCHOOLERS (3 TO 5 YEARS OF AGE)

This section provides a snapshot of some of the milestones your child should reach during the preschool stage. Once again, it is important to note that they will develop and achieve these milestones at their own pace. If you have any concerns regarding their progress, speak to your doctor or pediatrician.

From ages three to four, your child's intellectual development will become more evident. Their grammar will improve, and they will have a better understanding of the concept of time. They will also start sharing their ideas about story outcomes. Your preschooler will sing songs, memorize and recite poems. They will also be able to state their first and last name. They will use their learning, thinking, and problem-solving skills to understand the concept of 'same and different.' In addition, they will be able to draw a person with two to four body parts and understand basic counting. They can now copy capital letters using a crayon or pencil and participate in board and card games, creating opportunities for enjoyable family activities.

EARLY CHILDHOOD | WHERE THE MAGIC HAPPENS

At this stage, your child will prefer to play with other children than by themselves. They will understand the concept of sharing and taking turns and can now cooperate with other children. They are becoming more adept at resolving disagreements with others, making life a little easier for everyone. Make-believe plays a significant role in their life, and at times they will need your guidance to distinguish between reality and their imagination. For example, unfamiliar images may trigger unreal imaginations. Other social-emotional milestones at this stage include role-playing, such as pretending to be mom and dad. Your child will also start to identify personal interests and show enthusiasm for new experiences.

Preschoolers' physical abilities develop rapidly. They typically refine rudimentary skills such as using scissors, drawing circles and squares, hopping, standing on one foot, and catching a bounced ball. They can now kick balls and throw a ball overarm. At four years of age, your child will demonstrate increased dexterity. They can usually pour liquids and cut and mash their food with supervision.

By five years of age, your child will demonstrate many new competencies. From an intellectual perspective, they will become more confident and love to tell simple stories. Their speech is now clear and easily understood. They demonstrate a basic knowledge of grammar and an understanding of future tense, for example, *'Daddy will be here later.'* By this age, your child will typically know their name and address. They can usually count to 10 and draw geometric shapes like triangles. They will also be able to draw people with at least six body parts and write several letters and numbers. They can now understand basic daily needs, such as food for nourishment and money to buy things.

At this stage, your child's social-emotional development is characterized by a desire to please and be like their friends. They understand obedience and are more likely to agree with the rules. As a result, parents will feel more confident in allowing their children greater independence with appropriate supervision. However, depending on their mood and the situation, your child can be either demanding or cooperative. Another social-emotional milestone you will likely notice is your child's ability to differentiate between reality and make-believe. Creative interests like singing, dancing, and acting are all activities they may enjoy.

Your child's physical development is becoming more fine-tuned as their strength increases. Hopping and standing for 10 seconds or more on one foot is now achievable. Other possible physical activities include somersaults, swinging, climbing, and rhythm and movement routines. They may also be able to gallop and skip, leading with one foot, and begin attempting to catch a ball thrown to them. They are becoming more skilled at using a fork and spoon but still need additional practice with a table knife. They can independently use the toilet, which is timely given their upcoming transition to formal schooling.

More detailed lists of milestones for the three to five-year preschool age group can be found online (see, for example, [CDC Developmental Milestones](), [FFY Development Milestones 3-5 years]()). Parents with concerns about their child's developmental progress should seek advice from a healthcare professional.

ACTIVITIES FOR YOUR PRESCHOOLER

The preschooler activities are designed to build on and make use of your child's:

- Foundational knowledge and skills.
- Ability to communicate.
- Awareness and acceptance of social norms and expectations.
- Physical capabilities and stamina.

As with all planned activities, parents need to be well-informed. Your knowledge will play a crucial role in achieving successful learning outcomes. Therefore, undertaking background research becomes an essential part of the preparation for these activities. This research will ensure you can pass on factually correct answers to your child's questions.

Of course, there will be times when spontaneous activities and situations arise that are sparked by your child's curiosity. On these occasions, you will not have had the time to prepare and may need more information to respond correctly to your child's questions. If you are in this position, admit your lack of knowledge on the topic. Explain to your child that you will need to research the correct information to provide an accurate answer. Do this together so your child will understand how to search for information. The information you provide will serve as the foundation for all future learning on this topic. Therefore, it is important to ensure it is accurate.

Repetition is essential for reinforcing both new and previously learned skills and knowledge. Incorporating repetition into daily routines is easy to do. For example, when teaching the skill of setting the dinner table, use it as an opportunity to practice counting. Ask your child to count:

- How many people in their family will be coming to dinner,
- How many utensils will they need for each person, and
- How many utensils will they need in total. For example, for six people they will need six knives, six forks, six spoons, or twelve chopsticks.

To reinforce these skills, make this activity a daily responsibility for your child.

Parents can also introduce teaching activities for their children at the preschool stage to help cultivate the essential life skills summarized in the Table below. These include how to:

- Problem-solve and make choices,
- Share and take turns,
- Appreciate and accept diversity,
- Use good grammar,
- Ask curious questions,
- Appreciate the need for safety measures and rules,
- Understand sequencing and the concept of time,

- Understand the roles of leading and following,
- Demonstrate good behavior,
- Use polite language, and
- Understand emotions and learn how to manage feelings.

The importance of learning life skills in a child's early years cannot be overstated. The preschool years are ideal for introducing skills that foster independence, confidence, and responsibility. These traits are essential for daily life and becoming self-reliant adults.

Let me explain how easy it is to incorporate some examples of basic life skills into any activity. The following Table shows how to develop and reinforce these skills using a simple cooking activity as the vehicle.

LIFE SKILL	BASIC CONCEPT	PRACTICAL EXAMPLE
How to problem-solve and make choices.	Solving problems and making choices are an integral part of daily life. Parents should allow their children to develop and practice these skills (for example, what clothes to wear, what food to eat, and what games to play). Understanding how to use these skills will build their confidence, lead to more independence, develop their organizational skills, and give them some control over their future.	When preparing and cooking an evening meal, let your child know what is on the menu (for example, steamed fish and vegetables, with fruit for dessert). Outline the nutritional value of the fish and vegetables. Allow your child to choose which vegetables they would like to eat. Point out that different vegetables provide different nutrients. So, encourage your child to choose a variety. Explain that nutritious choices build their body and brain, keep them healthy, and give them the energy to run around each day. Highlight how adults will eat more food than children. Problem-solve together the specific quantities needed for a healthy serving for each person. Once determined, have your child count out the number of vegetables required. Encourage your child to develop problem-solving and decision-making skills as part of their daily routine. For example, explain that baking a cake in the park is impractical due to a lack of appropriate appliances. However, it is achievable in the kitchen, where all necessary equipment is available.

LIFE SKILL	BASIC CONCEPT	PRACTICAL EXAMPLE
How to share and take turns.	Sharing is an essential skill for the social-emotional development of preschoolers. When they develop even the most basic sharing skills, the positive effects on communication and socialization can extend well into the future. Learning to share will help your child form lasting friendships, play cooperatively, negotiate, and cope with disappointment. Sharing also helps teach your child to compromise and be fair-minded. These traits are important considerations when building and maintaining relationships with family, friends, and the broader community.	Your child may want to be involved in preparing the evening meal with you. However, some tasks, such as cutting vegetables with a sharp knife, will be out of the question. You will need to explain why it is risky for them to cut the vegetables. Engage in a discussion to identify a positive and safe way for them to participate. For example, sharing the responsibility and taking turns to mash the potatoes would be a practical alternative. This option can be implemented after you have demonstrated the technique. Sharing and taking turns must also be addressed when your preschooler interacts with other children. These occasions may involve some 'give and take' by the participants. So, provide opportunities for them to appreciate each other's points of view.

LIFE SKILL	BASIC CONCEPT	PRACTICAL EXAMPLE
How to appreciate and accept diversity.	The concept of diversity is broad. It encompasses the acceptance of, and mutual respect for, individuals with qualities and experiences that are different from our own. Your child is now aware of their physical characteristics and those of others. This awareness provides the perfect platform to continue a broader discussion of diversity and the importance of respecting and accepting all people.	Discuss the diversity of the food you intend to serve for the evening meal (for example, fish, vegetables, fruit). Draw attention to the different tastes, colors, shapes, textures, and nutritional value of each food item. Highlight the differences. Emphasize how each type of food contributes to good health and well-being. For example, calcium from fish strengthens bones and teeth, and carrots are good for eye health. Cooking, listening to music, reading, and watching television programs offer opportunities to embrace and promote diversity. These activities can help integrate physical, cultural, and linguistic diversity into everyday life. As a result, your child will become aware and appreciative of the diversity in the world.
How to use good grammar.	Grammar provides the building blocks for your child to express themselves in a more sophisticated manner. Good grammar helps to improve communication skills and convey clear messages.	Speak clearly and use good grammar when conversing with your child while preparing the evening meal. Your child will mimic your manner of speaking. They will also notice that when they talk in a similar way to you, others will understand and listen to them. For example, instead of saying, '*Mommy wants you to come here and mash the potatoes,*' you should say, '*I want you to come here and mash the potatoes.*'

LIFE SKILL	BASIC CONCEPT	PRACTICAL EXAMPLE
How to ask curious questions.	Questions are a mechanism for gathering information for cognitive development. Having the confidence to ask questions is fundamental for learning about life, acquiring new knowledge, and developing new skills. Your child is becoming more aware of the world around them, and their curiosity knows no bounds. Therefore, encourage them to ask questions that focus on the details. Parents can demonstrate their enthusiasm for learning by asking curiosity-driven questions. By doing so, they validate the fundamental role of questions in the learning process.	While preparing the evening meal, offer your child a small piece of raw carrot to crunch on. Ask thought-provoking questions that delve into the characteristics of the carrot. For example, *'Is the carrot crunchy, hard, juicy, and orange in color?'* This approach will motivate your child to ask questions as well. Consequently, they will have their curiosity satisfied and gain a deeper understanding of the subject. During the meal, when they are eating the steamed carrot, question their observations once more. You might say, *'Is the carrot still crunchy, hard, juicy, and orange in color?'* Discuss their answers and identify why particular characteristics of the carrot have changed. For example, steaming alters the texture and color of the carrot. You can follow this process with other meal ingredients, such as fish, potatoes, beans, broccoli, and squash.

LIFE SKILL	BASIC CONCEPT	PRACTICAL EXAMPLE
How to appreciate the need for safety measures and rules.	Safety measures and rules protect children from harm and keep them safe. These rules apply in the home (for example, use of utensils, equipment, and facilities) and in the community (for example, pedestrian and road rules, swimming at the beach, and traveling on public transport).	Preparing and cooking the evening meal offers practical opportunities to teach your child rules about using kitchen utensils and appliances, such as knives or a cooktop. Explain the dangers and risk of injury as you demonstrate how to safely handle and use a sharp knife to prepare the vegetables. Alternatively, you can give your child a Montessori Children's Knife to practice cutting a banana. This option will help them hone the skills required to use a sharper knife when they are older. When using the stove, ensure your child is a safe distance away. Explain the dangers and consequences of a hot gas flame or electric element. Close supervision of your child will always be necessary in the kitchen.

LIFE SKILL	BASIC CONCEPT	PRACTICAL EXAMPLE
How to understand sequencing and the concept of time.	Sequencing allows your child to recognize patterns that make the world more understandable and predictable. It helps them learn about routines and develops skills like reading and comprehension. Being involved with a familiar sequence of routines and schedules will enhance their awareness of time (that is, past, present, and future). Given its finite nature and the constraints it places on everyday life, time also has significant social importance and personal value.	The concepts of sequencing and time will become more apparent to your child when you provide explanations and practical demonstrations. For example, you could show the sequence of tasks for preparing the evening meal. Start by washing the vegetables, peeling them, cutting them into pieces, and finally cooking them. Explain how different vegetables take different amounts of time to cook. Use a clock or timer as an aid to demonstrate this clearly. Vegetables like carrots and potatoes take longer to steam than cauliflower and zucchini. To ensure all items are ready at the same time, you should stagger their cooking times accordingly. Incorporating words like 'first,' 'second,' and 'finally' into daily conversations will help your child grasp the concept of sequencing. Using these terms when discussing everyday activities can reinforce their understanding. Introducing words like 'morning,' 'afternoon,' and 'evening' or 'yesterday,' 'today,' and 'tomorrow' will further clarify their sense of time. These small language cues can enhance their comprehension of the order of events and the progression of time.

LIFE SKILL	BASIC CONCEPT	PRACTICAL EXAMPLE
How to understand the roles of leading and following.	Leading requires the development and use of imagination and communication skills. Learning to follow a leader requires attentive listening and recall of instructions.	After explaining the process and sequence of events for preparing the dinner in detail, your child will be able to lead. Role-playing will enhance this experience, as your child assumes the 'Head Chef' role and gives you instructions to follow. When preparing more complex meals, your child can contribute as part of the family group. They will need to listen carefully, recall, and follow your instructions to complete their tasks successfully. Playing simple social games such as 'Follow the Leader' or 'Simon Says' will reinforce these concepts and build your child's confidence.

LIFE SKILL	BASIC CONCEPT	PRACTICAL EXAMPLE
How to demonstrate good behavior and use polite language.	Good behavior and appropriate language will open doors for social engagements. Everyone will want to spend time and engage with your child if they are well-behaved and easy to be around. As a result, your child will likely receive positive feedback that will reinforce their good behavior and build their confidence and self-esteem.	If your child demonstrates good behavior, ask them to help you prepare the evening meal. Allow them to experience the treat of being invited to help. Your invitation will help them realize that you value spending time with them. Make it clear you are keen to do this activity with them because they are well-behaved and good company. Assign tasks to them that are necessary for the preparation of the meal. Praise your child for their efforts. Tell them how much you enjoy and appreciate spending time with them. Take every opportunity to routinely remind your child that their good behavior translates to happy times spent together. However, if your child displays bad behavior or uses impolite language, it is important not to overreact. Instead, explain why it is unacceptable. Highlight the negative consequences it could lead to, such as no one will want to spend time with them.

LIFE SKILL	BASIC CONCEPT	PRACTICAL EXAMPLE
How to understand emotions and learn how to manage feelings.	When your child can identify and understand their emotions, they will be better equipped to manage and express their feelings in a socially acceptable way. Children who develop these skills are more likely to become competent, confident, and empathetic. This foundation can lead to positive attitudes and behaviors later in life.	Your child may feel 'frustrated' because they are not allowed to cut or slice the vegetables for the evening meal with a sharp knife. Alternatively, they may be 'excited' when you allow them to mash the potatoes. They may not have the vocabulary to identify and express their emotions, such as frustration, fear, anger, nervousness, or excitement. This lack of vocabulary can sometimes lead to inappropriate or problematic behaviors. It is important for your child to recognize and name the emotions they are experiencing. Parents should talk about these emotions with their children and ask how they make them feel. These discussions will help them understand their emotions and those of others. With your guidance, they can learn the skills to manage their feelings in a positive and constructive way. The article, Helping Kids Identify and Express Feelings, posted on the Kids Helpline website, outlines several practical tips on this topic for parents. A helpful resource to complement this learning is the Junior Learning Emotion Dominoes game.

The following Table outlines a variety of activities to enhance your child's knowledge and skills. These activities are aligned with the developmental milestones typically expected of preschoolers. The purpose of these activities is to provide examples of accurate, age-appropriate information relevant to your child's development. This information builds on the foundational knowledge established in earlier years. Each activity is designed to spark deeper curiosity in your child and encourage their desire for new discoveries. The activities also encourage the pursuit of further knowledge. I encourage you to engage enthusiastically in these activities to nurture their interest and maintain their attention.

CODE	DESCRIPTION OF ACTIVITIES FOR PRESCHOOLERS
(I, P, SE)	Prepare and cook meals with your child. Draw attention to the nutritional value of the ingredients. This knowledge will help your child make healthy choices when they need to choose food for themselves. You may like to make Jamie Oliver's fresh pasta recipe. Add your favorite tomato sauce, herbs, and cheese to complete the meal. Involve your child in the cooking process and give them tasks they can manage. Identify the ingredients and remind your child of the country where the recipe for the meal was created—in this case, it would be Italy. Discuss the pleasant aroma of the sauce as it is cooking on the stove. Use a similar approach to introduce cuisine from other cultures, such as sushi, dumplings, or tacos. Examples of possible 'flashcard' words are *Italy, pasta, dough, eggs, flour, tomato, basil,* and *cheese*.
(I, SE, P)	Many countries now have a multicultural population. If you are fortunate to live in such a society, ask your child's friends over for lunch. Suggest they bring along some food to share which is representative of the cuisine from their culture. To enrich this cultural experience, you could play the national anthem of the country where the cuisine originated. For example, you might play the Japanese, Indian, or Papua New Guinean national anthem. While they enjoy the 'potluck' meal, use this opportunity to celebrate the unique aspects of different cultures. Encourage respect and appreciation for this diversity. Other ways of promoting different cultures include: • Attending festivals and events that celebrate other cultures, • Visiting the local library when they hold bilingual days for children, • Reading fairy tales and folklore from cultures around the world, and • Watching movies or TV shows that include characters from culturally diverse backgrounds, such as Sesame Street or Dora the Explorer.

CODE	DESCRIPTION OF ACTIVITIES FOR PRESCHOOLERS
Continued	Examples of possible 'flashcard' words are *Japan (sushi), Mexico (tacos), China (dumplings), India (curry puffs), Australia (Anzac biscuits), England (shepherd's pie),* and *America (cheeseburger).* > *'No one is born hating another person because of the color of his skin or his background or his religion. People must learn to hate, and if they can learn to hate, they can be taught to love. For love comes more naturally to the human heart than its opposite.'* > Nelson Mandela, Long Walk to Freedom
(SE, I, P)	Throughout the year, help your child understand the significance of special holidays and celebrations. These celebrations could include Christmas, Easter, Mother's Day, Father's Day, and family and friends' birthdays. These occasions will foster an appreciation of the important traditions and events in their lives. Your child's developmental stage will determine how much detail you include in your explanations of these events. It will also influence your choice of craft activities to reinforce their understanding. For example, at Easter time, you may like to decorate eggshells after removing the raw contents (see, for example, Blowing Out An Egg and Color the Egg Using Vegetable Dye). Alternatively, you may use craft supplies to create Tie-Dye Easter Eggs. Some simple generic craft activities are Finger Knitting and How to Make a Bookmark. You can easily adapt these activities for special occasions. For example, your child can use their finger-knitting skills to create a personalized bookmark for a birthday gift or craft a Christmas tree decoration. Once again, the activity will depend on the child's stage of development and possibly your religious beliefs. One example of a helpful resource for parents and caregivers is the activity book 365 Things to Make and Do by Fiona Watt.

Note: (I) = Intellectual, (P) = Physical and (SE) = Social-Emotional

CODE	DESCRIPTION OF ACTIVITIES FOR PRESCHOOLERS
Continued	There are also many country-specific holidays which you can highlight that hold significant cultural importance. Craft activities can provide meaning and understanding of the holiday and make it more memorable for your child. Examples of possible 'flashcard' words are *Christmas, Easter, mother, father, birthday,* and *holiday*.
(I, SE, P)	Teach songs that complement special occasions. For example, attend Christmas or Easter services at churches or town halls with your child. These outings will help them develop an understanding and appreciation of the meaning of these occasions. They will also become familiar with the associated music and songs, such as 'In Your Easter Bonnet,' 'Jingle Bells,' and 'Away in a Manger.' Examples of possible 'flashcard' words are *carols, manger, anthem, sing,* and *church*.
(I, P, SE)	Observe the four seasons—summer, autumn/fall, winter, and spring—with your child throughout the year. Each season has distinctive weather patterns uniquely determined by temperature, rainfall, wind, humidity, and air pressure. At the start of a new season, select a good vantage point in your home where your child has a clear view of the outside environment. Draw your child's attention to the unique conditions of each season. Discuss what they can see and ask questions to encourage their observational skills and build their knowledge. For example, you might say, *'Is it windy outside? Is it calm? Is it bright, dull, or dark? Is it cloudy, raining, or sunny?'* A fun poem to read during a thunderstorm is: **Thunder and Lightning** The thunder crashed The lightning flashed And all the world was shaken. The little pig Curled up his tail And ran to save his bacon. Anonymous

CODE	DESCRIPTION OF ACTIVITIES FOR PRESCHOOLERS
Continued	If the weather permits, go outside and experience the conditions. Draw your child's attention to what summer, autumn/fall, winter, and spring look, feel, sound, and smell like. Record the keywords your child uses to describe their observations and add them to their flashcard list. It will be helpful to take some photos and make audio recordings of weather conditions. These aids can be looked at or listened to multiple times to strengthen your child's new learning. A resource that you will find helpful throughout your child's early years is the Montessori Nature Resource. Reinforce your child's newly acquired knowledge with seasonally focused activities. For example, engage in making collages, painting, reading books and poetry, singing songs, or listening to music that reflects the atmosphere of each season. Activities such as listening to Vivaldi's Four Seasons can enhance their appreciation of music and nature. Examples of possible 'flashcard' words are *summer—hot, bright, humid,* and *dry; autumn/fall—colorful, crackling, cool,* and *pretty; winter—cold, rain, snow,* and *wet; spring—flowers, green, warm,* and *happy.*
(I, P, SE)	Demonstrate how to dry petals and leaves. Begin by having your child select the petals and leaves they would like to dry. Talk with them about the color and texture of their choices using descriptive language, such as smooth, bright, colorful, and soft. Place the petals and leaves between the pages of a book to dry. As the petals and leaves dry out, encourage your child to observe the changes in color and feel the changes in texture. Once again, use descriptive words like rough, brittle, faded, or dull when discussing these changes. These words will help your child express their observations more clearly. Once the leaves and petals are dry, they can be used to decorate handmade birthday and get-well cards. These personalized cards will be a thoughtful gift for the special people in their lives. Examples of possible 'flashcard' words are *petals, leaves, dry, color, rough, smooth, brittle, faded,* and *dull.*

Note: (I) = Intellectual, (P) = Physical and (SE) = Social-Emotional

EARLY CHILDHOOD | WHERE THE MAGIC HAPPENS

CODE	DESCRIPTION OF ACTIVITIES FOR PRESCHOOLERS
(I, P, SE)	Caring for a pet goldfish is a low-maintenance, allergy-free activity for young children and can provide a variety of learning opportunities. This activity will require background research so your child can learn how to care for a goldfish. Visit your local pet shop and let your child select a goldfish. Encourage them to take responsibility for feeding and caring for the fish according to the instructions. This long-term project will require your ongoing support and guidance to help your child stay motivated and remain engaged. Examples of possible 'flashcard' words are *goldfish*, *tank*, *water*, and *food*.
(I, P, SE)	Buy and familiarize yourself with a star chart relevant to your location (for example, National Geographic: The Ultimate Guide to the Night Sky). Show your child the stars in the sky and help them locate and name the star patterns using the chart as a reference. Purchase glow-in-the-dark stars and recreate star patterns on your child's bedroom ceiling to reinforce this new knowledge. Begin with familiar constellations, such as The Big Dipper in the Northern Hemisphere or The Southern Cross in the Southern Hemisphere. *Note:* Gazing at the night sky in a rural area, away from the city lights, is an incredible experience. Significantly, more stars are visible to the naked eye in rural areas compared to urban environments. Examples of possible 'flashcard' words are *star*, *sky*, *night*, *big*, *dipper*, *southern*, and *cross*.
(I, SE, P)	As an additional activity, visit an astronomical observatory to view the night sky through a powerful telescope. To reinforce this knowledge, also visit a planetarium, where stars, planets, and constellations are projected onto a dome-shaped ceiling. These experiences will enhance your child's understanding of the night sky. Examples of possible 'flashcard' words are *observatory*, *planetarium*, *telescope*, *astronomy*, *stars*, *planets*, and *constellation*.

CODE	DESCRIPTION OF ACTIVITIES FOR PRESCHOOLERS
(I, P, SE)	Purchase the book <u>Little Kids First Big Book of Space</u> to familiarize your child with the concept of planets. Construct a <u>Sun-Earth-Moon model</u> to demonstrate how their orbits relate to each other in space. For example, the Earth orbits the Sun once a year, while the Moon orbits the Earth once every lunar month. A resource that can promote more conversation on space-themed topics and illustrations is the Laurence King <u>Space Bingo</u> game. Examples of possible 'flashcard' words are *Sun*, *Moon*, and *Earth*.
(I, P, SE)	As an extension activity on planets and space, consider introducing the concept of space travel to enhance understanding and engagement. To become familiar with the topic, watch the movie <u>First Man</u>. This movie relates the story of the historic Apollo 11 mission when man first landed on the Moon. Outline the basic facts of the Apollo 11 mission for your child. Then, as a supporting activity, <u>build a rocket using a cardboard paper roll</u>. Act out the Moon landing with them, repeating the famous words spoken by astronaut Commander Neil Armstrong: *'The Eagle has landed. That's one small step for man, one giant leap for mankind.'* This re-enactment can help them connect with this historic event. When weather permits, and your child is old enough to stay up a little later, show them the moon in the night sky. Examples of possible 'flashcard' words are *rocket*, *planets*, and *astronaut*.
(I, P, SE)	To teach the colors of the rainbow, buy a glass prism and hang it at the window to allow the light to pass through it. Identify the colors that you and your child can see. Explain that these colors are the colors they will see in a rainbow. Use the acronym **Roy G. Biv** to quickly recall the sequence of colors in a rainbow (that is, red, orange, yellow, green, blue, indigo, and violet). When sunlight passes through water, such as a water droplet, it slows down and bends, causing the light to separate into its component colors. When the light exits, the droplet forms a rainbow. Rainbows are most common during summer after a storm. When the storm is over, sit outside with your child and check the sky for a rainbow (see, for example, <u>Rainbow Facts for Kids</u>).

Note: (I) = Intellectual, (P) = Physical and (SE) = Social-Emotional

CODE	DESCRIPTION OF ACTIVITIES FOR PRESCHOOLERS
Continued	As a follow-up activity, show your child a picture of a rainbow. Give them colored pencils to draw their impression of a rainbow on white paper. They can use the picture as a guide to replicate the colors and pattern they see. Then, suggest they use their rainbow creation to make a card for a special person in their life. Examples of possible 'flashcard' words are *prism, rainbow, storm, light,* and *water.*
(I, P, SE)	Finger painting is a creative activity. It allows your child to experiment with color and express themselves. When teaching the concept of colors, adopt a staged approach by initially introducing the three primary colors, red, yellow, and blue, individually. Red, yellow, and blue are called primary colors because they cannot be produced by combining other colors. Start by allowing your child to finger paint using only the red paint. After a day or two when your child can confidently identify the red paint, introduce the yellow paint. Let them paint exclusively with the yellow paint for the next couple of days. When your child can identify the yellow paint, introduce the blue paint in the same way. Once your child can confidently recognize the primary colors, encourage them to experiment by mixing two primary colors to create new secondary colors. For example, mixing red and blue creates purple, yellow and blue make green, and red and yellow combine to form orange. With further experimentation, your child will discover intermediate colors such as brown. To produce brown, mix one of the following combinations: red and green, blue and orange, or yellow and purple. As they experiment, encourage them to identify the colors they create. Explore your home for colored items or natural examples that match the colors they have created. For instance, you might find a green tablecloth, green leaves, a brown table, brown dirt, a purple dress or purple flowers. Examples of possible 'flashcard' words are *red, orange, yellow, green, blue, indigo, violet,* and *brown.*

CODE	DESCRIPTION OF ACTIVITIES FOR PRESCHOOLERS
(I, P, SE)	Buy several large sheets of thin cardboard. Place your child's hand on the cardboard and draw around the perimeter of the hand and fingers with a Texta/marker. Place your hand on the cardboard near the outline of your child's hand and draw around it as well. Draw around the hands of other family members and friends. Direct your child's attention to the different hand sizes on the cardboard. Emphasize that, despite the differences in size, all hands possess the same fundamental abilities. These abilities include performing tasks such as writing, drawing, cooking, feeding, picking up objects, washing themselves, and dressing. Expand this activity by tracing the feet of family and friends and discussing the various sizes of feet. Explain to your child that, although feet size may vary, everyone uses their feet for activities such as walking, running, jumping, hopping, skipping, and climbing. Examples of possible 'flashcard' words are *hand, feet, marker, outline*, and *size*.

The Magic of Music

Over the past 20 years, research has highlighted differences between musicians' and non-musicians' brains and behaviors. For example, Habibi (2016) notes that music training is related to better language and mathematical skills, higher IQ, and greater academic achievement. Also, differences between musicians and non-musicians have been found in areas of the brain related to hearing and movement, among others.

Habibi refers to a 2012 study by the Brain and Creativity Institute at the University of Southern California, examining the impact of group-based music training on child development. The study involved a group of 80 children aged 6 and 7 years. The findings suggest that music training, even for as little as two years, can accelerate brain development and improve the processing of sound.

Note: (I) = Intellectual, (P) = Physical and (SE) = Social-Emotional

CODE	DESCRIPTION OF ACTIVITIES FOR PRESCHOOLERS
(I, SE)	Plan to attend a symphony concert with your child. Before you go, spend some time watching the video George Meets the Orchestra. Event organizers generally hold 'child-friendly' symphony concerts during the school holidays. Time is usually taken at the commencement of these concerts to introduce the orchestral instruments individually. The First Book About the Orchestra is a helpful resource to read together. Examples of possible 'flashcard' words are *instruments, orchestra, conductor, baton, brass, woodwind, strings, percussion, concert,* and *symphony*.
(I, SE)	Play and listen to different genres of music at home, such as classical, pop, rhythm and blues, folk, or electronic. Try to identify the instruments while enjoying the music with your child. Examples of possible 'flashcard' words are *genre, music, classical, pop, rhythm, blues, folk,* and *electronic*.
(I, P, SE)	Making Music with Water is another fun activity to increase your child's musical awareness. Fill several glasses with varying amounts of water. Gently tap each glass with a pencil to hear the distinct tone produced by each one. Ask your child questions to spark their curiosity and help them learn from their observations. For example, you might ask, *'Do all the glasses produce the same sound when tapped? Which glass produces the lowest sound? Which one produces the highest sound? Does each glass contain the same amount of water? Do you need to add more water to your glass to create a higher sound?'* Examples of possible 'flashcard' words are *water, glasses, tap, sound, high,* and *low*.
(I, P, SE)	I encourage you to arrange music lessons for your preschooler, as research has shown that music training supports academic achievement. The well-known Suzuki and Yamaha Music programs are two of the most popular music education programs worldwide. The Suzuki Method is based on the fundamental belief that any child who is properly trained can develop musical ability. Dr. Suzuki's goal is to nurture a child's love and appreciation of music. At the same time, he aims to develop their character and teach them to play a musical instrument proficiently. Suzuki considers parental participation integral to a child's learning and enjoyment.

CODE	DESCRIPTION OF ACTIVITIES FOR PRESCHOOLERS
Continued	Suzuki classes are conducted as group sessions and include teacher-led activities. These activities involve singing, movement, counting, taking turns, and reading. They also explore pitch and rhythm using child-friendly instruments and listening to classical music to teach concepts and develop skills. Suzuki Early Childhood Education programs are available worldwide (for example, in Australia, the United States of America, and the United Kingdom).
	The design of the Yamaha Music program was a collaborative effort involving teachers, doctors, and psychologists. The program aims to uncover a child's musical potential by nurturing their abilities through music-based experiences. It focuses on developing fundamental music skills and cultivating a deep appreciation of music.
	The group classes are non-threatening and explore music through singing, movement, and keyboard use. A parent (or caregiver) is required to attend the class with their child. Two courses that cover the preschool years are Yamaha's Music Wonderland and Junior Music courses. These courses are available in over forty countries, including Australia, the United States of America, and the United Kingdom.
	Examples of possible 'flashcard' words are *music, sing, clap, dance, pitch*, and *listen*.
(P, I, SE)	Parents can introduce various child-friendly instruments to their children, such as a ukulele, harmonica, or drums. Consider selecting a ukulele that suits your child's age and size to engage them in music. This instrument is relatively easy to teach and can be purchased from your local music store. The Wiggles song, 'Ukulele Rock,' features the ukulele and is fun to listen to.
	If your child shows an ongoing interest in playing the ukulele, seek out age-appropriate, local tuition classes. Alternatively, you can keep it simple by buying an inexpensive ukulele tuner and a book on how to play the ukulele. This approach allows you to enjoy the learning experience together and encourage your child's interests.
	Examples of possible 'flashcard' words are *ukulele, harmonica, drums*, and *tuner*.

Note: (I) = Intellectual, (P) = Physical and (SE) = Social-Emotional

CODE	DESCRIPTION OF ACTIVITIES FOR PRESCHOOLERS
(I, P, SE)	Purchase a <u>magnifying glass</u> and use it to closely examine whatever interests or triggers your child's curiosity. Always discuss what they are looking at using descriptive language. Your purpose is to build their vocabulary and knowledge. Allow them to touch and feel the object of their attention unless it is potentially harmful, such as a thorn or spider. Discuss the object while they explore it. Ask them pointed questions to encourage closer examination to help them make detailed discoveries. For example, use the magnifying glass to examine leaves and together discover the veins. Discuss how the veins transport water and minerals from the plant's roots. Explain how they distribute these nutrients throughout the leaf to help it grow. You could then look at the veins in your child's arm. Discuss how the veins transport oxygen and nutrients in the blood to all parts of the body to keep it working efficiently. A fun game to support this learning is <u>Match a Leaf: A Tree Memory Game</u>. Examples of possible 'flashcard' words are *magnify* and *magnifying glass*.
(P, SE, I)	Buy an age-appropriate <u>basketball hoop with an adjustable stand</u> and a <u>basketball</u> for your child to enjoy with family and friends. This activity provides another opportunity to explore the concepts of distance and height, as well as counting (for example, the number of shots that go through the hoop). Examples of possible 'flashcard' words are *basketball*, *ball*, *bounce*, *shoot*, and *goal*.
(I, P, SE)	Buy an <u>Explorer Compass</u> and plan a walk with your child. Mark the starting point in your garden, then follow your written instructions, using the compass to determine the correct direction. You might walk five steps south, eight steps east, four steps north, and ten steps west. It will be fun to see where you end up. Encourage your child to discuss and plan their next walk while you write down their instructions. Examples of possible 'flashcard' words are *compass*, *explore*, *direction*, *north*, *south*, *east*, and *west*.

CODE	DESCRIPTION OF ACTIVITIES FOR PRESCHOOLERS
(I, P, SE)	Lie on your back in your garden or at a nearby park and invite your child to do the same. Spend time together observing and discussing the shapes and patterns of the clouds. For example, you might see the outline of a dog, a cat, a face, or a mountain. Encourage your child to use their imagination to interpret and describe the shapes they observe. Examples of possible 'flashcard' words are *clouds*, *shapes*, and *identify*.
(I, P, SE)	Identify recognizable clouds with your child, such as Cumulus, Cirrus, and Stratus. Discuss the uniqueness of the different types of clouds. Some clouds are full and fluffy, some are wispy, and some look like blankets. Photograph the clouds and draw pictures of them. Purchase a cloud chart with graphics and detailed information to enhance your child's knowledge. When outdoors, point out weather conditions that contribute to different cloud formations. For example, explain that wispy Cirrus clouds form when the weather is windy. Help your child create a collage using cotton wool to depict the different types of clouds they observe in different weather conditions. Poetry is an excellent complement to new learning. For instance, reciting a poem to your child while experiencing windy weather provides enjoyable repetition. *Who Has Seen the Wind?* Who has seen the wind? Neither I nor you But when the leaves hang trembling The wind is passing through Who has seen the wind? Neither you nor I But when the trees bow down their heads The wind is passing by Christina Rossetti The book Wind is a valuable resource for helping your child understand this aspect of weather. Examples of possible 'flashcard' words are *clouds*, *chart*, *cumulus*, *cirrus*, *stratus*, *calm*, and *wind*.

Note: (I) = Intellectual, (P) = Physical and (SE) = Social-Emotional

CODE	DESCRIPTION OF ACTIVITIES FOR PRESCHOOLERS
(I, P, SE)	The best way to learn about weather conditions is to experience them firsthand when it is safe. For example, take a walk in gentle rain with your child. Discuss raindrops with them and explain where they come from. Highlight the different sizes of raindrops, such as large, medium, and small. Explain that each raindrop has dirt at its center. Look at a raindrop's journey. After a rainstorm, discuss the process of evaporation with your child. Together, monitor the outdoor surfaces, such as the pavement, leaves, and grass to observe how wet they are. Note how long it takes for the water to evaporate. Explain that all living things, including people, animals, and plants, need water to survive. After a storm, look for a rainbow together. Sing a song about the rain, such as I Love It When It Rains by The Wiggles. Examples of possible 'flashcard' words are *rain, dirt*, and *evaporate*.
(I, SE)	Visit your local Bureau of Meteorology to enhance your child's understanding of the weather. Call ahead to enquire about arranging a visit and conversation with a staff member. Encourage your child to come up with a question about something they are curious to learn more about. Offer suggestions if they are having difficulty. For example: *'Why are some raindrops big and others small? Why does it get windy? Why do we have hailstorms?'* Examples of possible 'flashcard' words are *raindrop, windy*, and *hailstorm*.
(I, P, SE)	Encourage your child's curiosity about where their food, clothes, and belongings come from. For example: **Honey from bees**—Read books from the local library. One example might be Explore My World: Honey Bees. Or perhaps find a video that shows how bees collect nectar and convert it to honey. A local farmers' market, an agricultural high school, or a beekeeper may have honeycomb available for purchase. **Milk from cows**—Visit a dairy farm, hopefully at milking time. Let your child see how cream rises to the top of the bucket of milk. Buy or borrow the book Milk from Cow to Carton. This book explains the 'journey' of milk from the cow to a cool glass of milk on the table. Buy some cream and show your child how to make homemade butter.

CODE	DESCRIPTION OF ACTIVITIES FOR PRESCHOOLERS
Continued	**Water from rain**—Place empty buckets in the garden to measure how much water is collected during a rainstorm. After the storm, have your child check the buckets with you. This observation will give them a sense of how much rain has fallen. Visit places where water gathers, such as a dam, creek, pond, river, or the sea. Make a rain gauge and place it in your garden where your child can easily view it. Check the gauge with them after it has rained. Discuss how much rain has fallen in the previous 24 hours. **Glass from sand**—To learn about glassmaking and glassblowing techniques, watch a video on glassmaking as part of your preparation and research. Glass is made from ordinary sand. The sand is heated at a very high temperature until it melts and becomes liquid. As the liquid glass cools, it becomes malleable, allowing it to be shaped and colored into decorative and practical items. Look at all the glass items you have in your home. Explain to your child that glass, when first formed, is 'clear' and does not have a color. Look around your home and identify items made from clear and colored glass. If possible, take your child to a glassblowing demonstration. Take notice of the process used to add color to the glass. Glassblowers can mold glass into beautiful items. In Seattle, Washington, USA, there is a famous glass museum called Chihuly Garden and Glass. Here are some examples of Chihuly Glass Creations. **Tomatoes from seeds**—Grow, harvest, and use them in your salad or Bolognese sauce. Show your child how to save and prepare tomato seeds for growing in the springtime. You will need additional information on how a seed develops into a plant to answer your child's questions and successfully grow tomato plants. **Wool from sheep**—Sheep are a primary source of wool. Take your child on a farm excursion during the shearing season to observe how farmers shear sheep and prepare the raw wool for sale. As a follow-up activity, visit your local hand-weaving and spinning group. Watch the process of spinning raw wool into balls of yarn. The group may have items on display, such as jumpers, socks, or rugs they have created from previously spun yarn.

Note: (I) = Intellectual, (P) = Physical and (SE) = Social-Emotional

CODE	DESCRIPTION OF ACTIVITIES FOR PRESCHOOLERS
Continued	Discuss with your child how to transform the yarn into one of these items. Teach your child how to make creations with yarn. These creations could include DIY Pom Poms or other imaginative items using the Montessori finger knitting technique. Explore the local library or conduct an online search to find information on the origins of the various items of interest identified by your child. This information will support your child's learning, understanding, and knowledge development. Examples of possible 'flashcard' words are *glass, water, milk, honey, tomatoes,* and *wool*.
(I, SE)	I encourage you to read poetry to your child. For example, a collection of modern children's poetry can be found in the books 101 Poems for Children: A Laureate's Choice by Carol Ann Duffy and When We Were Very Young - a compilation of poems by A. A. Milne. This activity helps children develop their memory and encourages them to play with language and words. Examples of possible 'flashcard' words are *poem* and *poetry*.
(I, P, SE)	Buy magnets and magnetic toys to support interactive and educational activities at home. The book What Makes A Magnet? by Dr. Franklyn Branley provides simple instructions on how to make a magnet. Discuss and identify a magnet's North and South poles and show your child how opposite poles attract each other. Let your child try to join the two North or South poles together. Discuss the 'push and pull' exhibited by the magnets. The book What are Magnets?, published by Baby Professor, will help your child better understand this topic. Examples of possible 'flashcard' words are *magnet, pole, north,* and *south*.
(I, P, SE)	Introduce fractions by cutting fruit into halves, quarters, and eighths. Also demonstrate this technique when cutting string beans, sandwiches or any other items that require cutting. Always talk through what you are doing. For example, *'I am cutting this banana in half.'* Encourage your child to break the banana in half or quarters to share. Have a reason for the request, such as *'Please give your sister half of the banana.'* Examples of possible 'flashcard' words are *fractions, half, quarter,* and *eighth*.

CHAPTER 4 | CHILD DEVELOPMENT 'PLEASE EXPLAIN'

CODE	DESCRIPTION OF ACTIVITIES FOR PRESCHOOLERS
(I, P, SE)	When introducing something new to your child, aim for a location or venue with the best real-life experience. For example, visit a zoo or farm to learn about animals, an art gallery to explore art, or the beach to understand the sea. These experiences are highly effective when learning something new. Examples of possible 'flashcard' words are *zoo, art, gallery,* and *beach.*
(I, SE, P)	To introduce your child to the concept of history, visit a museum. There, they can explore exhibits featuring people, animals, artifacts, and cultural displays from the past. To help your child understand the historical timescale, explain that the exhibits on display are much older than their grandparents. This comparison will give them a clearer sense of the age of the items. The book <u>Beginnings and Endings with Lifetimes in Between</u> is a valuable resource for parents wanting to explain the concept of life and death to their children. This new knowledge will make your explanations of the museum exhibits more understandable. Examples of possible 'flashcard' words are *museum, old, artifacts,* and *history.*
(I, P, SE)	To introduce your child to science and engineering concepts, purchase an age-appropriate science activity book, such as the <u>Smithsonian 10-Minute Science Experiments</u> by Steve Spangler. This book introduces your child to the fundamentals of science, physics, chemistry, and engineering through simple, hands-on experiments. To further develop their interest, attend Interactive Science Fairs and Exhibition events in your country with your child (for example, <u>Science Alive</u> - Australia, <u>Science Kinetics</u> - USA, and <u>Spectacular Science Days Out in the UK</u> - UK). Examples of possible 'flashcard' words are *science* and *experiment.*
(I, P, SE)	A couple of simple experiments: Fill a clear glass vase with water and have your child choose a food coloring to tint it. Place a white <u>lily</u> in the vase. Let your child observe the lily's petals changing color over the next few days to 'match' the tinted water in the vase. This experiment demonstrates that flowers 'drink' and absorb water just as we do.

Note: (I) = Intellectual, (P) = Physical and (SE) = Social-Emotional

CODE	DESCRIPTION OF ACTIVITIES FOR PRESCHOOLERS
Continued	You could also do a simple floating and sinking experiment in the bath. Most bath toys float, so provide some items that won't float, like a spoon, a cake of soap, or a washer. Chat with your child about these items. In the first instance, let them experiment to find out what floats and sinks. The following day, you could draw pictures of the items that floated and those that sank. Ask your child questions about both experiments and discuss what they have noticed. Your intent here is to improve their observational skills. Borrow a book from the library or do your own research to explain the results they have observed. Examples of possible 'flashcard' words are *lily, vase, coloring, absorb, float, sink,* and *food*.
(I, P, SE)	Place a blindfold on your child and let them touch your face and the faces of various family members. Give them time to work out whose face they are touching. Ask leading questions to get them thinking. Encourage them to verbalize what they are feeling. For example, you might ask, *'Does that feel like Daddy's spikey beard or Mommy's soft, long hair?'* Examples of possible 'flashcard' words are *blindfold, touch, face, smooth, soft, spikey,* and *beard*.
(I, SE)	Promote an appreciation of time by giving your child a cardboard or plastic <u>clock face</u>. Initially, let them play with the clock hands and then teach them the numbers on the clock face. Once your child is familiar with the numbers, use daily activities scheduled at specific times to help teach them how to tell the time. The daily activities of breakfast, lunch, and dinner highlight the passage of time and offer context for this new information. If you start with breakfast time, set the clock hands to indicate when you usually eat breakfast. For example, if you typically have breakfast at 7am, position the clock hands to reflect that time. Show the clock to your child and explain, *'It is 7 o'clock in the morning, time for breakfast.'*

CODE	DESCRIPTION OF ACTIVITIES FOR PRESCHOOLERS
Continued	Repeat this activity each morning when you call your child for breakfast. Once they are familiar with the clock showing 7 o'clock, with the little hand on 7 and the big hand on 12, you can introduce other times. For example, at noon, you might say, *'It is now 12 o'clock, time for lunch.'* Review the specific times you have taught each day to reinforce your child's learning. With regular practice, your child will soon start telling you the time. Examples of possible 'flashcard' words are *breakfast, lunch, dinner, time, hands,* and *clock*.
(I, SE)	Start each day of the week by mentioning what day it is. *'Good morning, Millicent. It is Monday today. Let's think about what we usually do on Mondays.'* Jog their memory if they struggle to remember the regular activity for that day. For example, you might say, *'On Mondays, we go to playgroup. You will see your good friend Chloe there.'* With enough repetition, your child will easily recall this information. Make a habit of singing The Days of the Week often with your child. Examples of possible 'flashcard' words are *Monday, Tuesday, Wednesday, Thursday, Friday, Saturday,* and *Sunday*.
(I, SE, P)	Buy a wall calendar and turn to the page which displays the current month of the year. Discuss the number of days in the current month. Explain that not all months have the same number of days. The number of days will range from 28 to 31, depending on the month and the year. Count the days in the current month with them. Write the number of days at the bottom of the page for each month for easy reference. Once your child understands that there are 12 months in a year, you can teach them the following familiar rhyme: The Days of the Month 30 days has September, April, June, and November. All the rest have 31, except February, which has 28 days and 29 days each leap year.

Note: (I) = Intellectual, (P) = Physical and (SE) = Social-Emotional

CODE	DESCRIPTION OF ACTIVITIES FOR PRESCHOOLERS
Continued	If Daddy's birthday is in March, place a small headshot of him on the calendar on the date of his birthday. Discuss this with your child. For example, you might say, *'It is Daddy's birthday on the 31st of March, so we will need to bake his birthday cake on the 30th of March.'* Your child will enjoy assisting with birthday preparations, such as icing and decorating the cake and setting the table with party hats. They can also help select and wrap presents. These activities are also practical examples of how they can express love and care for others. Examples of possible 'flashcard' words are *January, February, March, April, May, June, July, August, September, October, November,* and *December*.
(P, I, SE)	Take a break from your everyday routine and organize a 'farm stay' experience to give your child (and you) a taste of country life. Farm activities may include feeding the animals, milking a cow, riding a pony, and collecting warm eggs from the chicken coop. Your child may also be able to pick fruit and vegetables and learn about a farmer's daily routine. If possible, prepare a meal using fresh produce from the farm, such as eggs, tomatoes, and oranges. Begin by cracking an egg into a cup and showing your child the raw egg. Encourage them to feel its texture as it slips through their fingers. Use descriptive language to help them articulate the experience, such as 'slimy,' 'slippery,' and 'gooey.' Next, crack open another egg to use for cooking. Explain how heating the egg in a frying pan causes it to firm up. Allow your child to safely observe the cooking process from a distance, noting the changes in color and texture as the egg cooks. Finally, serve the fried egg alongside fresh tomatoes, buttered toast, and a glass of freshly squeezed orange juice for a tasty breakfast. Examples of possible 'flashcard' words are *farm, animals, cows, hen, egg, slimy, slippery, gooey, rooster, pony, tomato, orange, toast, butter,* and *juice*.

CODE	DESCRIPTION OF ACTIVITIES FOR PRESCHOOLERS
(P, I, SE)	Visit a strawberry farm. Organize this activity in late summer, as strawberries need the summer heat to grow well. Picking strawberries is an easy and enjoyable activity for your child. Aside from humans, talk about the various creatures that enjoy eating strawberries. These include squirrels, possums, raccoons, birds, insects, deer, rabbits, marmots, tortoises, turtles, hamsters, and guinea pigs. If you have the opportunity, ask the strawberry grower to explain how they prevent these creatures from destroying their crop. Explain to your child that ripe strawberries are soft and sweet. They need to be handled gently to avoid bruising them. When you return home, discuss ways to prepare strawberries for eating or drinking. With your child's assistance, you could: <ul><li>Make a strawberry milkshake,</li><li>Add strawberries to a fruit salad,</li><li>Puree strawberries and add the puree to a small tub of cream cheese to create a delicious dip,</li><li>Dry your strawberries in the oven and create strawberry chips,</li><li>Make ice blocks by pureeing your strawberries and placing the puree in popsicle molds for freezing,</li><li>Make Strawberry Santas for Christmas, and</li><li>Make strawberry jam to have with scones and cream.</li></ul>Examples of possible 'flashcard' words are *strawberry, milkshake, dip, scones, cream,* and *ice block*.
(P, I, SE)	Teach your child simple gardening skills. A helpful book for this activity, published by Dorling Kindersley, is Let's Get Gardening. This book will help your child understand the concepts of sustainability, recycling, and conservation. It will also motivate your child to spend time outdoors learning about plants and wildlife. Provide your child with a hat, gardening tools, gloves, and footwear for use in the garden. Examples of possible 'flashcard' words are *gardening, hat, tools, gloves, boots, plants,* and *recycling*.

Note: (I) = Intellectual, (P) = Physical and (SE) = Social-Emotional

CODE	DESCRIPTION OF ACTIVITIES FOR PRESCHOOLERS
(I, P, SE)	Help your child set up a crop rotation project in your garden. This project will teach them which plants thrive during different seasons of the year. It will also help them understand the types of soil required, such as acidic or alkaline soil. The project will also teach them the importance of Companion Planting for managing pests. Growing and harvesting their vegetables will also give them great satisfaction. The article Crop Rotation from Academic Kids offers fundamental information to help you and your child get started. Examples of possible 'flashcard' words are *soil, crop,* and *harvest*.
(I, P, SE)	Visit an organic community garden in your local area where your child can see lots of insects at work. Talk to the gardeners to learn how they attract beneficial insects, such as ladybugs, praying mantises, bees, wasps, and dragonflies to the garden. Discuss the key roles each insect plays in pollination and pest control. Examples of possible 'flashcard' words are *organic, garden, ladybugs, bugs,* and *insect*.
(I, P, SE)	Look for opportunities to visit an orchard with your child to see the fruit growing on the trees. You might need to lift them up to pick the fruit if they cannot reach it themselves. Once again, discuss the season and weather conditions required to grow the fruit. For example, apple trees thrive during the winter season and the apples are typically harvested from late summer to early autumn/fall. The exact timing depends on the region and the specific apple variety. They grow best in full sunlight and need protection from strong winds to ensure healthy development. When you return home, demonstrate how to prepare and use the fruit in various ways. These preparations could include making fruit salad, juicing, pureeing, cooking, or drying the fruit. Singing The Wiggles song, 'Fruit Salad Yummy Yummy,' will add to the fun of this activity. Examples of possible 'flashcard' words are *orchard, fruit, pick, season,* and *harvest*.

CODE	DESCRIPTION OF ACTIVITIES FOR PRESCHOOLERS
(P, I, SE)	Visit a local farmers' market where your child can meet the farmers who grow the fresh fruits and vegetables for sale. They may also have the opportunity to interact with farmers who raise cattle, sheep, and chickens, and produce meat, milk, and eggs. Additionally, beekeepers may be present offering honey harvested from their bees. Examples of possible 'flashcard' words are *vegetables*, *fruit*, *eggs*, *milk*, and *honey*.
(I, P, SE)	When preparing for a beach outing, emphasize the importance of being SunSmart. Also, consider adding a book on beach and surf safety to your child's bedtime reading list. One example is At the Beach with Lizzie and Luke by Boyd Conrick. Start reading the book a week or two before the outing to give your child enough time to become familiar with the safety advice. It would also be interesting to explore books about creatures that inhabit the sea. On the day of your beach visit, review the role of a surf lifesaver before you leave home. Explain that lifesavers are experts in beach and water safety. They help with issues such as treating jellyfish stings and protecting swimmers from rips. Remind your child that lifesavers want to keep people safe in the water. Everyone must swim between the flags, as lifesavers have designated this area as the safest. This rule helps ensure a safer swimming experience for everyone. When you arrive at the beach, talk to your child about the behavior you expect from them. Ensure they understand they must remain close by and within your line of sight, especially when they are in the water. Explore the shoreline and photograph the shells and other sea 'treasures' they find. You may even discover a shell fossil. As a follow-up activity, visit your local library to find books to help identify and provide additional information about your child's findings. Use your photos as a reference. Examples of possible 'flashcard' words are *beach*, *surf*, *flags*, *rip*, and *lifesavers*.

Note: (I) = Intellectual, (P) = Physical and (SE) = Social-Emotional

CODE	DESCRIPTION OF ACTIVITIES FOR PRESCHOOLERS
(P, I, SE)	Go outside with your child on a windy day if conditions are not too blustery. Let them experience the sensation of the wind on their face and in their hair. A pinwheel demonstrates the power of the wind. Sit together and make a pinwheel. Once completed, take the pinwheel outside for a spin. Consider buying a Windsock and placing it outside where your child can see it. The windsock will visually indicate the wind's intensity and direction before they step outside and feel it for themselves. Follow up by making a paper airplane to demonstrate how a plane uses air to fly. A helpful book on how to make a plane is the Paper Air Plane Book by Ken Blackburn and Jeff Lammers. Conduct experiments to see how far the paper plane will fly on both windy and still days. With your child's help, measure and record the distances the plane travels. Compare and discuss the results with them. You can also make a Garbage Bag Kite for use at the beach to demonstrate the force of the wind. While at the beach, draw your child's attention to the effect of the wind on the sea surface, particularly where the ocean meets the shoreline. Read the classic A. A. Milne poem Wind on the Hill to your child at bedtime. Examples of possible 'flashcard' words are *wind*, *pinwheel*, *sock*, *airplane*, and *kite*.
(P, I, SE)	Help your child make origami creations. The book Easy Christmas Origami by John Montroll provides clear instructions to make this an achievable activity. Examples of possible 'flashcard' words are *origami* and *instructions*.
(SE, P, I)	When the opportunity presents itself, catch a ride on a bus, tram, train, plane, or ferry. Teach your child how to be safe in each circumstance. Insist that your child holds your hand when boarding and exiting each mode of public transport. Encourage respectful behavior, such as sitting quietly and speaking softly, to ensure a pleasant experience for all passengers. Examples of possible 'flashcard' words are *bus*, *tram*, *train*, *plane*, *safe*, *respect*, *transport*, and *ferry*.

CODE	DESCRIPTION OF ACTIVITIES FOR PRESCHOOLERS
(I, SE)	Encourage your child's imagination by asking them to predict the outcome of a story you are reading together. This activity will help develop their creative thinking and comprehension skills. Also, ask your child to create a story using the pictures in a storybook to inspire them. Show enthusiasm for their efforts. Examples of possible 'flashcard' words are *imagination*, *picture*, and *story*.
(I, SE)	Ask your child to tell you a story from their imagination, then write it down for them in large font. Large font makes it easier for them to follow along when you read the story back to them. Leave spaces to include your child's illustrations that will bring their story to life. You could read the story to the family later and include it in your child's bedtime stories. Examples of possible 'flashcard' words are *story* and *illustrations*.

Grit—The SUPERPOWER of Never Giving Up

So, what would happen if your child developed a mindset of never giving up?

Bestselling author Nikki Gemmell looks at the issue of grit and whether it is the greatest gift for kids. She writes, *'Ah, grit. That magical four-letter word so beloved of parents and educators. Otherwise known as tenacity, persistence, drive. A holy grail in terms of success in school and life beyond it. But how on Earth to instill that magic fairy dust of driven determination in our kids? They seem either to have it, or they don't, and a lot don't—and as a parent I've no idea how to bottle the success formula. Can you instill a sense of grit at twelve? seventeen?'* (Gemmell 2016).

Gemmell cites the experience of British educator Mark Maclaine, who thinks you can. Maclaine opposes the idea of parents telling their children they are clever, as he believes it may give the impression that hard work is unnecessary. Instead, he encourages parents to praise their children's efforts. This approach helps them understand that success is a result of hard work. However, success will look different for everyone. The outcome for each child is unique and shaped by their individual strengths and abilities. Recognizing this uniqueness helps children appreciate their individual progress and potential.

Maclaine believes intelligence is malleable, which means it is not static. It can increase or decrease over time. He also notes that *'research has shown that students who believe in a fixed view of intelligence are less likely to work as hard as those who see it as malleable.'*

Note: (I) = Intellectual, (P) = Physical and (SE) = Social-Emotional

CODE	DESCRIPTION OF ACTIVITIES FOR PRESCHOOLERS
	Once students believe in the malleability of intelligence, they will often make repeated efforts to succeed. This attitude embodies the definition of 'grit.'

We have all read success stories about discipline and tenacity bringing about success. Grit may have you climbing higher than the more naturally gifted who thought they would succeed just because they were clever. Let's model grit for our children. Let them know that we struggle to achieve in some areas, but we try and try again till we get there. Relate stories to your child that illustrate the achievements of people they know who demonstrate grit.

> *'If at first you don't succeed try, try, try again.'*
> William Edward Hickson |
| (P, I, SE) | Give your child opportunities to practice a new skill. Encourage their efforts and, if possible, practice with them. For example, learning an instrument or playing a new sport requires regular practice to build confidence and competency. Encourage your child to imagine what they can achieve if they don't give up!

Examples of possible 'flashcard' words are *practice* and *achieve*. |
| (I, P, SE) | Out of view of your child, cut a hole in the lid of an old shoe box and place an item inside the box. Allow your child to reach into the box and feel the item. Give them time to try and work out what it is. Ask questions to encourage them to think in detail: *'Is it smooth? Is it hard? Is it cold? Is it furry?'* Encourage them to articulate what they are feeling and discovering.

Examples of items to place inside the box could be a hard-boiled egg, strawberry jelly, a leaf, a flower, fresh parsley, a toothbrush, toothpaste, salt, flour, or a favorite soft toy. This game is enjoyable and suitable for the whole family to participate in.

Examples of possible 'flashcard' words are *feel, smooth, hard, soft,* and *rough*. |

CODE	DESCRIPTION OF ACTIVITIES FOR PRESCHOOLERS
(P, I, SE)	Encourage your child to build with Lego and other building blocks. Show your interest in your child's construction by asking questions about it. Be on the lookout for Lego exhibitions or events held in your area. Visiting one of these events will inspire your child to design creative constructions. Examples of possible 'flashcard' words are *Lego*, *build*, and *construction*.
(P, SE, I)	Buy a yoyo for your child and learn basic yoyo tricks with the help of the Beginner Yoyo Tricks videos. Examples of possible 'flashcard' words are *yoyo* and *tricks*.
(P, SE, I)	Buy your child some beginner juggling balls and learn the basic skills of how to juggle. Examples of possible 'flashcard' words are *juggle* and *balls*.
(P, I, SE)	Buy your child a small hula hoop and a larger one for yourself. The article on how to hula hoop provides step-by-step instructions for both basic and more advanced techniques. Examples of possible 'flashcard' words are *hula hoop*, *large*, and *small*.
(P, I, SE)	Buy several small bean bags. Ask your child to hold the small hula hoop vertically out to their side. Count out loud how many bean bags you or the caregiver can throw through the hoop. Then, take the larger hula hoop and stand nearer to your child than they stood to you. Once again, count out loud how many bean bags your child can throw through the hoop. Be enthusiastic and praise their efforts. However, remember this is not a competition. Examples of possible 'flashcard' words are *bean*, *bags*, *throw*, *catch*, *one*, *two*, *three*, and *four*.
(I, P, SE)	Teach your child to set the dinner table using a printable placemat as a guide. Examples of possible 'flashcard' words are *knife*, *fork*, *spoon*, *plate*, *glass*, and *napkin*.

Note: (I) = Intellectual, (P) = Physical and (SE) = Social-Emotional

CODE	DESCRIPTION OF ACTIVITIES FOR PRESCHOOLERS
(SE, I, P)	Teach your child the art of conversation, especially over a meal at the dinner table. Dinnertime is typically a time to relax and enjoy each other's company. Remind them to listen respectfully and with interest to each family member's contribution. As a parent, you can actively participate in the conversation without dominating it and model how to engage effectively. Parents can show interest and encourage their children to share their thoughts by asking follow-up questions. > *'Listen earnestly to anything your children want to tell you, no matter what. If you don't listen eagerly to the little stuff when they are little, they won't tell you the big stuff when they are big, because to them all of it has always been big stuff.'* > Catherine M. Wallace The Art of Conversation is a handy resource designed to revive and improve young children's conversational and language skills. Another helpful resource to promote conversation is Kids Talking Point Cards. Examples of possible 'flashcard' words are *conversation*, *listen*, *respect*, and *interest*.
(SE, I, P)	Learning to express good manners should be part of your child's daily routine. For example, activities that teach your child how to express gratitude could include rehearsing how to thank someone in person or over the phone. You could also make personalized thank-you cards together. Another option is to learn how to create a posy from the garden as a thoughtful thank-you gift. Examples of flowers that are thornless and easy to pick include nasturtiums, forget-me-nots, and violets. Examples of possible 'flashcard' words are *card*, *thank you*, *telephone*, and *posy*.
(SE, I, P)	There is an African Proverb that says, *'It takes a village to raise a child.'* Your child will benefit enormously from sharing their life with caring, extended family and friends. So, ask family and friends over regularly so your child can enjoy their company. Examples of possible 'flashcard' words are *Nan*, *Gramps*, *Uncle Pete*, *Auntie Taryn*, *Uncle Tim*, and *Auntie Alli*.

CODE	DESCRIPTION OF ACTIVITIES FOR PRESCHOOLERS
(SE, P, I)	Make playdough together using <u>homemade playdough recipes</u>. Encourage your child to add the food coloring of their choice and help them knead it through the dough. Discuss the feel of the dough, for example, *'warm and smooth.'* Use <u>cookie cutters</u> to cut out and name shapes. This activity can be fun by itself, or it could be part of their imaginative play. To expand this activity, encourage your child to mix various food colorings and create a unique color to add to the playdough mixture. Add various ingredients to the mixture, such as rice, split peas, or shredded coconut to create textured playdough. > *'We didn't realize we were making memories, we just knew we were having fun.'* > Winnie the Pooh, A.A. Milne Examples of possible 'flashcard' words are *dough, warm, color, smooth, shapes, rice,* and *lumpy*.
(I, SE, P)	Discuss <u>how to make a telephone with cans</u>. This activity is both simple and engaging. As your child grows older, you can expand their understanding of sound by discussing how it travels through vibrations. Examples of possible 'flashcard' words are *telephone, cans,* and *string*.
(P, I, SE)	Let your child gather fallen leaves to <u>dry/press and make a bookmark</u>. Examples of possible 'flashcard' words are *leaves, press,* and *dry*.
(SE, P, I)	Being responsible for something essential to family life gives your child a true sense of belonging. To achieve this, involve them in simple household chores. Emphasize that they are a vital part of the family team, and their contributions are crucial for the household to run smoothly. Hold them to it. Suggest chores, such as bringing in the dog's bowl, collecting mail from the letterbox, or watering the garden and potted plants. Always ensure the chores are age-appropriate and achievable. Examples of possible 'flashcard' words are *responsible, chores, contribute, bowl, hose,* and *garden*.

Note: (I) = Intellectual, (P) = Physical and (SE) = Social-Emotional

CODE	DESCRIPTION OF ACTIVITIES FOR PRESCHOOLERS
(SE, P, I)	Teach your child how to make hand shadow puppets. The whole family can enjoy this activity. Follow up this activity with the poem My Shadow by Robert Louis Stevenson. Examples of possible 'flashcard' words are *puppet*, *hand*, and *shadow*.
(SE, I)	Take your child to the library for 'story time.' This experience offers children the opportunity to sit quietly in a group setting and listen as the librarian reads a story. Since this may be a new experience for them, your presence will provide a sense of comfort and reassurance. Examples of possible 'flashcard' words are *story* and *Librarian*.
(P, I, SE)	Show your child how to make corner page bookmarks using the intact corners of used envelopes. If you are unable to finish reading a book to your child in one sitting, use one of their bookmarks to mark your place. This will make it easy to resume the story later and maintain their interest. Your child will be excited to see how helpful their bookmark is when used in this way. Examples of possible 'flashcard' words are *corner*, *page* and *bookmark*.
(SE, P, I)	Making finger puppets is a good 'rainy day' activity for your child. Start by taking an envelope and cutting off the two intact corners, usually the bottom corners. Have your child draw a face on one side and hair on the flip side of each corner. Place one corner on your child's index finger and the other on your index finger. Act out a conversation between the two finger puppets. Ask leading questions and see where the conversation goes. For more advanced examples of 'envelope puppets,' follow the link to Quick and Easy Envelope Hand Puppets. Examples of possible 'flashcard' words are *index*, *finger*, *puppet*, and *conversation*.
(SE, P, I)	To promote imaginative play, provide a dress-up box of clothes and other helpful support items for role-playing. For example, these items might include a white shirt, a toy stethoscope, and bandages for a doctor. The Montessori doctor's tool kit would enhance this experience. Engage with your child in role-playing. However, allow them to lead and direct.

CODE	DESCRIPTION OF ACTIVITIES FOR PRESCHOOLERS
Continued	Some simple suggestions for activity 'props' might be: Hairdressing Activity Provide the following materials to inspire imaginative play: • A cardboard tube, that can be decorated to resemble a handheld hairdryer. • A brush and comb for styling. • A spray bottle filled with water to mimic a hair styling spray. • Small cooking tongs to represent hair straighteners. Restaurant Activity Set up a 'pretend' restaurant with the following materials: • Cardboard boxes to use as tables. • Reusable cutlery, plates, cups, and jugs for serving and dining. • Playdough in various colors to represent different types of food, allowing your child to create and serve imaginative dishes. Car Design Activity Provide a lightweight cardboard box that your child can easily stand in and lift. Many supermarkets offer free cardboard boxes intended for recycling, which are perfect for this activity. • Remove the flaps from both the top and bottom of the box. • Invite your child to select a color for painting the exterior of the box. • Check out the family car together. Identify the key features that should be painted onto the box. These might include: four doors, four wheels, plus the headlights, braking lights and indicator lights. • Discuss your child's color choices for each of these components, encouraging creativity and thoughtful decision making. • Once the paint has fully dried, have your child step into the open section of the box. • Instruct them to lift the box by holding the sides firmly at waist height. • Encourage them to 'drive' their painted car around the house and garden. Examples of possible 'flashcard' words are *hairdresser*, *restaurant*, *food*, and *car*.

Note: (I) = Intellectual, (P) = Physical and (SE) = Social-Emotional

CODE	DESCRIPTION OF ACTIVITIES FOR PRESCHOOLERS
(I, P, SE)	Encourage your child to create a special-purpose vehicle such as a fire truck or a police car. Show them pictures of these vehicles to inspire their creativity. Ask probing questions to help them notice and understand the unique details of each vehicle. For example, you might ask, *'What color are they? Where are their lights? Does the fire truck have a siren? What does it sound like? Does the police car have a siren? What does it sound like? Do either or both vehicles have flashing lights? Where are they located on the vehicles?'* Examples of possible 'flashcard' words are *flashing, lights, fire, siren, police,* and *truck.*
(I, SE)	Follow up the previous activity with a visit to a Fire Station, but only after you have called to set up a convenient time to meet with the firefighters. Before visiting, read stories about firefighters and their role in the community. Encourage your child to think of questions to ask them. If they are having difficulties thinking of ideas, suggest they ask a firefighter, *'Is your uniform hot to wear? Do you slide down a pole in the fire station? Do you sleep at the fire station? How do you know when there is a fire?'* Examples of possible 'flashcard' words are *uniform* and *pole.*

Imaginative Play

Janet Doman, Director of the Institutes for the Achievement of Human Potential, has shared her thoughts on the benefits of imaginative play (Doman 2018).

She believes there are huge benefits from exercising our imagination through 'play' as it is the foundation for creativity. Music, poetry, writing, and art all start with our imagination. For example, Mozart's prolific imagination continually fed his musical genius. Our children are born with an imagination that we must appreciate and encourage for their creativity to flourish.

Doman notes that *'Play allows the child to exercise his cortical muscle. It allows the child to experiment with data that he already has, to find out what works for him and what does not.'* Children understand cause and effect, and 'play' allows them to experiment. They store this information in their memory for future use. If encouraged, your child will learn that exploration, discovery, and creativity are fun and will be keen to do more.

CHAPTER 4 | CHILD DEVELOPMENT 'PLEASE EXPLAIN'

CODE	DESCRIPTION OF ACTIVITIES FOR PRESCHOOLERS
(I, P, SE)	Visit your local park and encourage your child to observe and draw their surroundings. Participate alongside them by creating your own sketches, sharing your impressions of the environment. Your child will appreciate and enjoy your participation in the activity. Take crayons, paper, and clipboards to hold the paper in place. Sit with them and discuss what they are drawing. Ask questions to encourage their curiosity about the object of their attention. Discuss it in detail to enhance their knowledge. For example, look at the bark of the different species of trees. What do you and your child notice? You will find that the bark on each tree species is unique. Look out for a paper bark tree. If you find some paper bark lying on the ground, take it home to use for an activity based on Indigenous art. In Australia, First Nations People are famous for their dot paintings. Visit a museum or art gallery to view actual examples. Help your child consolidate this knowledge by allowing them to create their own Australian Aboriginal Dot Painting. Supply them with cotton buds, finger paint, paper bark, and a book showcasing First Nations People's art for inspiration, such as Aboriginal Art by Wally Caruana. Other book resources that may be helpful are Australian Aboriginal Art Coloring and My Culture and Me. Alternatively, if you live in the United States, you could engage your child in craft activities inspired by Native American traditions. For example, collect leaves with your child. Make a small hole in each leaf near the point where the stem is attached. Take a piece of string and have your child thread it through the hole in each leaf. Tie off the ends of the string and let them use their creation as a decorative bangle. If you find feathers on your walk, you could also show your child how to make a Native American Headband. Examples of possible 'flashcard' words are *Aboriginal, native, headband, culture, dot, string, bangle, feathers, leaf,* and *painting*.

Note: (I) = Intellectual, (P) = Physical and (SE) = Social-Emotional

CODE	DESCRIPTION OF ACTIVITIES FOR PRESCHOOLERS
(P, SE, I)	Are you looking for an adventure? How about camping overnight with your child in your backyard? Be sure to leave your mobile phone in the house and remember the mosquito repellent! Make this adventure 'tech-free' and all about having fun with your child. **Camping Activities for a Preschooler** As always, preparation is the key to the success of any activity. Before embarking on this adventure, consult a Scout or Girl Guide handbook, such as <u>The Scouting Guide to Survival</u> or <u>The Scouting Guide to Hiking</u>. These guides provide valuable information on current safety tips and instructions for practical camping activities. Involve your child in each stage of this adventure: the initial packing, setting up the tent, washing the dishes, creating a makeshift shower, and final pack-up. **Morning** <ul><li>Pack for your camping experience just as you would if you were going on an actual camping trip.</li><li>Don't forget to include your lunch and dinner for the first day and breakfast for the next morning.</li><li>Store all food in an Esky to keep it cool.</li><li>Erect the tent and make sure that you involve your child in the process.</li><li>Arrange the airbeds, sleeping bags, and pillows in the tent.</li><li>Make sure you place your torches, snacks, and bottles of water next to your beds.</li><li>Set up your camping table and chairs as you will need them when it is mealtime.</li><li>Place the washing bucket, detergent, and tea towel near a garden tap to use when you wash and dry the dishes and utensils.</li></ul>

CODE	DESCRIPTION OF ACTIVITIES FOR PRESCHOOLERS

Continued	**Evening**
	• After eating dinner and washing the dishes, it may be dark enough to do a little star-gazing. Use a star chart to help you and your child identify star patterns in the night sky (see, for example, National Geographic Stargazer's Atlas: The Ultimate Guide to the Night Sky). If you must wait for sunset, you could play a card game like Animal Snap.
	• When you have finished star-gazing, it will be time to prepare for bed and snuggle into the sleeping bags. Don't rush your child off to sleep. Instead, relax and enjoy this special time with them. Some quiet activities suitable for the cozy atmosphere created by the LED lantern might be:
	   o Long chats. So, when you snuggle into your sleeping bags, listen carefully to what your child has to say. You may be surprised by what is on their mind.
	   o Listening to the night sounds in your garden.
	   o Taking turns to make up your own bedtime stories once the light is off.
	Additional evening activities for an older child might include:
	• Building a campfire (see, for example, Build a Campfire - Boy Scouts of America Handbook Hacks). Refrain from building one if you doubt your child's ability to act safely around a campfire. *Note:* Your primary consideration should be to keep your child safe and protect them from danger. Always supervise your child near a fire, even if you believe they understand and can follow the safety guidelines.
	• Cooking some sausages over the fire and eating them wrapped in fresh bread with tomato ketchup (tomato sauce) and mustard.
	• Roasting marshmallows or preparing chocolate and marshmallow-stuffed bananas cooked in the hot coals for a delicious dessert.
	• Sitting around the campfire provides an opportunity to connect with your child and talk about whatever is on their mind.
	• Singing some of your child's favorite songs around the campfire, with or without instrumental accompaniment, will add to this fun experience.
	• The Night Sky or SkyView®Lite Apps are valuable tools to help your child become familiar with the stars and constellations.

Note: (I) = Intellectual, (P) = Physical and (SE) = Social-Emotional

CODE	DESCRIPTION OF ACTIVITIES FOR PRESCHOOLERS

Continued	**Next Morning**
	• After breakfast, ask your child to assist you in putting together a simple makeshift shower using the following steps:
	   o Cut the sealed end of a jumbo garbage bag so that both ends of the garbage bag are open.
	   o Puncture four holes equally spaced around the rim of one end of the bag. Thread a separate piece of string through each of the four holes. Tie one end to the garbage bag and the other to a low-hanging branch or the clothesline frame. The length of the string will depend on the height of the branch that you need to reach. You have now constructed a private shower cubicle.
	   o When it is time for your child to shower, insert the hose through the top opening of the garbage bag. Angle it downward while your child soaps up inside the shower cubicle. No doubt, there will be shrieks of delight as they try to dodge the cold water.
	• After showering and dressing, find your <u>Explorer Compass</u> in preparation for the planned treasure hunt. Read the instructions for the treasure hunt to your child - 20 steps west, 10 steps north, and so on. The hidden 'treasure' could be a board game perfect for playing inside your tent. If it is cold, you can snuggle into your sleeping bags and enjoy the game together.
	• After you have packed up the 'camping gear' and returned inside, ask your child to reflect on their experience. Encourage them to share what they enjoyed most about their camping adventure. Write down their thoughts about the experience, leaving space for them to add illustrations to accompany these written memories. You can add this story to their bedtime collection. It will help them relive the happy memories you have created together and remind them of the new skills they learned. Rest assured; your child will often recount the exciting story of their camping adventure.
	
	Examples of possible 'flashcard' words are *tent, campfire, compass, shower, hose, treasure,* and *banana.*

TIPS FOR PARENTS OF PRESCHOOLERS

When your child enters the preschool stage, they are more likely to engage and interact in group settings outside the home environment. Examples of situations they may encounter without you by their side could include preschool, kinder-gym, visits to the park with friends, and children's parties. Your child will need to display acceptable behaviors in these social settings. Parents can help their children develop these behaviors with specific guidance and opportunities to practice.

In this section, I highlight practical considerations and strategies to help children handle these situations more confidently. These include:

- Reinforcing values and building character,
- Following rules and teaching self-discipline,
- Promoting and encouraging sharing, and
- Assessing the impact of screen time.

REINFORCING VALUES AND BUILDING CHARACTER

As your toddler transitions to preschool, continue using activities and everyday interactions to reinforce positive values and acceptable behaviors. When parents consistently display these values and behaviors in their own lives, their children are more likely to comply. Chapter 2 provides general guidelines to assist parents with this process.

Teaching values at home is crucial. Their adoption will influence how well your child interacts with classmates and handles the dynamics of school life. Educators will also continue to reinforce important values and behaviors in the preschool setting. For example, adopting values such as *respect, kindness, tolerance, patience*, and *self-control* at preschool helps to maintain a safe, harmonious, and effective learning environment. This dual approach will establish a solid foundation for developing your child's character. Their responses to life's challenges, as observed and perceived by others, will be the outward expression of their character.

When your child commences formal schooling, they will encounter more complex issues and situations requiring nuanced value-based responses. Parents should seek out learning resources that address these potential issues and provide a range of appropriate responses that their children can rehearse. The following link [Books to Build Character and Teach Your Child Important Values](#) contains suggestions for books that can assist parents.

FOLLOWING RULES AND TEACHING SELF-DISCIPLINE

During the toddler stage, your child is expected to develop an initial awareness of the rules and values underpinning acceptable behavior. However, when they commence preschool, they will be expected to follow the rules and demonstrate self-discipline.

As parents, we want our children to follow the rules set by the family, school, and community. Adherence to these rules will help them live happy, safe, and respectful lives. Rules provide a sense of predictability and consistency, which will assist in safeguarding your child's physical and emotional well-being. Rules also help guide our actions toward a desired outcome and provide comfort and confidence to those who follow them.

So, how can we, as parents, teach our preschoolers to follow the rules? I recommend using 'effective discipline,' a disciplinary approach delivered with fairness, consistency, and respect. Effective discipline aims to teach and guide children in a loving and supportive manner rather than forcing them to obey. This approach provides the foundation for the development of self-discipline. A child who can follow the rules and demonstrate self-discipline is better prepared for the real world (see, for example, Canadian Paediatric Society 2004).

During your child's preschool years, you will offer more detailed explanations about rules, limits, and behaviors than you did when your child was a toddler. As with any new learning experience, your child will need regular reminders of your expectations to help them demonstrate appropriate behaviors and self-discipline. Continued modeling of acceptable behavior is necessary. This form of repetition is essential for your child to learn and achieve the desired outcomes.

When your child follows the rules, show your appreciation. Reiterate the positive impact their good behavior has on others and reward them with your attention and time. For example, you might say, '*Thank you so much for being responsible and packing your toys away. Now, we won't have to worry about tripping or falling over. Once you have finished, I will have time to play a game with you before dinner.*' If your child refuses to tidy up their toys, explain that you will need to do it yourself to prevent anyone from tripping or falling. As a result, you will not have time for pre-dinner games with them.

The above example demonstrates that your attention and time are their rewards for responsible behavior. This positive experience is likely to influence how they respond to your future requests, as children naturally seek their parents' attention, time and approval. However, it is important to use your common sense in situations where your child may be struggling due to ill health, tiredness, or hunger. In these circumstances, it may be impractical for them to meet your expectations. Your pragmatic response in these circumstances will demonstrate your empathy and care for them.

In his book Contact: The First 4 Minutes (1986), Leonard Zunin describes a story that illustrates an approach to teaching acceptable behavior within a different cultural context. The story relates to how the Babemba tribe of Southern Africa deals with its members when one acts outside the tribe's code of conduct. The tribe places the offending member in the center of the village without any restraints. The entire tribe, including children, form a circle around them. Each tribal member reminds the offending member of the good deeds and positive attributes they have previously demonstrated within the tribe. This ceremony lasts several days and concludes with a celebration, symbolically welcoming the member back into the tribe. The tribe has reminded the member of their positive character traits, and the values held and respected by the tribe.

I am not suggesting that you use this 'tribal' approach literally if your child's behavior does not conform with your expectations and societal rules. However, the fundamental principle of the tribe's positive intervention may influence your thinking and approach to discipline. For example, you may say, *'Tom, I was surprised to hear that you hit your friend. You are usually such a kind boy. I like it when you use words to sort out disagreements. Hitting someone is not acceptable and is not the way to fix problems. Let's talk about how to handle this situation in a more acceptable manner.'* In the first instance, explain that he has upset his friend and will need to apologize for his behavior. Ensure that both children understand the need for tolerance, fairness, and respect for each other. Their social-emotional maturity levels will dictate what you say, and expect from them, as they resolve this altercation.

Psychotherapist Amy Morin emphasizes that the primary goal in guiding your child to follow the rules is to foster self-discipline. This goal is true regardless of the disciplinary approach you choose to use. The Collins Dictionary defines self-discipline as *'the ability to control yourself and to make yourself work hard or behave in a particular way without needing anyone else to tell you what to do.'* Self-discipline is a crucial skill for becoming a responsible adult. It is a learned ability that evolves over time with practice and guidance.

When teaching your child self-discipline, it is important to offer opportunities for them to practice making responsible choices. As a parent, there are specific strategies you can implement to help instill self-discipline from an early age. Here are some examples:

- Children learn through observation, so it is important for parents to model self-discipline. When your child sees you completing your tasks, like household chores, before you relax and watch a movie, they will understand the value you place on self-discipline. Over time, they will learn to mirror this behavior in their own actions.

- Providing structure is essential for encouraging the development of self-discipline. A daily routine helps your child understand their responsibilities and what is expected of them. Tasks such as eating breakfast, getting dressed, and brushing their teeth become part of a structured routine that, over time, they can manage independently.

- Clearly explain the consequences of your child's actions. For example, constantly reminding your child to eat breakfast, brush their teeth, and get dressed is time wasting. Their tardiness may result in them being late for school and you being late for work.

- Teach problem-solving skills. For example, if mornings are rushed, teach your child to prepare the night before. This preparation may involve setting the table for breakfast, laying out their clothes, and setting an alarm to wake up on time. These measures will ensure there is enough time to complete all tasks before leaving for school.

- Clearly explain the reasons behind rules and the importance of practicing self-discipline. Rules are established to ensure your child's physical and emotional well-being. They are also put in place to embody societal expectations and clarify acceptable behavior. Without rules, people would lack guidance on how to act appropriately in various situations.

- Praise and reward self-discipline. If you notice your child brushing their teeth and getting dressed without being reminded, praise their efforts. You could reward them with a fun activity that they enjoy doing with you.

Teaching rules and acceptable behaviors will help instill positive values in your child, such as *responsibility, patience, empathy,* and *tolerance*. Well-behaved children are more self-confident and likable and find it easy to make friends. Typically, they exhibit greater self-control, are more self-sufficient, and understand the importance of being accountable for their choices. They are more likely to make positive decisions based on their internal motivation rather than a fear of punishment. The Australian Parenting Website, raisingchildren.net.au, provides valuable tips on discipline and guiding behavior for babies and children, as well as, requests and instructions for helping children cooperate.

> *'It is easier to build strong children than repair broken men.'*
> Fredrick Douglass

PROMOTING AND ENCOURAGING SHARING

Why should your child share?

Learning to share is a challenge for a young child. However, it is essential for fostering cooperation and getting along with others, both in the family and at school. Sharing offers numerous advantages. It assists children in cultivating friendships, honing negotiation skills, coping with disappointment, strengthening values, and comprehending concepts such as compromise and fairness (raisingchildren.net.au 2020a).

Realistic expectations for preschoolers

As mentioned previously, sharing is particularly challenging for toddlers because they are unable to understand their friend's perspectives. They also lack experience with the concept of time and have limited emotional control. At the toddler stage, a parent's role is to model sharing and suggest how to share.

Around three years of age, a child will begin to appreciate someone else's point of view. At this stage of their development, they will also start to grasp the concept of time. As a result, they will have a clearer understanding of the expected duration of their friend's turn. A three-year-old will also have more control over their emotions, making sharing easier.

By the time your child reaches four years of age, they will have developed an increased capacity for sharing.

Teaching strategies for parents

Parents can employ the following simple strategies to help manage and teach the concept of sharing:

- Model sharing behaviors consistently by using examples from your daily life. These examples could include taking turns with your partner to use the computer or walk the dog. For these demonstrations to be effective, your behavior must reflect patience, self-control, and respect.

- Provide your child with a simple strategy to help them manage waiting for their turn. When they want to play with a toy their friend is using, encourage your child to tell their friend politely they are waiting for their turn. This approach helps them express their needs while practicing patience. In the meantime, suggest they play with another toy while they wait.

- Give your child numerous opportunities to practice sharing through games and activities with their family and friends.

- To provide context, insert the language of sharing into everyday conversations. For example, you might say, '*It is your turn to use the bathroom as your sister has finished. It is your sister's turn to set the table, as you had your turn last night. It is your turn to water the pot plants, as your sister had her turn yesterday.*'

- Set a time limit for sharing, as this will reassure your child that their wait will eventually end. Time is best taught to a young child using an analog clock. Show them where the clock hands will be positioned when it is their turn. Together, watch the clock hands move toward the designated time. Watching them move will help your child to understand the passage of time. It will also reassure them that their turn is approaching.

- Before a play date, discuss with your child the importance of allowing their friend to play with their toys. Your encouragement will foster kindness and help your child to develop an understanding of sharing and consideration for others. If your child does manage to share their toys, be sure to praise them. You might say, '*I was very proud to see you share your toy with your friend. That was very kind of you.*'

    Side note: Play dates can cause stress, particularly if your child owns special toys and does not want to share them. To avoid conflict, put these toys away. Dr. Elizabeth Westrupp, clinical psychologist at Deakin University, suggests we consider our willingness to share prized possessions before expecting our children to share theirs. Setting aside special toys for the duration of the play date illustrates that you acknowledge the significance of certain toys in their life. This strategy empowers them to share at their own pace, ensuring they feel comfortable and ready.

- When visiting friends, encourage your child to seek permission before playing with their friend's toys. Instilling this practice during their early years helps them to develop good manners and fosters respect for others' belongings.

- Use sharing activities to cultivate and reinforce specific values, such as *patience, self-control,* and *respect.* Compliment your child when they demonstrate value-driven behavior. For example, when your child waits patiently for another child to take their turn without interrupting, they are exhibiting self-control and showing respect. This behavior also shows their maturity and encourages positive interactions with their peers.

Practical Application

Use the words 'sharing' and 'taking turns' in context to help your child understand these concepts clearly. Repetition is essential for reinforcing their learning and comprehension. Here are some simple games and activities that parents can use to teach their children the concept of sharing and taking turns.

- Snakes and Ladders, Snap, Pin the Tail on the Donkey, and Chess are examples of games where each participant takes a turn. These activities promote teamwork and enhance social skills in their interactions with peers. Furthermore, a game like Simon Says involves one child assuming the role of leader (Simon) while the other participants follow the leader's instructions. Negotiating turns will be necessary for those who wish to take on the role of Simon in the game. This process encourages communication and fairness among participants.

- Provide your child and their friend with a packet of multi-colored crayons to share. Ask each child to create a drawing that incorporates the use of all the colored crayons. They will need to cooperate and take turns with the crayons to accomplish this task. Discuss your expectations clearly and acknowledge their cooperative behavior when they have finished their drawings. Reinforce that they successfully completed the task by taking turns and working together collaboratively.

Other simple activities that you may wish to consider are:

- Bake cookies with your child and their friend. Allow them to take turns adding the ingredients, mixing the dough, and using the rolling pin and cookie cutter.

- Provide a box of dress-up outfits. Encourage your child and their friend to take turns wearing their favorite costumes. Examples of costumes might include Disney character outfits, a magician's cape, a doctor's white coat and stethoscope, and a chef's apron and hat.

- Use a <u>sand timer</u> to set time limits for activities that involve children taking turns. The visual cue helps the waiting child understand that their turn is approaching. This approach ensures each child is given an equal amount of time. It also helps to promote fairness and minimize impatience.

ASSESSING THE IMPACT OF SCREEN TIME

Medical doctors, educators, and psychologists are raising concerns about the impact of 'screen time' on a child's brain. As a result, international studies are being undertaken to understand the influence of digital exposure on child development. These initiatives are looking at the impact of digital media and technology on a child's well-being and learning.

The following examples highlight the concerns that researchers believe may impact your child's early development, particularly in the first three years:

- The time spent on a device deprives children of the time they could otherwise use to explore the real world. Exploration of their environment and interactions with their family and community provides vital stimulation for brain development. Margalit (2016) expresses concerns that the absence of real-life experiences during these early years may hinder the formation of necessary learning foundations.

- Equally, there are concerns that the time spent on a device may take up your child's available time. Your child needs free time to let their mind wander and for their imagination to develop (Ruder 2019). According to Dr. Michael Rich, Associate Professor of Pediatrics at Harvard Medical School, *'boredom is the space in which creativity and imagination happen.'*

- Another concern is that the blue light emitted from iPads and mobile phones suppresses the production of melatonin. Melatonin is a hormone essential for a good night's sleep (Chang et al. 2015). Therefore, allowing children to use devices before bedtime can negatively impact their ability to achieve restful sleep.

Sleep is vital for brain development (Alario 2020). When your child sleeps:

- Many connections in the brain are forming,
- Memories of newly acquired information are stored,
- They are better equipped to regulate their emotions,
- They can concentrate more easily,
- Their energy is replenished, and
- Their immune system, which fights infection, is activated.

The Growing Up Digital (GUD) Alberta Project looks at the overall effects of devices on a child's development. This project was initiated by Dr. Michael Rich and has since been implemented in Australia (Growing Up Digital (GUD) Australia, First Phase Results (GUD) Australia, Second Phase Results (GUD) Australia). Dr. Rich urges a balanced approach for managing 'screen use' and makes the following pragmatic statement:

> *'We have to be flexible enough to evolve with the technology but choose how to use it right. Fire was a great discovery to cook our food, but we had to learn it could hurt and kill as well.'*
>
> Dr. Michael Rich

PREPARING YOUR CHILD FOR SCHOOL

A SIMPLE, PRACTICAL APPROACH

> *'Give your child the opportunity to start strong!'*
> Margaret Larden

Facing new situations for the first time can be daunting, and starting school is no exception. Children will benefit from their parent's guidance when navigating this new experience. A lack of preparation for this important day could result in unintended negative consequences and feelings of apprehension and uncertainty. With minimal effort, you can prepare your child for the transition to school by explaining what to expect. This preparation will help them face new challenges with confidence. It will also ensure a positive start to elementary school and lay the foundation for future learning and growth.

Side note: Remind your child to use their manners at school and be respectful toward others.

KNOWING WHAT TO EXPECT

We can take a leaf out of the preparation routinely undertaken by elite sportsmen and women before a major competition. Competitors typically arrive early at the venue to adjust to the local environmental conditions. Early arrival also gives them time to familiarize themselves with the facility. This strategy aims to minimize any uncertainty the athlete may feel before the event. It also reduces any stress that could negatively affect their performance. Following years of training, athletes want to perform at their best. They do not want their performance hindered by unknown factors on the day.

Similarly, it is important to familiarize your child with the layout and features of the elementary school they will be attending. Help them understand its location in relation to their home. You can also boost your child's confidence by developing their proficiency in skills needed for their daily school activities. This preparation will ease the transition and enhance their overall school experience.

START WITH THE BASICS

Preparing your child for school is a gradual process that begins in infancy. For example, the foundational skill of counting can be introduced early by consistently counting your baby's fingers and toes. Since all learning progresses incrementally, it is advisable to start early and build gradually. Fostering the following foundational skills can help reduce apprehension and ensure your child approaches their school experience with confidence and enthusiasm.

PERSONAL INFORMATION

Name recognition

Teaching your child to recognize, read, and write their full name is a relatively simple task involving familiarization and repetition. The book How to Teach Your Baby to Read: The Gentle Revolution by Doman and Doman (2006) provides helpful instructions.

For example, one straightforward method involves the use of flashcards.

- Write your child's first name in large, lower-case letters on a white flashcard using a red Texta/marker. During the first week, show them the flashcard and simultaneously say their first name aloud at least three times a day.

- Throughout the second week, show them the flashcard often and simultaneously say their first name aloud. Prompt them to read and say it with you.

- During the third week, when your child can confidently read their first name, place the flashcard with their name on a table. Help them practice writing their first name using easy-grip colored pencils on a sheet of white cardboard. Cardboard is heavier and more stable than a sheet of paper. This stability makes it easier for a child to learn how to write. Repeat this activity as often as possible until your child can confidently read and write their first name.

- You can teach them to read and write their middle name and surname using this method.

Provide regular opportunities and settings for your child to practice writing their name. For example, encourage them to write their name in the sand at the beach or 'sign' their finger painting. They could also trace their name in a layer of flour on the kitchen counter while you are baking. Consistent practice of this new skill will help build their confidence and ensure their success.

Age and birthday

Age and birthdays are abstract concepts. They can be difficult for a young child to fully comprehend but are relatively easy to introduce. When introducing new knowledge, start at the beginning to give some context. Remember, it is more practical to teach these concepts during your child's preschool years when they are developing a basic understanding of time.

Good visual teaching aids, such as photos of birthday celebrations, offer details that can help explain the concepts of age and birthdays. First, show your child a photograph of their cake and candle from their first birthday celebration. The conversation that may follow could be, *'Milly, let's look at your birthday cake and count the number of candles on it. Do you see there is only one candle? One candle indicates that you were one year old when this photograph was taken. Now let's talk about how you looked when you were one year old.'*

At this point, draw Milly's attention to some of her 'age-defining' physical features evident in the photograph, such as her size, hair, and teeth. Use additional photos or videos of her at one year of age to identify other features or abilities that demonstrate her stage of development. For example, you might say, *'It looks like you could crawl and stand when holding onto furniture.'* Then add, *'You were making sounds and wearing baby clothes, including a nappy.'* Repeat this activity with photos and videos of subsequent birthday celebrations up to Milly's current age.

To explore other aspects of your child's progression in age, draw attention to the obvious changes in their appearance from year to year. Arrange a chronological sequence of birthday photos to highlight this. Discuss the physical changes visible in each photograph, such as height, size, hair growth, mobility, and teeth. A video would be helpful to draw attention to other developmental milestones, such as speaking, walking, or eating independently.

To provide additional context, discuss your child's age in terms of the age of other family members. Show recent birthday photos of family members and count the candles on their cake. Explain, for example, that *'Mommy had 38 candles on her last birthday cake, so she* is older than you. You had four candles on your last birthday cake, which indicates you were four years old. You are much younger than Mommy.'

Having established the age difference, continue the discussion and compare other physical differences between mother and child. For example, you might say, *'Mommy is taller, heavier, and stronger than Milly.'* Then add, *'Mommy has thicker hair and bigger teeth, with many more of them than Milly.'* Finally, explain, *'That's because Mommy is much older than Milly.'* This activity aims to help your child understand the connection between their age and the number of candles on their birthday cake. It also highlights the physical changes that become noticeable as they grow older.

A calendar is the ideal teaching aid to explain the concept of the date of a birthday celebration. It provides a framework for the number of days and months in a year. This framework also gives your child a visual representation of the time that will pass during this period. It is best to use a hard-copy version of a calendar with large print that is easy to read. Turn the pages of the calendar to reveal the 12 individual months in a year. Say the names of the months as you run your finger under the written name. Go through the calendar again and count the number of months in the year. Do this activity often to familiarize your child with this new information.

The primary purpose of this activity is to teach your child the date of their birthday celebration. To keep it simple, highlight the date your child will celebrate their birthday on the calendar. Circle the date and write their name next to it. Draw attention to the date rather than the day, as the day will change every year. For example, you might say, *'Your birthday is on the 9th of October, Milly.'* At this stage of their development, linking your child's birth year to their current age is more difficult for them to comprehend. Use repetition to teach this information effectively.

Frequently remind your child of their age and the date of their birthday to help them easily recall the information when asked. As their birthday approaches, raise their awareness of the celebration to build excitement. Highlight upcoming family birthdays on the calendar as well. This information will help your child anticipate these special events and feel more involved in the celebrations.

Address and phone number

An effective method for teaching key information, such as your child's home address and phone number, is to set the details to music or rhythmic percussion sounds. Several examples, such as The Alphabet Song and the Do-Re-Mi song, demonstrate the long-standing use of this practice. Studies in music neuroscience have shown that pairing music and singing with academic information can enhance a child's ability to recall the material later. This approach allows them to retrieve and apply the information when needed (see, for example, Cox 2025).

To help your child learn their home address, compose a simple melody to go along with the words of the address and sing it together regularly. This technique aids in reinforcing memorization, enabling them to recall the information readily. Using a similar method, have your child remember the mobile phone number of at least one parent or caregiver. Parents can teach their mobile number to the beat of a drum. Another method is to use a low tone for the first number and a high tone for the second, alternating sounds throughout. I recently asked my adult son if he could sing the address of his childhood home to me. Without hesitation, he sang the address to the melody we had created. That must say something about the effectiveness of this technique.

BASIC MATHEMATICS

Counting, addition and subtraction

The foundation for basic mathematics begins in infancy. When introducing counting, ensure your child can see and interact with the objects or actions being counted. Examples include fingers, toes, steps taken, bites of food, bubbles blown, or candles on a cake. Count aloud with your child, gradually encouraging them to count independently as their confidence grows.

Repetition is essential for reinforcing new knowledge. You can build your child's confidence by engaging in activities such as singing nursery rhymes like '1,2,3,4,5 Once I caught a fish alive', playing hide-and-seek, or arranging magnetic numbers sequentially on a magnetic board or refrigerator. Encourage your child to touch each number as you count together, helping them associate spoken numbers with their written forms. With adequate practice, most 5-year-olds can count to 100 and recognize and read numbers up to 20.

Once your child is proficient in counting, you can introduce the concepts of addition and subtraction through games and everyday practical activities. For instance, count the fruit in your fruit basket together. Ask how many pieces will remain if you each eat one piece. Suggest they eat a banana while you eat an apple, then recount the fruit together. For example, six pieces of fruit minus two equals four remaining. Practical demonstrations like these provide clarity and help reinforce mathematical concepts in a tangible way.

Fractions

Teaching fractions to your child should be done using familiar objects and by incorporating the language of fractions into everyday practical activities. This approach helps simplify what might otherwise seem like an abstract concept.

- You can teach your child fractions using everyday language and associated actions, for example, *'Let's cut this orange in half.'* Cut the orange in half and show your child that both pieces are of equal size. Bring the two halves together and point out that they form one whole orange. Extend this activity by cutting another orange into quarters and drawing their attention to each quarter being the same size. When you bring the four quarters back together, demonstrate that they form one orange. Then, let them play around with the orange pieces. Ask questions such as, *'How many quarters make a half?'*

and *'How many quarters make three quarters?'* and help them discover the answers. As they eat the quarters, comment on how much they have eaten. *'You ate one quarter, Daddy ate two quarters, and Mommy ate one quarter. Four quarters make one orange. We shared one orange between us.'*

Under your supervision, let your child cut a banana in half using a 'safe' knife, such as the Montessori Children's Knives. The soft texture of the fruit will make it easy for them to cut. Once they have cut the banana, compare the two pieces to ascertain whether they are of equal size. Give them opportunities to practice this activity often.

- Painting is another activity that can reinforce the concept of fractions. Take a large piece of white paper and explain that you are going to fold the paper in half. Demonstrate to your child how to do this. Lie the paper on a flat surface. Fold the paper, line up the edges carefully, and run your index finger down the fold to form a well-defined crease. Take a pencil and ruler and draw a line along the crease. Secure the paper on an easel using pegs. Explain that the crease divides the paper into two halves. Touch the paper on the left side of the crease as you say the word *'left.'* Reinforce the concept of left and right by identifying the right side in the same manner.

  Instruct your child to paint one side of the crease red. Clarify that they will have completed half of the sheet of paper when they have painted one side up to the crease line. Repeat this activity using yellow paint for the remaining side. After both sides are painted and the paint has dried, encourage your child to cut the paper along the crease line where the yellow and red paint meet. Ask your child to place the red half on top of the yellow half to demonstrate that both halves are of equal size. Extend this activity by folding another piece of paper into quarters. Then, use the same process to explain the concept of quarters.

- Cooking is another activity that can be used to demonstrate the concept of fractions. Find a simple recipe, such as lemonade scones. Read the recipe with your child, running your finger under the words as you read. Show your child the different dimensions of the measuring cups used for cooking and select the sizes required for this recipe. Help them fill the 1 cup and ½ cup measures with the necessary ingredients for this recipe. Make the scones with them following the simple instructions. While the scones are cooking, let your child experiment with the stack of measuring cups and water in the kitchen sink. Nurture their curiosity. You might ask, *'How many ½ cups do we need to fill a 1 cup measure? How many quarter cups are needed to fill a 1 cup measure?'* Remember, this is not a test.

- You can also use 'time' to introduce fractions to your child. Your child may have a TV Program that they are allowed to watch. If the Program is one hour long, mention this to your child at the start. To help them become familiar with the passing of time, set the alarm on an analog clock to sound in one hour's time. An analog clock gives you a visual representation of the passing of time. Explain that when one hour has passed, the alarm will sound. Show your child the position of the clock hands when the Program begins, such as at 4 o'clock. Explain that when the alarm sounds in one hour, the clock hands will display 5 o'clock. Show them that the big hand is pointing at the 12, and the small hand has moved from the 4 to the 5.

You can explain the concept of half an hour by referencing a TV Program that lasts for 30 minutes. For example, you might say, *'Your TV Program will start at 4 o'clock,'* while showing them the position of the clock hands. You can add, *'It will finish at half past 4. Look, the big hand is only halfway around the clock.'* When the Program concludes, point out the clock hands again to show your child their new position. Explain that the big hand has moved halfway around the clock while the little hand is positioned halfway between the 4 and the 5.

Explain to your child that two 30-minute programs are equivalent in length to a 1-hour program. If they are limited to 1 hour of television per day, they could choose to watch two 30-minute programs instead of a single 1-hour program. This comparison will help them understand their viewing options and also bring some clarity to the concept of 2 halves making 1 whole.

- Provide further opportunities for your child to apply the concept of fractions. For example, when they want a drink, you could ask, *'Would you like half a glass of orange juice?'* When you pass it to them, draw their attention to the half-filled glass of juice. Likewise, you can ask your child if they intend to eat their whole cupcake or share half with you. If they are willing to share their cake, show them where to cut the cupcake to achieve two equal halves.

FINE MOTOR SKILLS

Fine motor skills are essential for everyday tasks. To develop these skills, children need to strengthen the smaller muscles in their hands. The following activities create opportunities for your child to practice and develop their fine motor and visual perception skills.

- Show your child how to properly grip and use easy-grip colored pencils and toddler-sized paintbrushes to scribble, color, draw, write, and paint. Ensure that the pencils are the appropriate thickness for little hands; thicker pencils are suitable for younger children (see, for example, Kidsfirst.com.au 2014).

  You can determine your child's dominant hand by observing which hand they naturally use for various activities. For example, notice which hand they prefer when they paint, draw, pick up a toy, throw a ball, or feed themselves with a spoon. Once you have identified their dominant hand, you can refer to them as left-handed or right-handed. You might say, *'It looks like you are left-handed, Tim. Your brother, Peter, is right-handed.'*

- Show your child how to hold and use scissors correctly. Having established their dominant hand, buy the correct-sized left or right-handed scissors. Encourage them to use the scissors at home with you so that this skill is well-practiced. Recognizing their dominant hand will be helpful with practical decisions they must make when they commence school. For example, if your child knows they are left-handed, they will learn to select left-handed scissors. This information will also be useful when arranging classroom seating. For example, left-handed students should sit on the left side of a shared classroom desk, and right-handed students on the right side.

- Encourage their construction skills using, for example, Duplo, Lego, puzzles, or train tracks.

- Provide opportunities to develop practical life skills, such as working with screwdrivers using the Montessori Screwdriver Board.

- Introduce your child to the basic skills required for using a computer. For example, help them practice using the mouse and learn how to direct and position the stylus.

- Give your child opportunities to dress themselves or their doll or teddy bear. Encourage them to practice tasks such as tying shoelaces, fastening sandals, zipping jackets, buttoning shirts, securing belts, and using Velcro tabs. Approximately one month before starting school, encourage your child to consistently practice dressing in their school uniform and putting on their shoes. Mastering these tasks will help ensure a smooth and efficient morning routine before school.

- Give them opportunities to eat independently using cutlery and chopsticks.

- Buy a lunchbox and water bottle for your child to use at school. Leading up to the commencement of formal schooling, encourage your child to use these items daily at lunchtime. This practice will help them become familiar with their purpose and develop their proficiency in opening and closing them.

- Teach your child how to maintain their general hygiene. Establishing good habits will include washing their hands before eating and after using the toilet, cleaning their teeth, and brushing their hair. Also, remind them to cough and sneeze into their elbow or sleeve if a tissue is not available.

- Provide opportunities to engage your child in threading activities using beads and tubular macaroni (for example, penne, rigatoni). Store these items in a variety of containers. Opening and closing these containers will ensure your child has additional opportunities to strengthen their fingers and hands.

- Demonstrate how to use jumbo tweezers, mini tongs, or teabag squeezers to pick up small objects used in creating a collage.

- Create and play games with marbles. Use Marble Run toy sets to build marble runs of various designs.

- Play games like Connect 4, Pick-up Sticks, and Kids Darts.

- Give your child opportunities to mold playdough and clay.

- Offer your child materials such as old boxes, egg cartons, cardboard tubes, wool, string, paper, tape, crayons, paint, and brushes to construct 'creative' works of art.

- Teach your child to finger knit and participate in finger string activities together.

- Ask your child to cook with you. Many simple cooking activities can help develop your child's fine motor skills. These may include measuring a flat teaspoon of sugar, adding a pinch of salt, or kneading scone dough. Your child could also create small decorations from leftover pastry for the apple or pumpkin pie you are preparing.

- Create easy Christmas origami handmade ornaments together.
- Make paper airplanes from The New World Champion Paper Airplane Book.
- Provide hours of fun solving puzzles using connect the dot activities.

Fine motor skills also require additional independent skills, such as precise visual perception, to handle an object or perform a task (Kid Sense 2020). Visual perception is the brain's ability to understand what the eyes see (Bishop 2018). Enhance your child's perception by discussing what they see. For example, identify small holes versus large holes, straight lines versus curved lines, large blocks versus small blocks, and rough wood versus smooth wood. Ask them specific questions about what they see to develop their observational skills. Their ability to accurately interpret what they see will directly affect their fine motor skills.

Side note: Always remember to do activities *with* your child rather than *for* them.

> *'When you cut it for me, write it for me, open it for me*
> *Set it up for me, draw it for me, find it for me*
> *All I learn is that you do it better than me.'*
>
> Anonymous

SCHOOL FAMILIARIZATION

The more familiar your child is with the school's location and facilities, the more comfortable they will feel on their first day and afterward. To help address feelings of separation, consider reading The Invisible String by Patrice Karst to them. This book gently explores the emotions children may experience when they are left at school. Reading this book in the weeks leading up to the start of school can provide reassurance and help build your child's awareness and confidence.

Before commencing school, provide opportunities for your child to become familiar with the school's location relative to their home. This familiarity will help alleviate any anxiety they may have. If you live within walking distance, select the safest route and plan to use it consistently. Walk the route together, pointing out key landmarks to look for, such as a church, a shop, or a friend's house. Frequent repetition of the walk before the start of the school term will bolster their confidence and enhance their sense of direction.

Walking may not be a practical option for students who live a substantial distance from their school. Driving or using public transport is a more suitable alternative in these cases. To help your child feel confident, use the same route every time you drive or take the bus to school. Point out landmarks like shops or parks to help them remember the route. This familiarization will reassure them that they are on the correct route.

To further prepare your child for school, request permission from the School Principal to walk around the grounds to familiarize them with the layout. Visit key areas such as classrooms, play areas, the administration building, toilets, and the tuck shop. If there are any 'out of bounds' areas, explain to your child why these places are off-limits for students. If allowed, use weekends to visit the playing fields and engage in games or sports together. This enjoyable activity will boost your child's confidence and help them to become more accustomed to the school environment.

As your child engages with the school community independently, discussing the sensitive topics of body safety and consent is essential. Initially, this might involve a simple explanation of 'safe touch' and the circumstances when it is appropriate (for example, a doctor's examination). A valuable resource for addressing their questions on this topic is the ABC of Body Safety and Consent by Jayneen Sanders.

MORE THAN BARE BASICS

GENERAL KNOWLEDGE

Children gain numerous benefits from acquiring a broad range of general knowledge. For example, understanding facts, such as bananas are fruits, camels store water in their humps, and pollution adversely affects our health and the environment, can enhance their awareness of their world. Educators recognize that a grasp of general knowledge helps children form a sense of belonging, make friends, engage in learning, and feel understood. These attributes are essential prerequisites for their development and progress.

Building a foundation of general knowledge in your child's early years boosts confidence and enhances their reasoning skills. This knowledge will also inform them of our dynamic world and guide their decisions and actions. By the time your child is ready to commence school, you will have shared countless facts with them. For example, the following activities are a snapshot of some general knowledge you may wish to impart.

- Show your child a photo of the current Prime Minister, President, or Head of State. Discuss the leadership roles these individuals hold in governing and leading their countries. Similarly, explain that parents are responsible for nurturing, guiding, and protecting their family, just as a government is responsible for overseeing and managing the nation.
- Play the National Anthem and sing it with your child often until they memorize the lyrics and tune. Examples include:
    - Australia—Advance Australia Fair
    - United Kingdom—God Save The King
    - Canada—O Canada
    - New Zealand—God Defend New Zealand
    - United States—Star-Spangled Banner

- Buy a miniature replica of your country's national flag. Let your child use this flag as a guide while drawing the design on paper. Use sticky tape or staples to attach the paper flag to a straw or a stick. This activity would be appropriate to undertake on your country's National Day.

- Show your child a map of their country of residence and identify it by name.

- Print two copies of a non-colored map of your home country that defines the states, territories, or provinces (see Shutterstock Maps for some examples). Take one copy and ask your child to cut out the individual jurisdictions shown on the map along their respective borders. Identify each jurisdiction by name and then ask your child to color each one with a different color. Place a complete map of your home country in front of your child. Using this map as a reference, encourage them to reassemble the cutouts to form the shape of the country. Repeat the name of each jurisdiction as they assemble the map. Place a photo of your child on the State where they live.

- Show your child a world globe and help them locate their country.

Side note: Use these types of activities to build your child's knowledge of other countries, which are the birthplace of their friends and families.

A comprehensive example of suitable Resources for General Knowledge is available for purchase from The Institutes for the Achievement of Human Potential.

INTRODUCTION TO READING

Teaching a child to read primarily involves repetition. Doman and Doman (2006) have developed a simple, foolproof method for teaching reading using flashcards. They identified font size and color as important contributors to a successful learning outcome (see, for example, Flashcards with Big Red Words). The teaching sessions are quick and keep children engaged. Their book How to Teach Your Baby to Read: The Gentle Revolution explains this process clearly, as the following selected extracts from pages 118-121 outline:

'The first step in teaching your child to read begins with just fifteen words. Begin at a time of day when the child is receptive, rested, and in a good mood. Use a part of the house with as few distracting factors as possible, in both the auditory and visual sense; for instance, do not have on the radio or television, and avoid other sources of noise. Use a corner of the room that does not have a great deal of furniture, pictures, or other objects that might distract the child's vision.

Now, the fun begins. On the first day, simply hold up the word Mommy, just beyond his reach, and say to him clearly, "This says Mommy." Give your child no more description. There is no need to elaborate. Permit him to see it for no more than one second. Next, hold up the word Daddy and again enthusiastically say, "This says Daddy." Show three other words in precisely the same way as you have these first two.' This set will now be comprised of five words.

'It is best when showing a set of cards to take the card from the back of the set rather than feeding from the front card. This approach allows you to glance at the upper left corner of the back of each card where you have written the word. This means that as you say the word to your child, you can focus on his face. Do not ask your child to repeat the words as you go along. After the fifth word, hug your child enthusiastically and comment on how fantastic he is at sitting and looking at the words.'

Flashing these five words for one second each constitutes one session. You should allow at least 15 minutes to pass before flashing the cards again. Aim to have at least three sessions over the course of one day.

'On the second day, teach the set of words introduced on the first day and add a second set of five new words. This new set should be seen three times throughout the day, just like the first set, making a total of six sessions. At the end of each session, tell your child how proud you are of them, hug them, and move on to an unrelated activity.

On the third day, add a third set of five new words. Now, you are teaching your child three sets of reading words, five words in each set, each set three times a day. You and your child are now enjoying a total of nine reading sessions spread out during the day, equaling a few minutes in all.

The first fifteen words you teach them should be made up of the most familiar and enjoyable words around him. These words should include the names of immediate family members, relatives, family pets, favorite foods, objects in the house, and favorite activities.'

Every five days, retire one word from each set and replace it with a new word. Maintain enthusiasm throughout the process, and after each session, warmly hug your child and express how proud you are of their efforts in learning to read.

To provide the necessary repetition for learning, I created a duplicate flashcard for each retired word. Copies of these flashcards made it possible for my child and I to play multiple games of Snap, further reinforcing their learning. Once it became evident that my child recognized each word, I created smaller flashcards to make them easier to handle.

The program presented by Readingeggs.com.au is also a valuable complementary aid to help your child develop confidence in their reading ability.

ATTEND AN INTEREST GROUP

Starting school is a significant life transition for your child. It can be exciting but may cause anxiety, uncertainty, and confusion. One strategy I used to help facilitate a smooth transition was to attend interest groups with my children during their preschool years. These experiences provided a mini preview of what they could expect when they commenced school. In these settings, teachers and instructors required them to pay attention. My presence and confidence in the teacher were reassuring for them, which helped them to feel relaxed and happy.

Before attending the interest group, take time to prepare your child by outlining the expected standards of behavior. Explain that they must sit quietly, listen to the teacher, and follow the teacher's instructions. Also, remind them to raise their hand if they have a question. You can also discuss the purpose of the session and how they might benefit. For example, you might say, *'Your gym instructor, Mr. Bennett, will teach you how to do a forward roll.'*

The type of group I am suggesting could include a junior science group, music lessons, swimming lessons, or gymnastics. Storytelling sessions at the library would also be an ideal activity. You may need to try a few of these groups on a trial basis to determine your child's level of interest.

> *'The beautiful thing about learning is that nobody can take it away from you.'*
>
> B. B. King

CREATIVE TECHNIQUES TO ENHANCE LEARNING

As a new parent, I always sought innovative and unique ways to enhance my children's learning potential. Two complementary techniques that I embraced were Brain Gym exercises and the therapeutic benefits of Rosemary Oil. It was claimed that both techniques could stimulate the brain and improve a child's learning ability. I have provided a brief overview of the logic underpinning each technique.

Brain Gym

Brain Gym is an educational program I used with my children to enhance their ability to learn. Dr. Paul Dennison and Gail Dennison developed the program in the 1970s. The program involves engaging children in daily repetitive activities, such as crawling, yawning, and outlining symbols in the air. It also emphasizes the importance of drinking plenty of water to stay hydrated.

They designed twenty-six Brain Gym activities to integrate, repattern, and increase blood flow to the brain to improve its function (Dennison and Dennison 1992). These exercises (for example, Brain Gym: The Complete Brain Warm-Up) were initially developed to assist students experiencing stress, inactivity, or learning difficulties. In addition to Brain Gym movements, I included exercise breaks like running or playing ball games, particularly when teaching new information. I found my children could focus more effectively after enjoying a short 'active' break.

In her book Smart Moves: Why Learning Is Not All In Your Head, Dr. Carla Hannaford (2010) emphasizes the critical role of movement in enhancing the learning process. As a neurophysiologist and educator, she advocates incorporating Brain Gym exercises into children's daily routines. This approach aims to create a state of learning readiness. Hannaford cites case studies demonstrating significant academic improvements in children who practiced these movements regularly. This book is inspiring and worth reading.

Many countries around the world have adopted the Brain Gym program. Experts recognize it as a safe, effective, innovative educational and self-development tool that integrates body and mind. It brings about rapid and often remarkable improvements in concentration, memory, reading, writing, organizing, listening, physical coordination, attitude, and motivation (for example, The Brain Gym Program, Brain Gym Australia, Brain Gym UK). These websites provide various online resources (that is, courses, materials, activities) that parents can use to access more information about the Program and its applications.

Aromatherapy

Have you ever wondered why the ancient Greeks wore rosemary wreaths in their hair as part of their standard dress? Records from 500 BCE indicate that rosemary was used by ancient cultures to 'strengthen' their brains and 'enhance' memory. Around the 1600s, Shakespeare also wrote in Hamlet that '*rosemary is for remembrance*,' indicating that the idea still existed during his time.

Over the years, many studies have explored the benefits of aromatherapy on health, well-being, and memory (see, for example, Herz 2016). Dr. Mark Moss and Victoria Earle from Northumbria University conducted a study to examine the effect of rosemary oil on children's memory. The study involved a small sample of 40 students aged 10 to 11 years (British Psychological Society 2017). They concluded that children exposed to the scent of rosemary oil scored better when recalling words. This finding was consistent with earlier studies examining cognition in healthy adults. The researchers postulated that the scent of rosemary oil stimulated the brain, particularly the transmitters associated with memory. However, they did not offer conclusive evidence. More extensive trials would be necessary to verify these findings.

Despite the overall benefits of aromatherapy, other educators have been more skeptical about the positive effects of rosemary oil. For example, Dabell (2019) points to the review work of Herz (2016) and the lack of definitive evidence that rosemary, in and of itself, can increase memory. It was unclear whether rosemary oil specifically outperformed other scents in boosting memory retention. Nevertheless, I was curious to explore its potential benefits.

When I read about the 'potential' benefits of rosemary oil, my eldest son was four years old. At the time, I felt that if rosemary oil could do no harm and might help invigorate the mind, improve concentration, and stimulate clear thinking, it was worth a try. These seemed like sound prerequisites for enhancing learning. I rubbed rosemary oil through my boys' damp hair each evening after their baths. I repeated the process in the mornings as they dressed. It was both easy and inexpensive to do.

Side note: If your child suffers from allergies, asthma, or other breathing conditions, speak to your doctor before rubbing rosemary oil into their hair or adding it to a diffuser in your home.

OUTINGS—KEEPING TRACK OF YOUR CHILD

Of course, nothing beats holding your child's hand at a crowded venue or on an outing. However, this is not always possible. I have provided several suggestions to assist you in locating your child if they become separated from you.

Back then …

When my children were of preschool age, we had a unique method for locating each other. When a child loses sight of their parents and cries out for *'Mommy'* or *'Daddy,'* it is natural for all parents nearby to respond. To differentiate our call, our solution was to call out the word *'Cooee'* loudly if we couldn't see each other. *'Cooee'* is a word used by the indigenous people of Australia that means *'come here.'*

Of course, you can use any word that holds meaning for both you and your children. Rehearse a specific call with your child at home and during outings. This practice will help them feel prepared and they will understand how to use it if necessary. As my boys grew older, we created our own 'whistle call,' which they found slightly less embarrassing.

Now …

A more effective high-tech solution today would be a GPS tracking device. I have provided the link for a [GPS Child Tracker](#) as an example. This device is waterproof and shockproof and can be clipped to clothing or placed in your child's backpack. Improvements to the technology will undoubtedly occur, so staying informed about new developments will be necessary.

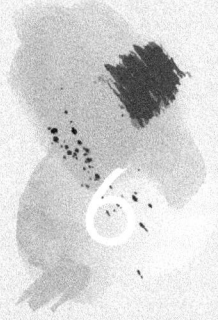

YOUR CHILD HAS STARTED SCHOOL WHAT NOW?

PARENTAL INVOLVEMENT AT SCHOOL

Parental or caregiver involvement in classroom activities at elementary school can facilitate a child's smooth transition into this new environment. Ask your child's teacher if they can suggest a way for you to be involved in the classroom activities. For example, the teacher may recommend reading with individual children once a week or accompanying the class on school excursions.

When a parent becomes involved in classroom activities, it usually telegraphs a message to their child that the classroom is a safe place. Through this involvement, children will see that their parents respect and value their teachers. This collaboration will also give the child a sense of belonging. Consequently, they should feel more secure, happy, motivated, and relaxed and have fewer behavioral issues (EarlyYearsCareers.com 2016).

EARLY CHILDHOOD | WHERE THE MAGIC HAPPENS

DO OUR CHILDREN LEARN IN THE SAME WAY?

> *'If a child can't learn the way we teach,
> maybe we should teach the way they learn.'*
>
> Ignacio Estrada

You may be worried that your child is not picking up a particular skill (for example, learning to read) as quickly as their friends. One possible explanation for this outcome is that the teaching method used by the teacher may not align with your child's specific learning style or intelligence profile. As a result, your child may be less receptive to the instruction. Teachers can address this problem by using alternative methods to present the information. Every child is unique. Therefore, it is unrealistic to expect a 'one-size-fits-all' approach to teaching and learning to be effective for every child (Gardner 2011a). Let me explain.

You may have heard of Harvard Professor Howard Gardner and his Theory of Multiple Intelligences and its profound impact on thinking and practice in education. His theory emerged from cognitive research in the 1980s, documenting how students' minds differ and learn differently. Each student has a unique profile and varying strengths across different intelligences. These differences influence how they approach tasks, solve problems, and progress in various educational domains (Gardner 2011a).

In his book Frames of Mind: The Theory of Multiple Intelligences, Gardner (2011b) introduced the idea that intelligence is multifaceted and should be recognized, nurtured, and valued as such. Initially, he identified seven intelligences—Verbal-Linguistic, Logical-Mathematical, Musical-Rhythmic, Bodily-Kinesthetic, Visual-Spatial, Interpersonal, and Intrapersonal—but has since suggested there are additional intelligences (see, for example, Edutopia.org 2013, Northern Illinois University Center for Innovative Teaching and Learning 2020). However, in this book, I have confined the discussion to the seven intelligences that Gardner initially identified.

Gardner believes that we all have multiple intelligences. One or two intelligences are usually more dominant than the rest, although that can change, certainly in early life (Gardner, personal communication, 2023). This dominance becomes evident when your child demonstrates superior ability in an area related to a specific intelligence. For example, excelling in a game that requires spatial thinking may suggest strong Visual-Spatial intelligence. Similarly, quickly learning a foreign language through cultural immersion may indicate strong Verbal-Linguistic intelligence. Gardner refers to multiple intelligences as the human intellectual toolkit. He believes that, barring significant disabilities, everyone has the potential to develop several intelligences. *'At any one moment, we will have a unique profile because of both genetic (heritability) and experiential factor*s' (Gardner 2013).

Historically, schools were biased toward the Verbal-Linguistic and Logical-Mathematical modes of instruction. This bias favored children who were strong in these 'valued' intelligences. It allowed them to excel and display what was perceived as the 'essence of intelligence.' Likewise, test designers primarily intended intelligence quotient (IQ) tests to assess Verbal-Linguistic and Logical-Mathematical intelligences and, occasionally, Visual-Spatial intelligence.

Results from IQ tests further reinforced the historical view of what it meant to be 'intelligent.' If your child's dominant intelligence is, for example, Musical-Rhythmic, Bodily-Kinesthetic, or Interpersonal, excelling on a traditional IQ test will be more difficult. This outcome arises from the fact that such tests often exhibit an inherent bias toward specific types of intelligence. As a result, your child will miss out on the recognition they rightfully deserve. Nor would they have been taught or assessed in a way that allowed them to use their dominant intelligence.

Gardner (2013) cautions against using specific tests to measure intelligence profiles. He maintains they would be challenging to design and implement and can lead to new forms of labeling and categorization of individuals. A critical limitation of such tests is their inability to assess and measure a child's specific intelligences through direct observation of performance. However, despite this limitation, he does not entirely dismiss the role that tests can play in assessing a child's intelligence profile.

Many other online tools, such as surveys, checklists, and questionnaires, are available to help parents assess and gain insight into their child's intelligence profile. One well-known test is the MIDAS test developed by Branton Shearer. This test provides a comprehensive description of the intellectual profile of a person from different age groups (miresearch.org 2021). The Connell Multiple Intelligence Questionnaire for Children (Scholastic.com 2023) is a similar test focusing on children.

Gardner's Theory of Multiple Intelligences has broadened our understanding of intelligence and encouraged educators to reconsider traditional teaching methods. The theory proposes two major transformations in the approach to teaching. Firstly, he emphasizes the need to 'individualize' (that is, personalize) teaching in the classroom. Tomlinson (2014) reasserts that educators should use detailed knowledge about each student's strengths, needs, and areas for growth to inform their teaching. Secondly, Gardner suggests the need for 'pluralization.' Pluralization means presenting the curriculum content in different ways so that each child can learn according to their intelligence profile.

Armstrong (2017, 2000), in two of his books, Multiple Intelligences in the Classroom and In Their Own Way, has reiterated Gardner's views. He suggests *'that teachers be trained to present their lessons in a wide variety of ways using music, cooperative learning, art activities, role play, multimedia, field trips, inner reflection and so much more so that each child has the opportunity to learn in ways harmonious with their unique minds.'* Teaching new information in this way gives each child the necessary repetition required for successful learning outcomes. In addition, it enhances their knowledge and offers opportunities to utilize and further develop their less-established intelligences. Your child will then be able to understand and interpret the new skill, concept, or topic from a different perspective. By presenting materials in various ways, you demonstrate what it means to understand something well (Gardner 2013).

If your child has difficulty understanding new material as it is presented in school, consider speaking with their teacher. Offering this feedback will encourage the teacher to tailor your child's learning experiences using alternative approaches to achieve positive outcomes. Also, ask how you can best support your child at home to build their confidence to ensure their in-school learning experiences are effective.

THE SEVEN INTELLIGENCES AND THEIR CAPABILITIES

To help you understand the uniqueness of each intelligence, I have summarized their characteristics and capabilities. I have also included some simple activities involving reading and mathematics that draw on the capabilities of each intelligence.

Engaging in these activities will provide you with insights into your child's intelligence profile. This insight will help you customize future learning activities that engage your child and develop their strengths. It will also allow you to focus on areas within their intelligence profile that may require growth. Parents can source additional ideas for activities that connect with the intelligences at Scholastic.com (2021) and Connell (2015).

> *'Everybody is a genius. But if you judge a fish by its ability to climb a tree, it will spend its whole life thinking that it is stupid.'*
>
> Anonymous

1. VERBAL-LINGUISTIC INTELLIGENCE

Verbal-Linguistic Intelligence relates to children who express themselves well through the spoken and written word. They can quickly grasp the intent of the viewpoints of others. Gardner suggests this type of intelligence is associated with the left side of the brain. These children prefer speaking and writing. They are sensitive to the meaning and order of words and love to tell stories and play word games. These might include Junior Scrabble and Jr. Boggle or more advanced versions like Spellie.

SIMPLE TEACHING IDEAS USING THE CAPABILITIES OF VERBAL-LINGUISTIC INTELLIGENCE

TYPE	ACTIVITIES
Reading	Teachers require children to learn new words. To help them learn quickly, parents should provide their children with opportunities for repetition at home.
	With a red marker, write each new word on a blank flashcard. Then, encourage your child to write the same word on another blank flashcard, using the one you wrote as a reference (that is, two flashcards for each new word). Repeat this process for each new word. After recording all the new words on flashcards, shuffle the cards and prepare to play a game of Snap with your child.
	As a separate activity, ask your child to incorporate one of the new words into a sentence. For example, if the new word is 'ball,' the sentence might be *'The dog ran after the ball.'* Record your child as they say their sentence to you. Demonstrate how to write the sentence on paper and encourage your child to do the same. Read the sentence aloud to them with expression while running your finger under each word as you pronounce it. Then, ask your child to read the sentence to you. Repeat this activity for each new word.
	Cook with your child but first record yourself slowly reading the recipe. Let them play it back as they follow the written recipe. Have them measure the ingredients and review the recipe together. For example, the recipe might include 1 cup of flour, ½ cup of honey, ¼ cup of milk, 2 eggs, and a pinch of salt.
Math	Hide and Seek is a fun game to play if you are trying to teach your child to count. First, let them hide while you cover your eyes and count out loud to 20. Record yourself counting on your phone. Then, switch roles. Leave your child to count along with the recording before they hunt you down.
	Encourage your child to jump rope while chanting One Potato, Two Potato. This activity will provide them with the necessary repetition to learn to count.

2. LOGICAL-MATHEMATICAL INTELLIGENCE

Children with this type of intelligence excel at understanding logical and mathematical problems, using a methodical approach to analyze and solve them effectively. They prefer using logic and reasoning. They enjoy working with numbers, analyzing patterns, and asking questions about how things work. They love sorting, classifying, and comparing. Games that may be useful for these children are The Gamesman-Children's Chess (Australia only), Magnetic Chess Set, Junior Monopoly, and Dominoes.

SIMPLE TEACHING IDEAS USING THE CAPABILITIES OF LOGICAL-MATHEMATICAL INTELLIGENCE

TYPE	ACTIVITIES
Reading	Write a word out in lowercase letters (that is, lowercase = cat, as opposed to uppercase = CAT). Sound the word using the individual phonetic letter sounds (not the letter's name). Let your child hear how the sound of the letters flow together. Seek advice from their teacher to clarify how best you can support their teaching methods to avoid confusing your child.
	Have your child copy each word from their reading list onto individual flashcards. Suggest how they can sort or categorize the words into different groups, such as words that start with 'a' or animal-related words. You can also encourage them to group words with similar spelling, like cat, mat, and rat.
	Discuss their logic and reasoning for the groupings. As you select each flashcard, ensure you say the word before placing it in its respective group. You can further reinforce this learning by applying the Doman method of instruction outlined in Chapter 5.
	Readingeggs.com.au is another helpful program to teach your child the individual letters of the alphabet, their associated phonetic sounds, and how to read.
Math	A practical way to introduce fractions is by cutting a banana into two halves. Highlight that each piece is equal in size and called a half. Have your child compare the length of each half to reinforce the concept. Then, observe together how the two halves form a complete banana when put back together.

TYPE	ACTIVITIES
Continued	Repeat this activity by cutting a second banana into four equal pieces. Explain that each piece represents one-quarter of the banana. When you place the four quarters back together, point out that they form a whole banana. Extend the activity by combining two quarters and one-half of a banana to make a whole banana. Discuss how many quarters of a banana are needed to make one-half of a banana. Frequent repetition of these activities will consolidate their understanding of fractions. You can easily integrate the basic concept of fractions into everyday conversations. For example, you might ask, *'Would you like half a glass of water? Would you like your sandwich cut into quarters? Would you please read half a page of your reader for me?'* <div align="center">**Halfway Down** Halfway down the stairs is the stair where I sit. There isn't any other stair quite like it. I'm not at the bottom; I'm not at the top. So, this is the stair where I always stop. A. A. Milne</div>

3. BODILY-KINESTHETIC INTELLIGENCE

Children with Bodily-Kinesthetic intelligence possess a strong sense of space, distance, depth, and size. They can demonstrate balance, coordination, and control of their body. They can perform complex movements easily and precisely. This characteristic is present in elite athletes in sports, such as gymnastics, diving, horse riding, cricket, soccer, basketball, and baseball.

These children prefer using their body, hands, and sense of touch to learn. They generally love to dance, act, and engage in mimes. Children with this intelligence enjoy learning through movement games. Playing games such as Twister and Simon Says would work well with these children. You could also use Charades to act out word meanings.

Children with Bodily-Kinesthetic intelligence will benefit from movement and exercise breaks throughout the day. Parents should encourage games using sporting equipment that is appropriate for their child's age and developmental stage.

SIMPLE TEACHING IDEAS USING THE CAPABILITIES OF BODILY-KINESTHETIC INTELLIGENCE

TYPE	ACTIVITIES
Reading	Teach your child to read at your local beach. Write a word in the sand taken from their reading list. Encourage them to practice writing the same word in the sand directly below where you have written the word. To make it more exciting, move close to the water's edge. Quickly write the word in the sand before a wave washes it away. Encourage your child to have their turn. Their excitement will mount as they rush to complete writing their word in the sand before the next wave washes it away. Another activity that draws on these capabilities could involve acting out verbs on the reading list, that is, doing words. Create flashcards with individual verbs, such as walk, skip, hop, yawn, gallop, bend, and jump. Make a game of it by showing and reading the word out loud to your child. Then, demonstrate the appropriate action. Have your child mimic the action while holding the flashcard and repeating the word.
Math	Parents can use everyday household items, such as spoons, straws, fruit, and crackers, to effectively teach basic math. Cut five pieces of cardboard in the shape of a dash to create the 'plus,' 'minus,' and 'equal' symbols. Teach addition and subtraction using fruit. For example, 4 oranges + 3 oranges = 7 oranges. Show enthusiasm and encourage your child to create their own math equations using the oranges. Count the fruit with them until they are confident and can count independently. Ensure you have access to a good supply of oranges before you commence this activity. Another fun idea is to bake cookies in the shape of numbers with your child. You could create cookie equations, such as 1 + 2 = 3. Alternatively, you could bake twenty of your child's favorite cookies. Count the cookies together and write the total number on a sheet of paper. Then, encourage your child to eat one. Count how many are left. Write down the equation that represents what has just occurred. That is, 20 - 1 = 19.

4. VISUAL-SPATIAL INTELLIGENCE

Children with heightened Visual-Spatial intelligence can create, imagine, and draw two-dimensional (2D) and three-dimensional (3D) images. This intelligence is evident in people with careers in, for example, gaming, architecture, and multimedia.

These children prefer using pictures and images. They enjoy puzzles and building with blocks and love to paint, draw, and mold playdough and clay. They enjoy pulling things apart and putting them back together. Displaying photos and images to these children will enhance their understanding of new material, complementing verbal explanations.

Provide art materials and books with bold graphics to assist this type of learning. When encouraging your child to use their Visual-Spatial intelligence, ask them to draw what they have learned. Suggest they create the drawings based on their observations.

SIMPLE TEACHING IDEAS USING THE CAPABILITIES OF VISUAL-SPATIAL INTELLIGENCE

TYPE	ACTIVITIES
Reading	Begin by writing a word from your child's reading list on a large sheet of cardboard. Instruct your child to shape each letter of the word using playdough. Then, guide them to place each playdough letter underneath the corresponding letters written on the cardboard. Photograph the playdough word and hang a printout of the image on their bedroom wall for regular checking.
	Use a finger-painting activity to demonstrate letter writing. Show your child how to draw letters in the paint using your finger and then encourage them to have a turn. Once the paintings are dry, hang them on your child's wall.
Math	Plan a treasure hunt for your child at your local park to encourage counting. Provide written instructions to guide your child to the treasure. Assist them in reading the instructions by running your finger under the words as you read together.
	Use an Explorer Compass to determine the directions outlined in the instructions (for example, 20 steps east, 40 steps south, 10 steps west, and 50 steps north). Make sure the step size is equal to your child's step size. Count the steps out loud together when following the instructions. Ensure the treasure is of sufficient value to warrant discovery.

5. MUSICAL-RHYTHMIC INTELLIGENCE

Children possessing Musical-Rhythmic intelligence can play music by ear, read and play from a musical score, and write music. They are receptive to melody, rhythm, pitch, and tone. They love listening to music, playing it, singing songs, humming, and moving to the rhythm of music. They enjoy creating tunes and trying to replicate tunes they have heard.

Playing music at home and exposing your child to various genres will help develop their musical intelligence. Attending musical activities such as concerts and musicals further enhances this growth. Activities like singing, dancing, and playing age-appropriate instruments like tapping sticks, maracas, triangles, and drums will foster their musical abilities.

Likewise, melodies, rhythm and clapping are great tools for these children to learn math facts and other content. Putting the Times Tables and Alphabet to music will make them easy to learn and remember. To further develop this intelligence, provide opportunities for your child to learn a variety of instruments (for example, Beginner Harmonica in the Key of C, How to Play the Harmonica, Kid's Ukulele, Ukulele Tuner, How to Play the Ukulele).

SIMPLE TEACHING IDEAS USING THE CAPABILITIES OF MUSICAL-RHYTHMIC INTELLIGENCE

TYPE	ACTIVITIES
Reading	Write each word from your child's reading list on individual flashcards. Show each flashcard to your child and pronounce each word for them. Use a variety of tones (for example, high or low) as you read each word on the list. Ask your child to join the game and read the words out loud.
	Encourage your child to write each word on a new flashcard, using your flashcard as a guide. After completing each word, suggest that they verbalize the word using either a loud or soft voice.
	Create a sentence that includes a word from your child's reading list. Repeat the sentence together to the regular beat of a drum or hand clapping. Repeat this activity for each word on their reading list.
	Frequently sing one of the many alphabet songs available online so your child can learn the name of each letter of the alphabet (for example, The ABC Song).

TYPE	ACTIVITIES
Math	Teach the <u>Times Tables</u> to music. This activity is easy to do while driving in the car since you will have a captive audience. Some simple home-based learning activities that can make use of your child's musical intelligence are: • Beating a drum and counting the number of sounds made. • Counting the number of black and white keys on their keyboard. • Ringing a bell a specific number of times to alert the family that it is time for dinner. Be ready to count along with your child as they engage in these activities.

6. INTERPERSONAL INTELLIGENCE

Children possessing Interpersonal intelligence are usually referred to as born leaders. They are generally pragmatic and very responsible. They are calm and good listeners, but their primary characteristic is their ability to use their knowledge to influence others. They are also able to identify strengths in others and encourage them to use these strengths.

Children with this intelligence prefer to learn through group activities or games. They are at their best when teaching others in a mentoring role. They enjoy interviewing, role-playing, and acting out stories. Make sure you have a dress-up box and other aids available to support their role-playing, as this activity will help to promote the development of this intelligence. Puppets are an excellent tool for children with strong interpersonal intelligence, serving as a medium for them to express themselves effectively.

SIMPLE TEACHING IDEAS USING THE CAPABILITIES OF INTERPERSONAL INTELLIGENCE

TYPE	ACTIVITIES
Reading	An ideal time to engage in a group activity that supports your child's reading development is after dinner while the family is still gathered around the table.
	In this activity, your child will play the role of the teacher. They will aim to teach all the family members the word on each flashcard taken from their reading list.
	Begin by saying the word quietly to your child and then sound it out phonetically to them. Have them repeat this process while showing each family member the word on the flashcard. At your child's request, each family member will repeat this process back to them.
	These activities will provide the necessary repetition for your child to learn each word on their reading list. It will also allow them to assume a mentoring role. In this role, they can teach others and shift the focus off themselves as they acquire new knowledge.
Math	Play a favorite board game, such as Monopoly, that relies on each player reading and interpreting the instructions on the cards. Additional assistance will be necessary to help with the game's financial aspects, such as addition and subtraction.
	Your child will be excited to play a board game with their family. The focus will be on the game rather than the learning that will occur. With your assistance, they can practice reading and math without feeling stressed and have fun in the process.

7. INTRAPERSONAL INTELLIGENCE

Children with Intrapersonal intelligence are reserved by nature. They have a deep connection with themselves and may hide their moods and feelings. They prefer to work alone and use self-study, and they are usually admired by their peers. A child with this intelligence views others through the lens of their own emotional life. They are happiest when observing, listening, and working on their own. This intelligence is the rarest of the intelligences.

A camera or drawing pad is a useful aid for a child with this intelligence to record their work. If you have a phone with a camera, encourage your child to take photos of their activities. Creating a photo scrapbook enables your child to reflect at a later time. Paper and art supplies are also helpful tools for your child to document their activities. This documentation will enable your child to revisit and recall their new learnings.

SIMPLE TEACHING IDEAS USING THE CAPABILITIES OF INTRAPERSONAL INTELLIGENCE

TYPE	ACTIVITIES
Reading	When you start teaching your child the alphabet, write each letter on a large sheet of cardboard and then pronounce its name. Ask your child to repeat the name. Give your child a glue stick to hold in their dominant hand. Guide their hand with the glue stick and trace the letter you have written on the cardboard. Affix split peas, rice, or sequins onto the letter. Repeat this process to reinforce this new learning. Encourage your child to undertake this activity independently. Ask them to pronounce the name of the letter often while completing the task. Be available to help if needed. Hang your child's collage on their bedroom wall at eye level. Continue practicing the name of the letter together. Ask your child how working independently on this activity made them feel. Take their feedback into account and identify any improvements you can make to enhance their next experience.
Math	Subtraction can be taught while playing a game of <u>ten-pin bowling</u> at home. Start by counting the 10 pins. Have your child arrange them in the required triangular formation for the game. Encourage your child to draw the 10 pins in formation on the left side of a large sheet of cardboard. Commence the game by having your child roll the ball toward the pins and observe how many pins they knock over. On the cardboard, draw a minus sign (-) to the right of where your child has drawn the 10 pins.

EARLY CHILDHOOD | WHERE THE MAGIC HAPPENS

TYPE	ACTIVITIES
Continued	Walk over to the pins together and count the number knocked over (for example, 5 pins). Return to the drawing on the cardboard. Have your child draw to the right of the minus sign the 5 pins they knocked over. Draw an equal sign (=) on the cardboard to the right of where your child has drawn the 5 pins.
	Walk back to the pins and count the number of pins together that are still upright. Return to the pictorial equation on the cardboard and have them draw the 5 pins still standing.
	Underneath this pictorial equation, write the equivalent equation using the actual numbers. Count the number of pins drawn on the cardboard with your child and write down the equivalent equation (for example, 10 - 5 = 5).
	Ask your child if they want to repeat the activity, but this time by themselves. Be around to assist if they need help. However, remember they may enjoy having the space to try it independently.
	Take a photo of your child playing this game. Print it off so that you can talk about the activity at bedtime.
	Ask your child how they felt while learning this new concept. For example, were they happy, confused, confident, or nervous? Consider their response and identify any improvements you can make to ensure their next experience is even more positive.

It is important to accept that we all learn differently. If your child is not responding to a particular teaching method at home or school, consider the Theory of Multiple Intelligences. This theory offers parents and teachers a range of alternative approaches to explore. So, be creative at home and present new material in multiple ways (Gardner 2013). Use meaningful activities to help your child understand the new material. These activities will build their confidence and the necessary skills before they advance to the next stage of knowledge development.

Gardner explains that *'instruction designed to help students learn material in multiple ways can trigger their confidence to develop areas in which they are not as strong'* (Northern Illinois University Center for Innovative Teaching and Learning 2020). Edutopia.org (2021) offers insight into different learning approaches and techniques to keep children engaged.

LEARNING SHOULD BE A POSITIVE EXPERIENCE

To achieve successful learning outcomes, the teaching activities at home must be enjoyable. Implement the following tips to maximize your child's learning outcomes, regardless of the subject you are teaching. Make every endeavor to:

- Participate in the activity with your child. Demonstrate the activity and support their efforts. For example, draw the letters, read the words, and write the numbers.

- Teach your child the new material in various ways. Ensure they understand the information and provide them with the repetition necessary to achieve competency.

- Engage your child's senses to make the experiences more meaningful. For example, you can put the words you are teaching to music, write new words in gritty sand, and teach counting to the beat of a drum.

At all times, remember you are teaching and not testing. Your child will learn more quickly if you are patient and avoid negativity in response to their efforts.

> *'If to correct you must humiliate, you don't know how to teach.'*
> Joe Becigneul

DEVELOPING A GROWTH MINDSET AND THE KEY ROLE OF PRAISE

The early chapters of this book emphasize how parents can nurture their child's curiosity, resilience, and grit. These qualities are essential for helping children explore their world and engage in meaningful learning. I have also alluded to the importance of *praising* effort. In this section, I explore the key role of praise and its potential to motivate, guide, and nurture the development of a *growth mindset* in young children.

After years of research, eminent Stanford University psychologist Professor Carol Dweck identified a simple yet ground-breaking idea about the power of the human mindset. In her book *Mindset: The New Psychology of Success*, Dweck (2006) introduced the concept of two mindsets: *fixed* and *growth*. She explained how these mindsets shape people's beliefs about their intelligence and abilities and ultimately influence life outcomes.

A person's mindset refers to an established set of attitudes, beliefs, assumptions, and perspectives that shape how they think, interpret situations, and approach life. It influences how they perceive the world, relationships, and personal development, as well as their approach to learning and response to challenges. Additionally, their mindset affects decision-making and how they handle success and failure.

> *'Dweck illuminates that our beliefs about our capabilities exert tremendous influence on how we learn and what paths we take in life.'*
> Bill Gates

A parent can shape their child's mindset through guidance, experiences, and intentional efforts. This approach can lead to different outlooks and behaviors in their child's life. Dweck explains how a *fixed* mindset (that is, believing abilities are inborn and unchangeable) can limit achievement. In contrast, a *growth* mindset (that is, believing abilities can be developed and improved) fosters resilience and learning.

Dweck's research on mindsets began in the 1980s when she became interested in student attitudes toward failure. She observed that while some students rebounded quickly from setbacks, others were deeply discouraged by even minor setbacks. This observation led her to explore people's beliefs about learning and intelligence. She concluded that children praised for being smart often focus on performance, avoid taking risks, and experience anxiety about failure (see, for example, Mindsetworks.com 2017). These children have a *fixed mindset*.

In contrast, children who are praised for behaviors that lead to growth rather than for their innate abilities tend to put in more effort. They are more likely to try harder and dedicate extra time to their tasks. This persistence often leads to higher levels of achievement. When parents explain that the brain functions like a muscle that requires exercise to grow, children start to grasp this concept. They understand that their intelligence can improve through intentional actions and behaviors. This analogy helps them recognize the importance of effort in their learning process. This understanding fosters a thirst for mastering new skills and knowledge. These children have a *growth mindset* marked by resilience and grit when they falter.

Research conducted by Dweck and her colleagues at the University of Chicago has shed some light on the early development of fixed and growth mindsets. Their findings focus on how these mindsets emerge in young children (Gunderson et al., 2013). The study examined how mothers praised their infants at ages one, two, and three, with follow-up assessments conducted five years later. The results revealed that toddlers whose parents praised their efforts and actions, rather than praising them as individuals, developed a more positive and confident approach to new challenges. These children believed they could improve their performance through hard work. The study also indicated a correlation between having a growth mindset in second grade and subsequent academic performance and success in fourth grade. This finding highlights the significance of developing a growth mindset early in a child's life.

PRACTICAL STRATEGIES FOR FOSTERING A GROWTH MINDSET

Young children naturally gravitate toward a *growth mindset* from birth. They curiously explore their environment using their senses to learn through trial and error, observed modeled behaviors, and instruction. Parents can use these early years to actively cultivate a growth mindset in their children by encouraging their learning efforts. Positive encouragement will significantly enhance a child's willingness to take on challenges and persist in learning.

At some point in their development, many children make the unfortunate shift from a *growth mindset* to a *fixed mindset*. The cause of this switch is unclear. However, I believe this shift is influenced by several factors. These factors include the expectations established by parents, teachers, and others who prioritize outcomes instead of the processes used to achieve them.

Dweck (2006) outlines ways to cultivate the development of a growth mindset. These include emphasizing the importance of encouraging children to embrace challenges and learn from mistakes and setbacks. Parents should nurture their children's belief in their ability to grow and improve across different areas of life. In his book, *The Agile Learner: Where Growth Mindsets, Habits of Mind and Practice Unite*, Anderson (2023) highlights that our mindset can lie on the continuum between *fixed* and *growth*. Put simply, developing a growth mindset is a journey that requires reinforcement and encouragement from parents. This support enables children to cultivate habits that promote a growth mindset.

Here are some simple strategies to foster a growth mindset compiled from Dweck's (2006) work and other practitioners (see, for example, Millacci 2021):

- **Explain the Concept**—To adopt a growth mindset, children must first understand the concept. A practical way to introduce this concept is to compare the brain to a muscle that gets stronger when you use it. For example, lifting weights will build arm muscles just like the learning process will exercise and strengthen the brain. Emphasize that their ability to learn is not fixed but can develop throughout their life. When your child shares something they have learned, reinforce that their knowledge and skills are growing. For example, you might say, *'With all the effort you're putting in, you're getting smarter every day.'*

- **Use growth mindset language**—Every day, take a moment to ask your child what they have learned. Infuse growth mindset language into your conversations with them. Young children are deeply interested in vocabulary, so use this interest to embed words, such as *strategy, behavior, growth, brain, effort, stronger,* and *feedback*. Incorporating these words in your conversations can organically encourage a growth mindset. The Growth Mindset Conversation Cards are a beautifully illustrated deck designed to inspire meaningful conversations. They feature engaging questions that help parents and children discuss topics like growth mindset, kindness, resilience, and gratitude.

- **Praise growth mindset behaviors**—Your praise should be directed at your child's behaviors and actions that lead to growth and indicate a *growth mindset*. For example:

    o Taking on challenges—Praise your child for attempting problems that are slightly too difficult for them.

    o Setting goals—Praise your child for deciding to learn a new skill, such as swimming.

    o Planning—Praise your child for asking to attend swimming classes.

    o Being persistent—Praise your child for continuing to attend their class even though they sometimes do not feel like it.

    o Using creative and innovative strategies—Praise your child when they are prepared to use innovative strategies to solve a problem. For example, if your child cannot attend swimming class but needs to practice, they could work on their strokes while lying on a narrow bench. This alternative approach will allow them to practice their technique even when they cannot access a pool.

- **Facilitate reflective thinking**—When your child encounters difficulties progressing with a challenge, prompt them to reflect on their unsuccessful strategy. Encourage them to discuss what they think went wrong. Rather than suggesting solutions—which is always a temptation— collaborate with your child and provide support as they brainstorm ideas for a new strategy.

> *'Everyone learns in a different way.*
> *Let's keep trying to find the way that works for you.'*
>
> Carol Dweck

- **Celebrate mistakes**—Encourage your child to view mistakes as opportunities to learn and develop. Promote a culture of embracing risks and learning from mistakes. Allow your child the space to make mistakes, as this experience imparts essential life lessons. It builds resilience, which strengthens their growth mindset. Remind them that learning involves making and accepting mistakes and facing challenges. Emphasize that these experiences are crucial to growth.

    Avoid criticism and excessive assistance, as these responses undermine your child's confidence. They will also hinder the development of perseverance and belief in their ability to achieve success through hard work. Encourage your child to reflect on their mistakes and what they have learned from them. Make this a regular topic of conversation and sharing.

> *'Your best teacher is your last mistake.'*
>
> Author uncertain

- **Cultivate a positive attitude toward the learning process**—Model how to embrace challenges and persist through difficulties to inspire your child to adopt a similar mindset. Set an example of resilience, grit, and problem-solving. Discuss your challenges and successes. Being humble and 'upfront' with your child is incredibly powerful. Encourage your child to share their own experiences with you and the family. These honest discussions will help your child develop a positive attitude toward learning and help them understand that it is a lifelong endeavor.

  Set a positive example for your child by taking on a new, challenging task yourself. Your actions will inspire them to take risks, embrace new experiences, and persevere when faced with challenges. Typically, children will experience the most growth in the presence of adults who embrace a growth mindset.

- **Recognize hard work**—Encourage your child to share a task they worked hard on today. Acknowledge their effort and dedication and reinforce the importance of their commitment. For example, you might say, *'I can see this was a challenging task, and I'm proud you stuck with it. It seems your approach didn't give the desired result this time—what other strategies might you try?'* This response avoids labeling or judging their work. Your feedback will help your child understand that their hard work is valued. They will also learn that improvement comes through effective effort and perseverance.

- **Introduce the power of 'yet'**—When faced with discouragement, remind your child of the transformative potential of the word 'yet.' 'Yet' reinforces a mindset that ongoing development and improvement are possible with time and continued effective effort. For example, your child might say:

  o *'I can't do this'* …your response should be *'You can't do this, yet.'*
  o *'This doesn't work'*…your response should be *'This doesn't work, yet.'*
  o *'I am not good at this'*…your response should be *'You are not good at this, yet.'*
  o *'I don't know how to'*…your response should be *'You don't know how to, yet.'*

- **Foster independence and collaboration**—Encourage your child to solve problems individually or collaboratively with friends when appropriate. Promote teamwork, idea-sharing, and mutual learning by teaching them to celebrate each other's successes. Be ready to offer guidance during challenges if the team is collectively stuck. This approach will help your child develop empathy, teamwork skills, and a shared sense of growth.

- **Encourage and demonstrate positive 'self-talk'**—Positive self-talk refers to the internal dialogue or stream of thoughts we use to interpret experiences, cope with challenges, and reinforce good thoughts about ourselves. It involves self-encouragement, believing in one's abilities, maintaining hope, and staying positive even when things are tough.

  Positive self-talk is informed by the strategies a parent uses to encourage their child's growth mindset. As a result, a child might express thoughts like, *'I can learn to do it if I practice'* or *'I can fix this if I try a different strategy.'* They may also say, *'I can't do this yet, but with time and practice, I will succeed.'* Positive self-talk shapes a young child's attitudes, emotions, and well-being.

For example, it can:

o Help reframe negative thoughts and promote a more optimistic outlook.
o Empower children to face challenges with a more positive attitude.
o Foster resilience, help children bounce back effectively from setbacks, and navigate difficult situations.
o Help to develop a problem-solving mindset.
o Help to develop a can-do attitude and minimize self-doubt.
o Have a positive impact on physical health.
o Serve as a powerful motivator for pursuing goals with determination.
o Create a positive mindset that enables clear and rational thinking.
o Contribute to an overall sense of well-being and happiness. Children who consistently reinforce positive thoughts are more likely to experience joy and contentment.

Some examples of negative and positive self-talk:

INSTEAD OF THINKING	TRY THINKING
'I'm not good at this.'	'What am I missing?'
'I give up.'	'I will use a different strategy.'
'This is too hard.'	'This may take some time and effort.'
'I can't make this any better.'	'I can always improve, so I will keep trying.'
'I just can't do math.'	'I am going to train my brain in math.'
'I made a mistake.'	'Mistakes help me learn.'
'She is so smart. I will never be that smart.'	'I am going to figure out how she does it so I can try it too.'
'It is good enough.'	'Is it my best work?'
'Plan A didn't work.'	'Good thing the alphabet has 25 more letters.'

It is important to note that while positive self-talk is valuable, it is not a cure-all. Additionally, promoting a balance between positive self-talk and realistic self-appraisal is crucial for your child to understand what is possible. For instance, it is unrealistic for a young child to expect to handle the demanding task of chopping wood. They would need more physical strength and maturity for such a task. Only when they are much older and stronger will they be capable of learning this skill. No amount of positive self-talk can change this reality.

- **Acknowledge the process**—Parents should acknowledge the process their child uses to tackle a task, not the outcome or the person. Highlight the importance of the journey. Recognize and praise your child's efforts. When providing your child with feedback, focus on the learning process. For example, you might say, '*You worked very hard on that,*' or '*That seems to have been a challenging task, but you stuck with it.*' Let them know you are proud of them for not giving up.

  Ensure your feedback is constructive and supportive and offer guidance on areas for improvement. Be specific about what your child did well and how their effort contributed to the outcome. Be sincere about what you appreciate and mean what you say. Specific feedback helps children understand the connection between their actions and results.

  Acknowledge a job well done and encourage your child to take pride in their personal growth achieved through their efforts. For example, you might say, '*I have noticed how much better you have become at dressing yourself. You have been practicing, and it is paying off. You should be proud of yourself for not giving up.*' Acknowledge their progress and improvement over time. Your acknowledgment will help them understand that growth and learning are important and take time.

- **Read books about a growth mindset**—This activity will help your child become more familiar with the strategies for developing a growth mindset. The following list of books and resources is a good starting point for parents who want to create and encourage a growth mindset in their child (see, for example, The Girl Who Never Makes Mistakes, Mistakes Are How I Learn, Your Fantastic Elastic Brain, The Power of Yet, I Believe I Can, Big Life Journal Resources for 4 to 6-year-olds, Growth Mindset Poster).

In summary, here are some fundamental guidelines to help parents stimulate a growth mindset in their children:

- Emphasize that their brain is growing rather than telling them they 'tried their best.'
- Accept mistakes rather than criticize them for making mistakes.
- Ask them for explanations rather than telling them the answers.
- Acknowledge the amount of work they put in rather than labeling or judging the work.
- Praise their effort rather than praise the outcome.

Cultivating a growth mindset in preschool children helps them unlock their potential, fostering cognitive and emotional development. This investment in their future is crucial. Parents can accomplish this by:

- Encouraging effort,
- Nurturing a love for learning,
- Teaching the concept of 'yet',
- Embracing mistakes and challenges,
- Modeling a growth mindset,
- Offering constructive feedback, and
- Promoting collaboration.

Such an environment develops resilience, curiosity, and a lifelong enthusiasm for learning.

> *'I am still learning.'*
> Michelangelo, at age 87

HOW TO PRAISE YOUR CHILD'S LEARNING ENDEAVORS

In nurturing growth mindsets, Dweck emphasizes the importance of 'praising effort.' However, she does not mean praising just any effort. Her focus is on praising the behaviors and actions that lead to growth. Anderson (2023) points out that not all types of effort produce growth outcomes. He warns that praising effort that does not lead to growth can be counterproductive to developing a child's growth mindset.

Unfortunately, Dweck's original intention behind praising effort has been misinterpreted by some parents and teachers. This misinterpretation has led to unintended consequences when the wrong type of effort is praised. Children have received inappropriate feedback such as, *'You did your best,' 'At least you tried,'* or *'Great effort'* (Dweck 2015). This misguided praise, intended to inspire children to extend their knowledge and skills, inadvertently encourages a *fixed mindset* rather than a *growth mindset*. Children may interpret this feedback as a sign that their parents and teachers doubt their ability to improve. It can cause them to lose confidence, stop trying, and eventually give up.

Anderson (2023) clarifies 'effort' by identifying four distinct types: *low, performance, ineffective,* and *effective* effort. He emphasizes that *effective* effort should be promoted and encouraged, as it fosters growth and facilitates new learning. Children who engage in *effective* effort through using specific behaviors and actions will develop and master new skills.

The following table summarizes the four types of effort and emphasizes the distinctions between them. These distinctions will help parents respond appropriately and effectively. Anderson's suggestions for feedback serve as a guide for parents whose children are starting formal schooling.

FOUR DIFFERENT TYPES OF EFFORT
(from Anderson 2023)

LOW EFFORT - TAKING THE EASY ROAD

Description	Suggested Feedback
When children engage in low effort, they choose tasks that are too easy and only require basic skills. While they may appear busy and focused, they are not acquiring new skills. Because the work is easy, the quality is likely to be high. Any mistakes tend to be careless and lack learning value. They are not being challenged or learning anything new in content or the learning process.	Praising low effort will only lead to further underperformance. However, we should reinforce the commendable actions and behaviors associated with this type of effort. For example, you might wish to highlight the time and focus they devoted to a task. It is also important to help them understand that they are not learning anything new because they are not challenging themselves. Thus, we should direct them to pursue more challenging tasks that will lead to growth.

PERFORMANCE EFFORT – DOING YOUR BEST

Description

Performance effort involves delivering your best work consistently while operating comfortably within your established skill set. This level of effort is suitable for performance-oriented situations, such as exams or exhibitions. While energy and skill levels are high, children remain within their comfort zone and are not experiencing the stretch required to grow. Mistakes are typically avoided in this context, limiting the potential for learning and improvement.

Suggested Feedback

There will be times when the focus should be on mastery, and you should congratulate your child for their achievement. However, when children are praised only for their high performance, they tend to concentrate on the required standards. This focus may lead them to overlook the actions and behaviors necessary for ongoing learning and growth. If you suspect this is happening to your child, your response should consider the following:

- Acknowledge and show appreciation for the hard work and learning contributing to their skill proficiency. Ensure they link these actions and behaviors to their current achievements.

- Emphasize that achieving mastery or meeting a standard is a positive accomplishment. However, it is essential to recognize that this represents just one step in the continuous process of learning and growth. Encourage your child to consider 'What's next?' in their learning process.

- Facilitate future learning by identifying opportunities and setting appropriate goals together. For instance, emphasize the importance of tackling more difficult tasks to foster your child's learning and growth.

For example, you might say, *'You have done so well learning all this! You have worked very hard. It is amazing to see how much you understand now! Now, let's think about even more fun things to learn. Let's set some goals to ensure you continue learning.'*

Side note: Praising children for their achievements can sometimes make them feel comfortable and only showcase what they already know. This validation may cause them to avoid new challenges that could encourage growth. Remind your child that school is not just a place to showcase existing knowledge but is primarily a platform for ongoing learning.

INEFFECTIVE EFFORT - WORKING HARD BUT GETTING NOWHERE

Description

Children who display ineffective effort are being challenged and expend lots of energy. However, they lack the skills to meet these challenges. Even though they work hard, they make very little progress. As a result, they experience frustration and negative self-talk, often saying, *'I can't do this!'* In this circumstance, parents might feel inclined to praise their children for *'trying their best,'* but doing so only perpetuates a cycle of ineffective effort.

Suggested Feedback

Instead of praising ineffective effort, parents should guide their child to more effective ways to address challenges rather than saying, *'You tried your best.'* If your children are struggling with a particular challenge, the feedback we give them should have the following qualities:

- Recognize the hard work and persistence your child is investing in the task and acknowledge the challenge they are taking on. Encourage and commend the actions and behaviors that underpin their effort.

- Acknowledge that the current behaviors and actions appear to be ineffective. Prompt your child to explore other existing strategies or learn new ones. Guide them towards a more *effective* approach.

For example, you might say, *'It is great to see how much effort you have put into this challenging task. I appreciate that you have worked hard but are not getting the desired results. Let's look at some other strategies that might help with this challenge. It is not just about working hard. I want to see you move forward and continue to learn.'*

Side note: Sometimes, your child may undertake a challenge that is far too difficult for their current abilities. In this circumstance, their efforts are likely to be ineffective. Parents should encourage their children to take a step back and focus on mastering previous knowledge and skills before progressing further.

EFFECTIVE EFFORT - LEADING TO GROWTH AND NEW LEARNING

Description

Effective effort is the kind of effort that Professor Dweck refers to when discussing the importance of 'praising effort.' A child operating at a level slightly beyond their current abilities, both in terms of behaviors and understanding, is engaging in effective effort.

Effective effort leads to a growth in skills and knowledge and is essential to developing a growth mindset. Mistakes made at this level, known as 'stretch mistakes,' hold significant learning potential. They identify areas where a child's learning may be insufficient and where minor adjustments can lead to steady, incremental growth.

Suggested Feedback

Praising the specific actions and behaviors that constitute effective effort is essential. Parents should commend their children for embracing challenges just beyond their current capabilities. It is vital to help your child understand that these challenges might lead to mistakes. However, it is important to emphasize that these mistakes are valuable learning opportunities.

By directing praise towards the specific actions and behaviors that foster continuous growth, parents can:

- Motivate their child to keep stretching their learning boundaries and attempt slightly more difficult problems.

- Build their child's resilience and determination in the face of mistakes.

- Focus on the successful strategies they have used to address and learn from these mistakes.

- Highlight the new skills their child has developed and discuss how they can apply these skills to new learning challenges.

Effective effort is central to the development of a growth mindset. A growth mindset is based on the premise that determination and hard work can enhance intelligence and abilities. Like Dweck, Anderson emphasizes the importance of praising the actions and behaviors that exemplify effective effort rather than focusing on outcomes or innate ability. This approach is crucial in positively shaping a child's learning experience. By praising *effective* effort, the focus shifts from fixed abilities to the ongoing learning and improvement process.

Acknowledging and praising your child's behaviors and actions during a task motivates them to strive for improvement. Your encouragement fosters perseverance, even in the face of challenges. This mindset also helps children view mistakes and challenges as valuable opportunities for growth and learning. Instead of perceiving these experiences as obstacles, they learn to embrace them as key elements of their development.

Children are willing to step out of their comfort zone when parents reassure them that their behaviors and actions can lead to growth. They will become more resilient, embrace new challenges, and take risks. They will start believing in their ability to change, overcome obstacles, achieve goals, and ultimately take responsibility for their own growth.

> *'If parents want to give their children a gift, the best thing they can do is to teach their children to love challenges, be intrigued by mistakes, enjoy effort, and keep on learning.'*
> Carol Dweck

Parents are responsible for praising behaviors and actions that foster growth. They must also be clear and specific in how that praise is delivered. Education is fundamentally about growth. As Dweck (2006) points out, we should attribute that growth to what a child does rather than their inherent ability or the outcome achieved. Recognizing the different types of effort underlines the importance of acknowledging and fostering the right kind of effort.

ENCOURAGE YOUR CHILD'S INTERESTS AND STRENGTHS

One way of encouraging your child's interests and strengths is to examine your home environment and routine and adapt it to support their interests. For example, if your child is interested in music, give them access to musical instruments to experiment with at home. Encourage them to use their instruments to play along with the music they are listening to, such as songs by The Wiggles. You can also use music to enrich your child's experience during different activities. For example, you could play music while they are learning new skills, completing chores, or getting dressed.

I recently read an interesting story about English biologist Charles Darwin. He told of how he loved poetry and music as a young man but completely neglected them due to his devotion to biology. As a result, poetry meant nothing to him as an adult, and music was merely noise. Darwin wished he could relive his youth to enjoy his early interests and continue appreciating them into adulthood. His reflection serves as a reminder for parents to cultivate a variety of their children's interests, both in their early years and as they grow.

WHAT IF NONE OF THIS WORKS?

A fundamental belief that should underpin your relationship with your child is to accept that they are 'unique and enough.' This principle becomes especially important if your child encounters developmental challenges at school, and all avenues of support have been explored. This support may include teacher advice and professional involvement.

In his best-selling book, The 7 Habits of Highly Effective People, Stephen Covey (2013, p. 24-28) gives a personal account of how he and his wife dealt with the difficulties experienced by one of their sons during his early school years. The following story is a message for all of us. It emphasizes that our children are unique and worthy of our love exactly as they are. They will thrive when we release them from the stranglehold of comparison.

> 'Enough'—just as you are!
>
> Stephen's son was having a difficult time academically, socially, and on the sporting field at school. As with any loving parent, Stephen agonized over his son's unhappiness. He and his wife wanted to help him. They made a concerted effort to offer guidance and 'psych him up.' However, the more he failed to achieve, the more he was ridiculed by others. These circumstances led Stephen and his wife to defend their son, which caused him to feel embarrassed and sad.
>
> Their approach, while born out of love, was not helping. After making this discovery, they decided to let their son know that he was 'enough' and that they loved him just the way he was. They stopped defending him and giving him advice. They realized their role was to affirm, enjoy, and value their son. They stopped comparing him to his siblings, to themselves, or against societal expectations. Instead, they just relaxed their grip and enjoyed him.
>
> He experienced a period of withdrawal, as they had always protected him. However, over time, he came to believe their unspoken message that he was indeed 'enough.' Slowly, his confidence grew as his fear of failure to meet the expectations of others diminished. As the months and years passed, he began excelling in all areas of his life. His quiet confidence enhanced his ability to connect with others as he understood his own uniqueness and value. This awareness allowed him to appreciate others in the same way.

Interesting fact: Atychiphobia, that is, an extreme fear of failure, describes how we act when fear gets in our way. This feeling prevents us from taking the necessary steps to progress and accomplish our goals. It can be linked to many causes, such as critical or unsupportive parents (Peterson et al. 2025).

THE BENEFITS OF CHESS

Many benefits exist for children who enjoy playing board games, especially the game of chess (see, for example, The Gamesman-Children's Chess (Australia only), Magnetic Chess Set). Interest has surged in recent years (Keener 2022), and chess is now used as an educational tool in many schools worldwide (Chessineducation.org 2023).

Chess has long been referred to as the *'game of kings,'* as it requires strategic thinking, forecasting, and decision-making. It also sharpens problem-solving skills, making it an intellectual challenge that has endured through the ages. The ability to play this game relies heavily on the Logical-Mathematical and Visual-Spatial intelligences, which encapsulate these skills. Participation in the game inevitably strengthens these intelligences and, to a lesser extent, some of the others that Howard Gardner has identified.

Martin Pein, an International Chess Master and journalist, reminds us that chess is an affordable activity that cuts across many barriers. These include language, age, gender, race, religion, physical ability, and social status. It is a game played by millions worldwide and can promote inclusion, mutual respect, tolerance, and fairness.

Educators worldwide generally acknowledge that playing chess is an effective way to develop numerical, verbal, thinking, and creative skills. It also helps improve memory. Over the past two decades, several studies have focused on whether chess instruction can enhance academic performance in primary and middle school students (Sala et al. 2017). These studies have also examined the impact of chess on cognitive abilities. The results show that students' achievement, especially in mathematics and general cognitive ability, can improve with as little as one hour of training per week (see, for example, Deary et al. 2007). It was also noted, although to a lesser extent, that reading ability was enhanced.

These findings are not surprising, as chess is a cognitive (brain-based) activity that engages working memory, reasoning skills, and concentration. These key factors contribute to success in mathematics. The level of impact appears to be more significant among younger students and is linked to the amount of instruction and training they receive (Rosholm et al. 2017).

For me, the decision to invest time and effort to learning chess in order to teach my children was straightforward. It was guided by the research available at the time. The results suggested that playing chess provided opportunities to develop a range of skills and offered several key benefits (see, for example, Gardinerchess.com.au 2023, Kingslandchess.com 2023). It will:

- **Exercise both sides of the brain**—your child will need to use both logical and creative thinking when playing the game.

- **Improve memory**—your child will need to recall past moves that they and others have successfully used as part of their strategy to win games.

- **Enhance problem-solving and spatial awareness skills**—your child will have to strategically consider the options available for their next move, given the position of the remaining chess pieces on the board.

- **Prolong concentration**—your child will need to concentrate for long periods. They must remember their opponent's last move and evaluate the current state of play before making their next strategic move.

- **Cultivate planning and foresight**—your child will gradually learn to think ahead and plan tactical moves to place them in a winning position.

As with many board games, chess also offers the opportunity to develop your child's social skills and awareness. Some examples are:

- Actions have consequences that may have either positive or negative outcomes.

- Everyone needs to learn how to win and lose. You will be able to teach your child how to be a good sport and congratulate their opponent on a good game, whatever the result. As your child matures, they will appreciate how both winning and losing can inform improved performance in future games.

- Chess can relieve stress and have a calming effect as your child focuses on the game.

- With chess as the vehicle, making friends is a less threatening exercise. Chess gives your child something to discuss and allows their friendships to grow organically.

- Chess is an inclusive and intergenerational game that everyone can enjoy.

- Playing chess as part of a school team can nurture a sense of belonging in your child. It is well-known that children who feel they belong are generally happier, more relaxed, learn more efficiently, and have fewer behavioral problems.

- Chess provides an opportunity for your child to learn how to play by the rules.

Introducing your child to chess at home before they begin formal schooling will boost their confidence. This early exposure will also ensure that playing the game at school will be a more enjoyable experience for them.

If you are new to chess, consider purchasing the book Chess for Children by Murray Chandler and Helen Milligan. This resource clearly explains the game's rules and basic moves. I also recommend Chess for Children Activity Book by Sabrina Chevannes. This book uses creative activities to further enhance your child's interest and understanding of the game.

THE BENEFITS OF BOREDOM

> *'Imagination is more important than knowledge.'*
> Albert Einstein

Throughout this book, I encourage parents to embrace learning opportunities inspired by their child's natural curiosity. Equally, young children should be given time to entertain themselves without parental input. Your responsibility is to foster their imagination and creativity while they are young. These opportunities will help your children become self-sufficient and able to entertain themselves independently. They will be more equipped to handle potential boredom with creativity and confidence. However, parents often make the mistake of believing they should fill every minute of their child's day with structured activities.

During my childhood, there were many occasions when I was expected to entertain myself. I continue to use this skill to this day. However, I understand that in today's world, it is more challenging to step back and allow your child to have unstructured time. Allocating unstructured time is particularly difficult for parents, given the increasing pressure on children to excel at school. As your child grows, it is unlikely that their day will finish when the school bell rings. For example, after-school activities such as music lessons, sports practice, swimming lessons, or language classes will leave little time to relax and use their imaginations.

Colier (2018) notes that children today often have overly busy schedules, which cause them to feel uncomfortable when faced with unstructured time. She suggests that this discomfort stems from a fear of boredom. Parents are under pressure to address this situation or risk being criticized by their peers. When a child is bored, it is perceived to be a time when there is nothing to do, nothing to think about, and nothing to learn. Colier reports that two positive outcomes can occur when your child is bored, which can be beneficial throughout their life. Firstly, your child will learn to use their imagination to entertain themselves. Secondly, they will learn to enjoy their own company.

The issue magnifies when your child starts formal school. In his book <u>The Art Of Growing Up</u>, award-winning author and respected educator John Marsden (2019) emphasizes the importance of allowing boredom to be part of our children's lives. He is critical of the modern parenting approach of tightly controlling every minute of a child's day and advocates for more unstructured time. Marsden opposes filling after-school hours with numerous 'must-learn' activities. He contends this practice is suffocating and sets our children up to feel helpless, hopeless, and angry. He argues that children need time to relax, experience boredom, and be imaginative and creative without parental pressure. Imagine your frustration if your boss insisted you stay behind and learn a new skill after a busy day at work.

My Childhood Days—A Reflection

I grew up in a loving home in Sydney, Australia, where money was scarce and only used for essential needs. My father's long workdays meant weekends were dedicated to home maintenance, leaving little time for relaxation. My mother, a full-time homemaker, used her dressmaking skills to provide clothing for the family. Back then, communities were supportive and helped each other in times of need. As a result, my parents were very busy and had little time to focus on child development activities.

Toys were scarce, and extracurricular activities only became an option once I was old enough to travel independently. This era was a time without televisions, iPads, mobile phones, or computers. We had many books which we read and reread. I quickly learned to entertain myself, especially after school.

The backyard was my playground, particularly during the summer months. I remember building cubby houses under trees and walking along two-meter-high paling fences on our boundary, which, in hindsight, was quite dangerous but, at the time, so much fun. This latter activity was my version of tightrope walking. My favorite pastimes were organizing and participating in running races, obstacle courses, and musical plays with my neighborhood friends.

Lying on the back lawn and gazing at the clouds in the sky was an activity I enjoyed. Time passed slowly as I pondered what the cloud formations resembled - animals, humans, or make-believe characters. Sometimes, my mom would join me, and we would chuckle at each other's suggestions.

My friends and I picked grapes from the garden vines and stomped on them in large plastic bowls with our bare feet. We were proud of the juice we produced and loved how the juice stained our feet. I spent many hours perched on a branch in our old fig tree, feasting on the delicious figs while acting out my version of the Swiss Family Robinson tale. Running through the sprinkler on hot, humid days was another exhilarating experience. My recollections are of afternoons filled with laughter and sunshine, utterly oblivious to anything outside my safe and happy world.

Revisiting these childhood memories reminds me of how fortunate I was to have had opportunities to entertain myself. I feel grateful for those carefree days, a relaxed childhood, unhurried play, and the time to unwind and let my imagination run free.

A PARENT'S ADMISSION

When my children were growing up, I fell into the trap of attempting to develop *all* their talents, which was fashionable then. It was, and still is today, a very competitive world for our children to navigate. After school, it was a logistical challenge to ensure my children arrived on time at their extracurricular sports training and music classes. They were exhausted, but I was determined to give them every opportunity to develop their interests and nurture their talents.

That was until one afternoon when I raced to pick up my 8-year-old son from cricket practice to drive him to his music class. Snacks, a change of clothes, wet washers, and towels lay on the back seat of the car. It was 4.45 pm, and he had been at school since 8.30 am. He would not arrive home until 6.45 pm if he attended his music class. He dragged himself into the car and looked at me, his face drawn in exhaustion. Then he said, *'So if I'm good at something... does that mean I have to do it?'* He was referring to the after-school classes I had enrolled him in. I was shocked to realize that while I wanted him to excel in everything, he wasn't interested. He was worn out.

We did not attend his music class that night. Instead, we drove straight home. After he had showered and pulled on his 'PJs,' we chatted over dinner about the activities he wanted to pursue. It turned out that despite the required practice, he enjoyed his music classes and looked forward to Saturday morning swimming. This revelation was a pivotal moment, as I had genuinely believed that my actions were in his best interest.

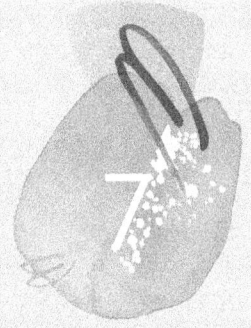

THE EXERCISE CONNECTION

The positive impact of regular exercise from an early age on a child's overall development is well established (Rowley and Williams 2015). Exercise offers greater benefits when performed outdoors (Bento and Dias 2017). Outdoor environments provide the space for children to experience freedom in a dynamic setting, where they can be energetic, playful, and connect with nature. Additionally, exposure to sunlight and fresh air supports strong bone development and boosts immune function.

Children have a natural inclination for physical activity during early childhood. However, a concerning trend has emerged in modern society that was not present a generation ago. Technology now dominates many aspects of our lives. Parents have become increasingly reliant on technology as a substitute for direct caregiving.

Today's economic pressures often require both parents to work outside the home. In addition, they must also manage household duties and care for their children. These responsibilities leave parents with limited time and can create considerable stress, often resulting in their use of technology as a substitute for active parenting. While this is understandable, reliance on technology can have negative ramifications. For example, it can rob young children of their parents' attention and valuable exercise time. I would advise parents to make every effort to ensure their children engage in adequate exercise.

During my children's early years, I aimed to create a healthy balance between relaxation and active play for them. I was mindful of establishing good sleep patterns and providing activities that would stimulate their brains and foster holistic development. General exercise was encouraged, but I also focused on three specific activities: vestibular activities, swimming, and walking. These activities were easy to implement and, according to research, could support key developmental outcomes.

This chapter explores the benefits of integrating general exercise, vestibular activities, swimming, and walking into your child's daily routine.

GENERAL EXERCISE

PHYSICAL BENEFITS OF EXERCISE

Regular aerobic exercise, the kind that gets your heart and sweat glands pumping, has many physical benefits for children (Healthdirect.gov.au 2020), such as helping to:

- Build strong bodies,
- Maintain a reasonable body weight,
- Increase lung capacity,
- Improve coordination and strengthen muscle control,
- Increase flexibility,
- Develop good posture and balance, and
- Improve sleeping habits.

Establishing good sleeping habits will have lifelong benefits, as sleep is essential for optimal learning, memory function, general health, and well-being (see, for example, Gehrman 2022).

INTELLECTUAL AND EMOTIONAL BENEFITS

Regular aerobic exercise has many intellectual and emotional benefits for children (see, for example, Health.harvard.edu 2014, Health.harvard.edu 2016, Postal 2009), such as:

- Boosting the size of the area in the brain, that is, the hippocampus, which helps a person's ability to remember what they read or hear,
- Regenerating brain cells,
- Supporting new learning and the ability to concentrate and think, and
- Increasing happiness by reducing stress and anxiety.

The book Spark! How exercise will improve the performance of your brain by Ratey and Hagerman (2013) provides an excellent summary of the effect of exercise on the brain.

HOW CAN YOU PROMOTE EXERCISE?

It is important to prioritize exercise in your child's life as a necessary component of each day. Establishing this habit at an early age will motivate your child to make exercise a vital part of their daily routine. You can promote exercise in several ways:

- Be active, so your child can see the value you place on exercise.

- Incorporate exercise into their daily routine by engaging in activities such as walking to the shops together, gardening, or completing household chores.

- Take notice of activities that interest your child. Check if these activities are age-appropriate and safe, and if so, encourage your child's involvement.

- Provide opportunities to try a variety of exercise activities.

- Use exercise as a treat or reward for your child instead of sedentary activities like screen time. For example, reward them with a swim at the beach.

WHEN TO COMMENCE EXERCISE

Exercise should start when your child is a baby. The Australian 24-Hour Movement Guidelines for the Early Years (birth to 5 years) gives general recommendations for the length of time your child should be physically active each day. You can find more detailed guidelines for physical activity and exercise for infants, toddlers, and preschoolers on the Health.gov.au (2021) website. Encourage your child to move; the more, the better.

BABY—BIRTH TO 1 YEAR

Allow your baby floor time in a safe place where they can move their limbs freely, such as on a fixed play mat. This activity should include 'tummy time'. However, speak to your healthcare professional for guidance on when to start. Get down on the floor with your baby so that they can see you clearly and you can communicate effectively with them. As your child grows, create additional safe areas for crawling, walking, and running (Health.harvard.edu 2017).

The Australian Parenting Website, raisingchildren.net.au, provides extensive play ideas to encourage movement for your 0 to 12-month-old baby.

TODDLER—1 TO 3 YEARS

Experts recommend that toddlers engage in at least three hours of physical activity throughout the day, including light and energetic play. These activities may include walking, throwing and catching balls, dancing, hopping, skipping, jumping, flying kites, and swimming. Toddlers also enjoy running games such as 'chasey' and 'hide-and-seek' or visiting the playground at the local park.

PRESCHOOLER—3 TO 5 YEARS

Experts recommend preschoolers engage in at least three hours of physical activity throughout the day. Of this time, 60 minutes should consist of energetic play. In their book—Fit Baby, Smart Baby, Your Baby! From Birth to Age Six —Doman, Doman, and Hagy (2012) explain the stages of mobility from birth to 6 years of age. The authors outline how to design a learning environment that will enable your child to reach each stage.

Consider how to integrate age-appropriate exercise into your child's daily routine. For example, if your child enjoys creative/artistic activities, consider a walk in a park to collect leaves, twigs, and stones for them to use in a collage. Find your nearest jungle gym or climbing wall if they like to climb. If they enjoy books and reading, walk or ride to your local library. If your child is interested in music, play the music they choose and dance with them.

THE BALANCING ACT

Have you ever had an ear infection and experienced difficulty with balance or dizziness? The reason is your ears serve not only for hearing but also as centers for balance and the body's orientation in space. Your ears provide vital information that enables the brain to interpret the body's orientation and movement within its environment. This information signals whether the body is stationary or in motion, along with the speed and direction of movement.

VESTIBULAR PROCESSING SYSTEM

The Vestibular Processing System is the mechanism within the ear for monitoring body movements and sensations. Whenever we move our head, the inner ear's receptors in this processing system send input to the brain.

The complex structure of the inner ear plays a central role in processing this information (neuroscientificallychallenged.com 2023). This system consists of canals containing fluid and lined with tiny hairs. The fluid moves around in the canals and touches the hairs each time we move. Signals are transmitted to the brain, providing information on how and where to move. Greater movement generates more input to the brain as the fluid moves vigorously and stimulates more hairs.

The vestibular system plays a vital role in everyday life. It connects and interacts with other sensory systems, including sight, hearing, and proprioception. Proprioception is our body's ability to sense its position, movement, and orientation in space without relying on vision. This system supports multiple functions that help us maintain balance and stabilize the head and body during movement. It also plays a crucial role in maintaining the correct posture.

In simple terms, the vestibular system supplies the brain with information about the body's motion, head position, and orientation in space. This information is essential for normal movement and equilibrium. Developing these abilities enhances your child's overall well-being and ability to learn. It also supports the development of speech, hearing, and the interpretation of language (Williams and Grigg 2019, Rowley and Williams 2015).

Every child requires vestibular stimulation to achieve the independence necessary to explore the world around them. Vestibular stimulation should involve activities suited to your child's age, preference, and unique capabilities. From birth, children gradually develop self-awareness and an understanding of the world through involvement in multi-sensory experiences and physical interactions.

Sandler and Coren (1981) noted that vestibular stimulation during infancy can enhance brain function and body development, including improvements in muscle tone. Their research indicates that this stimulation significantly influences several key areas:

- Visual alertness,
- Rousing levels,
- Visual tracking behavior,
- Motor development, and
- Reflex development.

> *'Our children who roll and tumble are engaged in their first lesson towards becoming the Einsteins of the future.'*
>
> Sally Goddard-Blythe

If your child's vestibular system is underdeveloped, you may observe delays in their motor skills, balance, and coordination. These delays may cause your child to bump into furniture, struggle with walking, and have difficulty sitting still (ilslearningcorner.com 2016). Including vestibular activities in your child's daily routine may help meet these challenges. However, always seek professional advice if you have any concerns.

WHAT ARE VESTIBULAR ACTIVITIES?

Traditionally, parents have played with their children by moving them through space in various ways and at different speeds. These movements are fundamental to vestibular stimulation. They include rocking, rolling, swaying, tumbling, bouncing, swinging, and spinning.

Children crave activities that are developmentally good for them, and swinging is one of them. Swinging provides excellent stimulation for both the body and brain. It can occur when you hold your child in your arms, dance with them, or gently rock them to sleep. This stimulation also occurs when we swing them back and forth on swings or in hammocks. Eventually, when they are strong enough, they can practice brachiating across overhead ladders with your assistance (Williams 2021).

These activities can be calming and soothing, making them ideal for pre-sleep or after-school relaxation. For example, you might gently rock your baby or have your toddler or preschooler rock slowly in a hammock (see, for example, Stetka 2019). These slow, quiet activities will give your child the opportunity to relax. Conversely, some vestibular activities can energize your child if they feel lethargic and need a boost. For instance, you can rock back and forth with your toddler while singing Row, Row, Row Your Boat or encourage your older child to enjoy brachiating. Each child will respond uniquely to these activities. Incorporating these activities into your child's daily routine will nurture their healthy development.

Before beginning vestibular activities, consider these practical suggestions to ensure a positive experience for both you and your child (see, for example, Activebabiessmartkids.com.au 2021):

- Keep vestibular stimulation games short. It is also important to remember that slow, gentle movements give the brain time to recognize the action and to respond accordingly.

- Only do these activities when you and your child are well and relaxed. Mothers should refrain from getting involved until they have fully recovered from giving birth to their baby.

- Ensure you feel confident about the activities by practicing with a doll before engaging with your child.

- Only do the activities if your child is enjoying them.

- Bend your knees when lifting your child, as this will protect your back from injury.

- Be cautious when engaging in spinning activities with your child. Limit the duration to brief intervals, such as 10 seconds clockwise, followed by 10 seconds counterclockwise (Grogan 2023). Spinning provides children with an intense sensory experience. However, exceeding the recommended time limits can cause nausea or even vomiting.

VESTIBULAR ACTIVITIES FOR BABIES OR TODDLERS

Young babies need sensory experiences to help organize, develop, and strengthen their vestibular system. This growth supports their social-emotional and intellectual development (Rowley and Williams 2015). Therefore, parents should be purposeful in their interactions with their baby or toddler and dedicate a few fun-filled minutes each day to vestibular stimulation. This approach ensures that the development of their balance and coordination is intentional, not left to chance.

The following activities are taken from the work of Williams and Grigg (2019). They are intended to send sensory information to your baby's brain. These activities will help them understand how it feels to move through space and orient themselves in various positions:

- Gently 'fly' your baby around like an airplane, holding them firmly under their arms. Keep them in a horizontal position and orient their face toward the ground. This position will help them feel secure and allow them to see everything 'below.'

- Dance with your baby. Find a song with a good beat and moderate tempo. Bounce, turn, swoop, and move around as you hold the baby close to you.

- Lie on your back on the ground, bend your knees, and place the baby on top of your shins. Rock the baby backward and forward. If your abdominal muscles can manage it, rock them from side to side. While working your baby's vestibular system, you are safely strengthening your core muscles, which is a bonus!

- If two adults are present, place your baby on a blanket and have each adult hold two corners. Gently swing the baby from side to side, mimicking the motion of a hammock.

- Lie your baby over an exercise ball or similar. Gently rock them backward and forwards. Put a toy on the ground for them to look at and possibly pick up.

- Take your toddler to the park and let them play on an age-appropriate swing and slide.

- Bounce your baby or toddler on your knee. Many rhymes can accompany this activity, for example, Yankee Doodle Went to Town and The Grand Old Duke of York. Rhymes are helpful for language development and are even more effective when combined with vestibular activities. For example, you can rock back and forth with your baby or toddler while singing Hickory Dickory Dock.

- Hold your baby or toddler and slowly turn in a small circle one way and then the other.

Activities like these will stimulate the balance areas of the brain and help accelerate motor development in your baby or toddler.

VESTIBULAR ACTIVITIES FOR PRESCHOOLERS

As your child develops and becomes more physically stable, they can undertake more independent activities. Here are a few examples that you can easily implement and integrate into your preschooler's daily routine:

- Ask your child to lie on their side at the top of a grassy slope. Position them so they can roll down to the bottom safely. Before they start rolling, demonstrate how to make fists with their hands, cross their arms over their chest, and then begin rolling down the slope.

- Choose an appropriately sized and weighted hoop and practice in the sunshine. The video Teaching Your Child to Hula-Hoop explains how to determine the size and weight of the hoop and demonstrates how to get started.

- If you are lucky enough to have a rocking chair, let your child use it under your supervision.

- Find a grassy area where your child can safely spin in circles with arms outstretched for a brief period.

- Enjoy swaying with your child in the wind.

- Help your child use an age-appropriate swing and slippery dip at the park.

- Dance with them to their favorite music or song.

- Buy a skipping rope. If you do not have assistance, tie one end of the rope to a well-secured post. Hold the rope parallel to the ground at a height of about 2.5 cm (1 inch). Encourage your child to jump over it from a standing position. As your child gains confidence, gradually increase the height of the rope.

- Teach your child to do Preschool Handstands and, eventually, a cartwheel under the guidance of their gymnastic coach.

- Play Pin the Tail on the Donkey when your child and their friends are comfortable with being gently spun around while wearing a blindfold.

- Practice Juggling Balls with your child.

- Teach your child to toss a small beanbag above their head. Show them how to track the beanbag's movement with their eyes to make catching it easier.

- Set up an obstacle course in the garden for your child, requiring them to crawl, climb, and jump.

For additional vestibular activities that will provide more variety for your preschooler, visit the following website (Grogan 2023).

VESTIBULAR ACTIVITIES FOR SCHOOL-AGED CHILDREN

A well-developed vestibular system will greatly benefit a child starting formal schooling. It helps them manage the physical, intellectual, and social-emotional challenges and expectations of school life.

> *'The vestibular system is said to be the most important influence for everyday functioning. It is the unifying system that directly or indirectly influences nearly everything we do.'*
>
> Carla Hannaford

This finding suggests there is justification for continuing vestibular activities during your child's school-age years. Therefore, I encourage you to explore additional activities for them to participate in. I selected three activities with vestibular benefits for my children: brachiating, basic gymnastics, and trampolining. Each of these activities provided many valuable developmental benefits. I have highlighted brachiation here as the benefits are significant.

Brachiating is the ability to swing on an overhead ladder from one rung to the next. The ladder should be positioned parallel to the ground at a suitable height.

This equipment can be purchased online from the following websites for assembly and use at home (see, for example, funkymonkeybars.com, foreverredwood.com, and armagado.co.uk). The book Fit Baby, Smart Baby, Your Baby! From Birth to Age Six by Doman, Doman, and Hagy (2012) provides instructions on introducing and teaching your child to brachiate.

The benefits of brachiation include (Stevens-Smith and Murdock 2021):

- Providing vestibular stimulation by having your child swing from rung to rung helps them develop spatial awareness. This activity also helps them understand personal space and move without bumping into objects.

- Stimulating both sides of your child's brain for greater integration and learning,

- Creating greater lung capacity, which allows your child to breathe more deeply,

- Strengthening your child's hands and arms,

- Assisting with fine motor development, which helps with coloring, cutting, writing, and painting,

- Improving eye-hand coordination, which helps with reading, writing, and problem-solving,

- Strengthening the upper body, which is necessary for good posture while sitting, and

- Developing communication skills as children negotiate turn-taking.

Side note: Signs of an immature vestibular system in school-age children can include poor posture while seated and difficulty with balance. They may struggle with tasks that require fine motor skills, such as writing. They may also struggle to maintain attention in class and find learning challenging. If you have any concerns about the challenges your child is experiencing, consult a professional for guidance.

SWIMMING

Research tells us that activities such as swimming may increase the production of the brain's 'feel-good' neurotransmitters (that is, endorphins). Endorphins make you feel happy. Swimming regularly, as with any exercise, can increase self-confidence and improve mood. As your child matures, swimming laps can help them relax. This activity encourages them to concentrate on their strokes, leaving no room to dwell on any worries. This type of exercise can lead to a feeling of calm (Mayoclinic.org 2020). An intense swimming workout can stimulate the growth of new brain cells in the areas of the brain affected by stress.

The freestyle swimming stroke requires both sides of the body to work together. Researchers have found that this action enhances communication between the left and right hemispheres of the brain. This left-right brain communication results in increased awareness, which can make it easier to learn new information. Additionally, swimming increases blood flow to the brain, helping us think more clearly (Lepore 2019).

In addition to the obvious physical and health benefits, swimming promotes happiness and relaxation and enhances learning abilities (Borreli 2016).

WHEN SHOULD YOUR BABY LEARN TO SWIM

Most experts agree that babies should only be exposed to chlorinated water after six months of age. This caution is primarily due to their immature immune systems (Healthline.com 2020). Check with your pediatrician or baby health care nurse on the specific recommendations for your child.

Side note: Newborns and infants should never be left alone near a body of water (for example, puddles, bathtubs, or pools). It is essential to understand that a child can drown in as little as 2.5 cm/1 inch of water (Healthline.com 2019).

Harvard Medical School notes that children under four years of age usually struggle to listen to a swimming instructor, follow their instructions, and retain the information provided (Health.harvard.edu 2024). Parents are encouraged to take their little ones into the pool once they reach six months of age. With the guidance of a swimming instructor and the presence of a parent, these early water experiences can help children develop confidence in the water.

Of course, some children may be ready to learn to swim before age four. So, be prepared to encourage them if they show an interest and are cognitively and physically ready.

SWIMMING BENEFITS FOR BABIES

Infant swimming classes typically include activities centered around water play and promote skin-to-skin contact with the parent. At this stage of their development, your baby will participate in these activities alongside other babies and parents. Being involved in these classes and developing skills may help their confidence and self-esteem (Healthline.com 2019).

According to Swim England, the national governing body for swimming, there are a number of swimming benefits for babies (Swimming.org 2020). These benefits include:

- Building water confidence,
- Providing quality bonding time,
- Building and strengthening muscles and gaining control of their movements,
- Improving coordination and balance,
- Improving heart, lung, and brain function,
- Increasing appetite, and
- Encouraging sleep.

Side note: This unique group environment can provide an early opportunity for your baby to socialize.

SWIMMING BENEFITS FOR TODDLERS AND PRESCHOOLERS

Studies have shown that once your child begins formal schooling, the benefits of preschool swimming are measurable and can provide a competitive edge. For example, a four-year international study by Jorgensen (2013) showed that children who swam could achieve a wide range of developmental milestones earlier than their non-swimming peers. This pioneering research was led by the Griffith Institute for Educational Research in partnership with Swim Australia and the Laurie Lawrence Kids Alive swim program.

A core group of 176 children aged three, four, and five years old underwent an intensive assessment process using internationally approved testing methods. The research found that children across these age groups who swam regularly were ahead of their non-swimming peers when it came to:

- Physical development—on average, 7 months ahead.
- Cognitive development—on average, 10 months ahead.
- Social-Emotional development—on average, 15 months ahead.

The results also revealed that children who swam regularly were ahead of their non-swimming peers when it came to:

- Oral expression—on average, 11 months ahead.
- Mathematical reasoning—on average, 6 months ahead.
- Reading—on average, 2 months ahead.
- Story recall—on average, 17 months ahead.
- Understanding directions—on average, 20 months ahead.

These results confirm that the advantages of learning to swim before the age of five are more than just water safety. They reveal that swimming offers children direct and indirect developmental benefits, aiding their transition to school. Learning to swim before five years of age provides the perfect foundation for a lifetime of healthy, non-impact exercise.

WALKING

Since the mid-twentieth century, many studies have explored the health benefits of regular walking and aerobic exercise (Morris and Hardman 1997). For example, the medical profession now advocates walking as a key strategy for improving adults' physical and mental health. Further studies suggest that physical activity, such as walking, may positively affect children's brain health and cognitive function (Khan and Hillman 2014). Professor Tomporowski from the University of Georgia notes that exercise has *'a more long-lasting effect on brains that are still developing'* (cited in Tumbokon 2020). These findings suggest that taking regular walks with your children from an early age could be beneficial.

The most effective way to ensure your child walks regularly is to integrate it into their daily routine. To ensure these walks fit into the daily routine, you must plan and allocate time for their duration in advance (Feigelson 2016). Accompany your child along the routes to their term-based activities, such as playgroup, kindergarten, or school. This planning will help you predetermine the time required for each walk. Take a light stroller in case your child cannot walk the entire distance.

Factor in time for your child to explore the surroundings and satisfy their curiosity as they walk along the route. It may not be apparent, but a walk can provide many teachable moments, particularly as seen through the eyes of a small, curious child. Their view of the world differs from ours as they are much closer to the ground. When you allow unhurried time for your child to make exciting discoveries, you effectively validate these learning experiences.

Walking together also provides opportunities for you to spend quality time bonding, communicating with your child, and interacting with neighbors and friends. These interactions will further establish your child's sense of community. Walking is a spontaneous, inexpensive, and environmentally friendly activity requiring no equipment other than a good pair of walking shoes. It is an activity that can be done virtually anywhere.

THE BENEFITS OF WALKING FOR CHILDREN

Researchers have studied the physical, intellectual, and social-emotional benefits of regular walking, and the results show promise. They show that the benefits of daily walks can extend to every age group.

The acknowledged benefits of walking for adults may also positively impact children. These include:

- Enhanced learning and memory capacity by increasing mental alertness and focus, which improves concentration (Ratey and Hagerman 2013, Khan and Hillman 2014),

- Improved cognitive performance by stimulating brain function for processing knowledge and gaining understanding through thought, experience, and sensory input (Aberg et al. 2009),

- Improved cognitive flexibility, fostering new ideas and original thoughts through increased creative thinking (Oppezzo and Schwartz 2014),

- Positive effects on health and metabolism (Belcher et al. 2015),

- Increased strength, flexibility, and stamina to meet physical demands, and

- Improved mood and self-esteem, reduced stress through balanced body chemicals and hormones, and improved sleep quality (Health.harvard.edu 2011, Mayoclinic.org 2020, Psychologytoday.com 2020).

Taking the time to make walking a regular part of your child's daily routine will help maintain and safeguard their physical and mental health.

TIPS AND IDEAS TO ENCOURAGE WALKING

When parents participate in a daily walk with their child, they demonstrate the value they place on the exercise. Your enthusiasm and interest in the surroundings during your walk will inspire your child's curiosity.

Initially, accompanying your child on walks to specific destinations—such as visiting family, friends, school, shops, or the local park—adds purpose to the activity. This approach can encourage their participation and make the experience more enjoyable. The following tips and ideas will help your child develop a love for walking, both as a physical exercise and a learning experience.

Babies

When you feel up to venturing out with your newborn for a walk, it would be advisable to keep the outing short. Limiting it to around 30 to 45 minutes will give both of you a chance to get used to this new experience. Ensure you dress your baby appropriately for the weather and protection from the sun (Babycentre.co.uk 2023). Consult your healthcare nurse for advice on age-appropriate prams and strollers for your baby. As they grow, you will need to upgrade the strollers to accommodate their changing physical needs.

When a healthcare professional recommends it, transition your baby to a forward-facing baby carrier or backpack. The forward-facing position allows your baby to take in their surroundings and engage with people they see on the walk. Constantly talk to your baby about what is in their line of sight. Whenever possible, move close to the object you are describing. Enhance your baby's walking experience by encouraging them to smell and touch objects that are safe and suitable. These experiences help them explore their surroundings and stimulate their sensory development.

Toddlers

When your child is physically capable of participating in a short walk with you, be careful to choose a distance that is achievable for them. Hold their hand to ensure stability and safety when near roadways and traffic. Don't worry about cutting the walk short. It is important that they enjoy the outing rather than return home exhausted. This approach will ensure your child will want to participate in the activity again. Increase the length of their walks over time and try to choose a time of day when your toddler is fresh. Always take a stroller with you in case they need a break from walking.

Explain new experiences and the expected behaviors when necessary and appropriate. For instance, you might say, *'Let's cross the road, but first, we need to stop here on the sidewalk. Take a good look both ways and wait until there's a clear gap in the traffic since there's no pedestrian crossing nearby. If we do not take these precautions, we risk being hit by a car.'* Repeat this experience frequently to give your child the opportunity to learn and understand your expectations and the underlying reasons.

Preschoolers

The following suggestions aim to encourage preschoolers to participate in walking activities that stimulate, provide experiences, build knowledge, and enhance spatial awareness.

Note: Each activity can be scaled back slightly for your toddler.

- Take a leisurely walk with your child around the local neighborhood to help them become familiar with the area. Point out various landmarks along the way to enhance their awareness of their surroundings. These landmarks will be points of reference when they are older, more independent, and walking to and from school. Take this opportunity to teach them pedestrian and road safety rules. Discuss where to walk, when to cross the road, and where to cross safely. Refer to resources such as Pedestrian Safety and Road Safety for Kids in Australia, Road Safety and Pedestrian Safety in the USA, and Rules for Pedestrians in the UK for country-specific guidance.

- Organize a treasure hunt in your local park. Use a homemade map of the park with walking instructions that lead to the location of the treasure.

- A forest or a park with many trees is the perfect location to play 'Hide and Seek.' Your child can play this game with their friends or just you.

- Undertake 'adventure' walks with your child. For example, these walks could be along a beach or in a forest. Make exploration the focus and see what they can discover. Be sure to take a small bag to carry their discoveries. While walking along the beach, they may come across small shells to use later to make a seashell necklace or bracelet. While exploring the forest, suggest they collect some small rocks with at least one flat surface suitable for 'rock art' paintings (see, for example, How to Paint Rocks, Images of Rock Art in Newfoundland).

We have all experienced the feeling of calm as we stroll along a beach or in a quiet forest. These 'chill-out' moments are beneficial for both parents and children. They help to bring balance to our busy lives. Natural environments, even when experienced through images alone, can enhance mood. When multiple senses are engaged in natural settings, including visual, auditory, and aromatic experiences, there are significant improvements in well-being. Interestingly, beaches and forests are where we inhale an abundance of negative ions that some say positively impact our mood and energy levels (Mann 2003).

- Organize a bush walk for your family. Take an Explorer Compass and a walking trail map with you. Examples of maps are Best Kid Friendly Trails in Australia, Best Kid Friendly Trails in England, and Best Kid Friendly Trails in the USA. Discuss the function of both aids and use them with your child on your hike. Show your child your current location on the map and give them the option of choosing which route to follow next. Selecting the route will stimulate their curiosity and make the walk more interesting. Bring a picnic and enjoy the scenery while you have your lunch. Draw attention to the sounds, smells, and feel of the surrounding environment. Talk with them about what they can see around them. Encourage your child to take photos to help them recall this experience when they return home.

- The beach or the park are also great locations for ball or frisbee games. If you have a family dog, they usually enjoy participating in these games, which adds to the overall fun.

- Provide your child with a <u>pedometer</u> or a <u>Surveyor's Measuring Wheel—Imperial, Surveyor's Measuring Wheel—Metric</u>. This equipment will help them track the number of steps taken or the distance walked to reach their destination. Encourage your child to use a small notebook to document their walk. Assist them in recording the number of steps taken, their starting point, destination, and their favorite part of the experience.

POINTS TO REMEMBER

Before engaging in any exercise activity, it is essential to establish suitable protective measures and prioritize safety to minimize the risk of injury to your child.

These considerations should include:

- Protecting your child from the sun with sunscreen and a hat.
- Keeping your child well hydrated with water.
- Ensuring they are wearing protective shoes appropriate for the activity.
- Ensuring the environment is safe, the equipment is appropriate, and the conditions are acceptable for your child's age and fitness level.
- Accounting for any medical conditions that may affect your child's ability or safety when participating in an activity. If necessary, seek medical advice relevant to your child and the activity to enable appropriate preparation (for example, EpiPen, mosquito repellent, Insulin).

Walking is a straightforward yet essential aerobic activity. It helps maintain a child's physical fitness, promotes cognitive development, and improves overall health and well-being. It is essential for parents or caregivers to actively engage in a diverse range of physical activities with their children. This commitment will encourage their children to embrace exercise as a lifelong habit.

KEY TAKEAWAYS

- If possible, prepare before your baby is born, as you will never again have as much free time as you do right now. Build your confidence with knowledge.

- Keep in mind your baby is born ready to learn, so carefully consider what it is you want to teach them. Whatever it is, will be the foundation on which they build their lives.

- Be the person you want them to be. They are always watching and will definitely mimic you.

- Always, tread gently with them. They are new to this world, and they are waiting on you for cues.

- Hold them, love them unconditionally, be proud of their efforts and always encourage their curiosity. Provide them with accurate information and opportunities to practice so that they can gain competency and confidence.

- Let them know they are unique and perfect in your eyes, as this will influence how they see themselves.

- I can guarantee that this will be the most demanding and most rewarding role of your life. At times you will feel totally overwhelmed and underprepared. At these times reach out, seek answers, and accept help. No-one knows it all.

- Above all though, in the midst of all the busy days and nights, try to remember just how fortunate you are and enjoy your parenting journey.

Margaret Larden

APPENDIX 1—REFERENCES

This bibliography below has been compiled from a variety of reputable sources. It contains extensive knowledge and information that supports an evidence-based approach to the learning methodologies used in early childhood education and presented in this book. These sources include published books, academic journal papers, articles from leading universities, government organizations, professional societies and conference proceedings. Also included are results from research projects, blogs by qualified specialist experts and practicing consultants, contributions from early childhood and parenting websites, and insights from a modern AI-powered research assistant tool https://delvy.ai

The links to the References will be maintained and accessible via the References and Resources page on the author's website marglarden.com. If you have any issues or questions, please do not hesitate to contact the author at marglarden@gmail.com.

APPENDIX 1 | REFERENCES

CHAPTER 1

American Montessori Society 2020, *Education that Transforms Lives*, viewed 3 July 2020, <https://amshq.org/About-Montessori/History-of-Montessori/Who-Was-Maria-Montessori>

delvy.ai 2025, *An AI-powered, evidence-based research assistant*, delvy is built by Reforged, Copyright © 2025 Reforged LLC. All rights reserved, viewed 5 January 2025, <https://delvy.ai>

Institutes for the Achievement of Human Potential 2019, *A Gentle Revolution in our Own Home*, viewed 12 May 2020, <https://www.iahp.org/mother-of-six-success-story/>

Institutes for the Achievement of Human Potential 2021a, *The Newborn Course*, viewed 13 April 2021, <https://iahp.org/well-children/course-programs/>

Institutes for the Achievement of Human Potential 2021b, *How to multiply your baby's intelligence*, viewed 12 May 2020, <https://iahp.org/well-children/course-programs/>

Seldin, T 2017, *How to Raise an Amazing Child the Montessori Way: A Parents' Guide to Building Creativity, Confidence, and Independence*, 2nd edn, Paperback version, Dorling Kindersley Ltd, accessed 10 April 2023 from Amazon.com

Selhub, E 2022, *Nutritional psychiatry: Your brain on food*, posted 18 September 2022, viewed 5 November 2024, <https://www.health.harvard.edu/blog/nutritional-psychiatry-your-brain-on-food-201511168626>

US National Academies of Sciences, Engineering, and Medicine 2016, *Parenting Matters: Supporting Parents of Children Ages 0-8*, Washington, DC: The National Academies Press, viewed 5 January 2024, <https://doi.org/10.17226/21868>

CHAPTER 2

Centerhealthyminds.org 2024, *What is Innate Kindness?* viewed 29 April 2024, <https://centerhealthyminds.org/join-the-movement/innate-kindness>

Cherry, K 2022, *What is Self Esteem?* updated 7 November 2022, viewed 3 April 2023, <https://www.verywellmind.com/what-is-self-esteem-2795868>

Dewar, G 2023, *Teaching self-control: Evidence-based tips*, viewed 24 May 2024, <https://parentingscience.com/teaching-self-control/>

Johansson, E 2018, *Values Education in Preschool*, in Johansson, E and Einarsdottir, J (eds.), Values in Early Childhood Education, Citizenship for Tomorrow, 1-16, Paperback version, 1st edn, Routledge Publishers, New York, accessed 12 June 2024 from Amazon.com

Lovat, T and Hawkes, N 2013, *Values Education: A Pedagogical Imperative for Student Wellbeing*, Educational Research International, 2(2), 1-6, viewed 13 June 2024, <http://www.erint.savap.org.pk/PDF/Vol.2(2)/ERInt.2013(2.2-01).pdf>

Making Caring Common Project 2022, *7 Tips for Raising Caring Kids*, Harvard Graduate School of Education, viewed 21 July 2024, <https://mcc.gse.harvard.edu/resources-for-families/7-tips-raising-caring-kids?>

Thekindnesscurriculum.com 2020, *An Introduction to the Kindness Curriculum (Prior to School)*, viewed 4 August 2022, <http://thekindnesscurriculum.com/prior-to-school/>

The Resilience Project 2022a, *The Resilience Project*, viewed 20 May 2020, <https://theresilienceproject.com.au>

The Resilience Project 2022b, *References and Readings*, viewed 20 May 2020, <https://theresilienceproject.com.au/presentation-slides-references/>

ValuesbasedEducation 2021, *Values-based Education (VbE): The beating heart of education*, Newsletter, viewed 16 June 2021, <https://valuesbasededucation.com>

CHAPTER 3

BabySensory.com.au 2020, *The power of touch*, viewed 6 July 2020, <https://www.babysensory.com.au/power_of_touch>

CogniKids.com 2021, *Important Milestone—CRAWLING*, posted 18 March 2021, viewed 25 July 2025, <https://cognikids.com/movement-milestone-crawling/>

Developingchild.harvard.edu 2018, *Brain Architecture*, Center of the Developing Child, Harvard University, viewed 10 July 2021, <https://developingchild.harvard.edu/science/key-concepts/brain-architecture/>

Doman, G and Doman, J 2006, *How to Teach Your Child to Read: The Gentle Revolution*, Paperback version, revised edn, Square One Publishers, accessed 11 April 2023 from Amazon.com

Eliot, L 2000, *What's Going on in There? How the Brain and Mind Develop in the First Five Years of Life*, Paperback version, Bantam Doubleday Dell Publishing Group Inc, accessed 15 July 2021 from Amazon.com

Eliot, L 2012, *Pink Brain, Blue Brain: How Small Differences Grow into Troublesome Gaps—And What We Can Do about It*, Paperback version, Oneworld Publications, accessed 15 July 2021 from Amazon.com

Eliot, L, Ahmed, A, Khan, H and Patel, J 2021, *Dump the "dimorphism": Comprehensive synthesis of human brain studies reveals few male-female differences beyond size*, Neuroscience and Biobehavioral Reviews, 125, 667-697, viewed 8 July 2021, <https://www.sciencedirect.com/science/article/pii/S0149763421000804?via%3Dihub>

HelpGuide.Org 2019, *What is secure attachment and bonding?*, viewed 6 July 2020, <https://www.helpguide.org/family/parenting/what-is-secure-attachment-and-bonding>

Kidspot.com.au 2015, *Six Reasons Why Crawling is Important*, posted 20 November 2015, viewed 7 July 2020, <https://www.kidspot.com.au/baby/baby-development/six-reasons-why-crawling-is-important/news-story/d95b4e7b765c817b85dbd1b8f5fdc249>

Knost, LR 2013, *Whispers through Time: Communication Through the Ages and Stages of Childhood*, Paperback version, Little Hearts Books, LLC, accessed 27 April 2023 from Amazon.com

National Scientific Council on the Developing Child 2009, *Young children develop in an environment of relationships*, Working Paper No. 1, retrieved 6 July 2020 from <https://developingchild.harvard.edu/resources/wp1/>

Perry, PD and Szalavitz, M 2011, *Born for Love: Why Empathy is Essential—and Endangered*, Paperback version, HarperCollins Publishers Inc., accessed 27 April 2023 from Amazon.com

Rosalind Franklin University of Medicine and Science 2021, *Massive study reveals few differences between men's and women's brains: Neuroscientists conduct meta-synthesis of three decades of research*, ScienceDaily, posted 29 March 2021, viewed 8 July 2021, <http://www.sciencedaily.com/releases/2021/03/210325115316.htm>

Rippon, G 2020, *The Gendered Brain: The New Neuroscience that Shatters the Myth of the Female Brain*, Paperback version, Vintage Publishing, accessed 27 April 2023 from Amazon.com

Winston, R and Chicot, R 2016, *The importance of early bonding on the long-term mental health and resilience of children*, London J Prim Care, 8(1), 12-14, viewed 5 July 2020, <https://www.ncbi.nlm.nih.gov/pmc/articles/PMC5330336/>

ZerotoThree.org 2010, *Tips on Nurturing Your Child's Curiosity*, viewed 25 September 2020, <https://www.zerotothree.org/resource/tips-on-nurturing-your-childs-curiosity/>

CHAPTER 4

Alario, C 2020, *Sleep and Brain Development: an important connection*, posted 1 March 2020, viewed 19 November 2020, <https://www.nestedbean.com/blogs/zen-blog/sleep-brain-development-for-babies>

Canadian Paediatric Society 2004, *Effective Discipline for Children*, Paediatrics and Child Health, 9(1), 37-41; viewed 16 August 2022, <https://www.ncbi.nlm.nih.gov/pmc/articles/PMC2719514/>

Chang, A-M, Aeschbach, D, Duffy, JF and Czeisler, CA 2015, *Evening use of light-emitting eReaders negatively affects sleep, circadian timing, and next-morning alertness*, Proceedings of the National Academy of Sciences of the United States of America, 112(4), 1232-1237; viewed 19 November 2020, <https://www.pnas.org/content/112/4/1232>

Colab.thekids.org.au 2024, *Five Top Tips To Build Young Brains from Professor Donna Cross*, Telethon Kids Institute, Minderoo Foundation, viewed 15 November 2024, <https://colab.thekids.org.au/siteassets/media-images---colab/campaign-brighter-tomorrows/tki1173---colab-telethon-handout-final.pdf>

Doman, G and Doman, J 2006, *How to Teach Your Baby to Read: The Gentle Revolution*, Paperback version, revised edn, Square One Publishers, accessed 25 November 2020 from Amazon.com

Doman, J 2018, *Imaginative Play: Does it Really Matter?* E-Newsletter, The Gentle Revolutionary—Helping Parents to Help Children, The Institutes for the Achievement of Human Potential, 27 July 2018.

Famlii.com 2020, *The Basics of Child Development: How Children Think, Feel and Grow*, viewed 8 July 2020, <https://www.famlii.com/basics-child-development-social-emotional-physical-cognitive-development/>

Firstfiveyears.org.au 2019, *How and when to teach your child to share*, posted 14 March 2019, viewed 10 October 2020, <https://www.firstfiveyears.org.au/child-development/how-and-when-to-teach-your-child-to-share>

Gemmell, N 2016, *Mark Maclaine, grit—and the greatest gift for kids*, The Australian, 5 February 2016, viewed 5 November 2020.

Habibi, A 2016, *Music training speeds up brain development in children,* The Conversation, posted 4 August 2016, viewed 16 July 2020, <https://theconversation.com/music-training-speeds-up-brain-development-in-children-61491>

Juntti, M 2019, *Want to Raise a High-Achieving Kid? Talk to Your Toddler Like This,* posted 17 December 2019, viewed 28 September 2020, <https://www.fatherly.com/health-science/raise-high-achieving-test-taker/>

Klein, TP 2020, *How Toddlers Thrive: What parents can do for children ages 2 to 5 to plant the seeds of lifelong happiness*, Paperback version, Profile Books Ltd, London, accessed 13 October 2021 from Amazon.com

Layton, J 2009, *Does singing make you happy?—Physical Effects of Singing*, posted 2 June 2009, HowStuffWorks.com, viewed 15 July 2020, <https://science.howstuffworks.com/life/inside-the-mind/emotions/singing-happy.htm>

Mancini, M 2020, *12 Fascinating Facts About Crows*, updated 30 September 2020, viewed 18 October 2020, <https://www.mentalfloss.com/article/504722/12-fascinating-facts-about-crows>

Margalit, L 2016, *What Screen Time Can Really Do to Kids' Brains—Too much at the worst possible age may have negative consequences*, posted 17 April 2016, viewed 18 July 2020, <https://www.psychologytoday.com/us/blog/behind-online-behavior/201604/what-screen-time-can-really-do-kids-brains>

Markham, L 2012, *Peaceful Parent, Happy Kids: How to Stop Yelling and Start Connecting*, Paperback version, Penguin Putnam Inc, accessed 7 October 2020 from Amazon.com

Montessori Academy 2017, *The Importance Of Repetition In Early Childhood*, posted 4 May 2017, viewed 26 July 2025, <https://montessoriacademy.com.au/repetition-child-development-montessori/>

National Scientific Council on the Developing Child 2007, *The Timing and Quality of Early Experiences Combine to Shape Brain Architecture*, Working Paper No. 5, retrieved from <https://developingchild.harvard.edu/resources/working-paper/the-timing-and-quality-of-early-experiences-combine-to-shape-brain-architecture/>

Nelsen, J, Erwin, C and Duffy, RA 2015, *Positive Discipline: The First Three Years,* Revised edn, Paperback version, Random House USA Inc, accessed 7 October 2020 from Amazon.com

Raisingchildren.net.au 2020a, *Sharing and learning to share,* posted 23 November 2020, viewed 5 October 2021, <https://raisingchildren.net.au/toddlers/behaviour/friends-siblings/sharing>

Ruder, DB 2019, *Screen Time and the Brain: Digital devices can interfere with everything from sleep to creativity,* posted 19 June 2019, viewed 28 April 2023, <https://hms.harvard.edu/news/screen-time-brain>

Siegel, DJ and Bryson, TP 2011, *The Whole-Brain Child: 12 Revolutionary Strategies to Nurture Your Child's Developing Mind, Survive Everyday Parenting Struggles, and Help Your Family Thrive,* p.139, Delacorte Press, viewed 3 July 2020, <https://www.azquotes.com/quote/484387>

Zunin, L 1986, *Contact: The First Four Minutes—A practical approach to meeting the right person for you,* Mass Market Paperback version, Ballantine Books, accessed 16 July 2020 from Amazon.com

CHAPTER 5

Bishop, D 2018, *What are Visual Perceptual Skills?,* viewed 2 December 2020, <https://www.continued.com/early-childhood-education/ask-the-experts/what-are-visual-perceptual-skills_22984>

British Psychological Society 2017, *Rosemary aroma can aid children's working memory: Exposure to the aroma of rosemary essential oil can significantly enhance working memory in children,* Science Daily, posted 2 May 2017, viewed 15 July 2020, <https://www.sciencedaily.com/releases/2017/05/170502204545.htm>

Cox, J 2025, *Music makes it memorable,* posted 5 March 2015, viewed 23 January 2025, Penn State Extension Better Kid Care, The Pennsylvania State University, <https://extension.psu.edu/programs/betterkidcare/news/2015/music-makes-it-memorable>

Dabell, J 2019, *Forget the Rosemary Oil,* posted 20 November 2019, viewed 19 February 2023, <https://johndabell.com/2019/11/20/pass-the-rosemary-oil/>

Dennison, PE and Dennison, GE 1992, *Brain Gym: Simple Activities for Whole Brain Learning,* Paperback version, Edu Kinesthetics, accessed 27th November 2020 from Amazon.com

Doman, G and Doman, J 2006, *How to Teach Your Baby to Read: The Gentle Revolution,* Paperback version, revised edn, Square One Publishers, accessed 25 November 2020 from Amazon.com

Hannaford, C 2010, *Smart Moves: Why Learning Is Not All In Your Head,* Paperback version, 2nd edn, Great River Books, accessed 28 April 2023 from Amazon.com

Herz, RS 2016, *The Role of Odour-Evoked Memory in Psychological and Physiological Health,* Brain Sci., 6(3), 22, viewed 19 February 2023, <https://www.ncbi.nlm.nih.gov/pmc/articles/PMC5039415/>

Kidsfirst.com.au 2014, *Pencils or Crayons? What should kids use first,* posted 6 August 2014, viewed 22 July 2020, <https://kids-first.com.au/pencils-or-crayons-what-should-kids-use-first/>

Kid Sense 2020, *Fine Motor Skills,* viewed 17 August 2020, <https://childdevelopment.com.au/areas-of-concern/fine-motor-skills/>

CHAPTER 6

Anderson, J 2023, *The Agile Learner: Where Growth Mindsets, Habits of Mind and Practice Unite*, Digital version, Kindle edn, published by James Anderson, accessed 10 February 2024 from Amazon.com

Armstrong, T 2000, *In Their Own Way: Discovering and Encouraging Your Child's Multiple Intelligences*, Paperback version, revised and updated edn, Tarcher Perigee, accessed 28 April 2023 from Amazon.com

Armstrong, T 2017, *Multiple Intelligences in the Classroom*, Paperback version, 4th edn, ASCD Books, accessed 28 April 2023 from Amazon.com

Chessineducation.org 2023, *Chess in Education—An international perspective*, viewed 10 March 2023, <https://chessineducation.org/home-int>

Colier, N 2018, *Can I Let My Child Be Bored? How to effectively handle your child's boredom*, posted 23 January 2018, PsychologyToday.com, viewed 4 August 2020, <https://www.psychologytoday.com/au/blog/inviting-monkey-tea/201801/can-i-let-my-child-be-bored>

Connell, JD 2015, *Brain-Based Strategies to Reach Every Learner*, Paperback version, XanEdu Publishing Inc., accessed 6 March 2021 from Amazon.com

Covey, SR 2013, *The 7 Habits of Highly Effective People: Powerful Lessons in Personal Change,* Paperback version, 25th Anniversary edn, Simon & Schuster UK Ltd, accessed 29 April 2023 from Amazon.com

Deary, IJ, Strand, S, Smith, P and Fernandes, C 2007, *Intelligence and educational achievement*, Intelligence, 35(1), 13-21, viewed 10 August 2020, <https://www.sciencedirect.com/science/article/abs/pii/S0160289606000171?via%3Dihub>

Dweck, CS 2006, *Mindset: The New Psychology of Success*, Hardcover version, 1st edn, Random House Publishing, accessed 10 January 2024 from Amazon.com

Dweck, CS 2015, *Carol Dweck revisits the 'growth mindset,'* retrieved from <https://www.edweek.org/leadership/opinion-carol-dweck-revisits-the-growth-mindset/2015/09>

EarlyYearsCareers.com 2016, *Promoting a sense of belonging in your baby room: Why is it important for babies to experience a sense of belonging?*, posted 30 December 2016, viewed 26 July 2020, <https://www.earlyyearscareers.com/eyc/ways-to-help-continuous-improvement/promoting-a-sense-of-belonging-baby-room/>

Edutopia.org 2013, *Multiple Intelligences: What Does the Research Say?,* posted 8 March 2013, updated 20 July 2016, viewed 1 August 2020, <https://www.edutopia.org/multiple-intelligences-research>

Edutopia.org 2021, *Brain-based learning*, viewed 5 March 2021, <https://www.edutopia.org/topic/brain-based-learning>

Gardinerchess.com.au 2023, *Why do we believe in chess?*, viewed 29 April 2023, <https://gardinerchess.com.au/about-us/>

Gardner, H 2011a, *The Unschooled Mind: How children think and how schools should teach*, Paperback version, 2nd edn, Basic Books, accessed 28 April 2023 from Amazon.com

Gardner, H 2011b, *Frames of Mind: The Theory of Multiple Intelligences,* Paperback version, 3rd edn, Basic Books, accessed 28 April 2023 from Amazon.com

Gardner, H 2013, *Frequently Asked Questions—Multiple Intelligences and Related Educational Topics*, viewed 27 February 2021, <https://scholar.google.com.au/scholar?q=Gardner,+H+2013,+Frequently+Asked+Questions—Multiple+Intelligences+and+Related+Educational+Topics>

Gunderson, EA, Gripshover, SJ, Romero, C, Dweck, CS, Goldin-Meadow, S and Levine, SC 2013, *Parent praise to 1 to 3-year-olds predict children's motivational frameworks 5 years later*, Child Development, 84(5), 1526-41, viewed 8 February 2024, <https://srcd.onlinelibrary.wiley.com/doi/epdf/10.1111/cdev.12064>

Keener, G 2022, *Chess is Booming*, The New York Times, 27 September 2022, viewed 29 April 2023.

Kingslandchess.com 2023, *10 Big Brain Benefits of Playing Chess*, viewed 29 April 2023, <http://www.kingslandchess.com/why-learn-chess.html>

Marsden, J 2019, *The Art of Growing Up*, Paperback version, MacMillan Australia, accessed 29 April 2023 from Amazon.com

Millacci, TS 2021, *How to Nurture a Growth Mindset in Kids: 8 Best Activities*, post modified 30 June 2025, viewed 5 August 2025, <https://positivepsychology.com/growth-mindset-for-kids/>

Mindsetworks.com, 2017, *Decades of Scientific Research that Started a Growth Mindset Revolution*, viewed 11 January 2024, <https://www.mindsetworks.com/Science/Default>

Miresearch.org 2021, *Multiple Intelligences Developmental Assessment Scales*, viewed 28 April 2023, <https://miresearch.org>

Northern Illinois University Center for Innovative Teaching and Learning 2020, *Howard Gardner's theory of multiple intelligences*, In Instructional guide for university faculty and teaching assistants, viewed 10 July 2020, <https://www.niu.edu/citl/resources/guides/instructional-guide/gardners-theory-of-multiple-intelligences.shtml>

Peterson, ER, Sharma, T, Bird, A, Henderson, AME, Ramgopal, V, Reese, E, and Morton, SMB 2025, *How mothers talk to their children about failure, mistakes and setbacks is related to their children's fear of failure*, British Journal of Educational Psychology, 95, 124–142, <https://doi.org/10.1111/bjep.12685>

Rosholm M, Mikkelsen MB and Gumede, K 2017, *Your move: The effect of chess on mathematics test scores*, PLoS ONE 12(5): e0177257, viewed 10 August 2020, <https://journals.plos.org/plosone/article?id=10.1371/journal.pone.0177257>

Sala G, Foley, JP and Gobet, F 2017, *The Effects of Chess Instruction on Pupils' Cognitive and Academic Skills: State of the Art and Theoretical Challenges*, Frontiers in Psychology, viewed 10 August 2020, <https://www.frontiersin.org/articles/10.3389/fpsyg.2017.00238/full>

Scholastic.com 2021, *Activities and Printables*, viewed 27 July 2025, <https://www.scholastic.com/parents/kids-activities-and-printables.html>

Scholastic.com 2023, *Multiple Intelligence Questionnaire*, viewed 26 July 2025, <https://teachables.scholastic.com/teachables/books/multiple-intellgence-questionnaire-9780439590204_001.html>

Tomlinson, CA, 2014, *The Differentiated Classroom: Responding to the Needs of All Learners*, Paperback version, 2nd edn, ASCD Publishing, accessed 28 April 2023 from Amazon.com

CHAPTER 7

Åberg, MAI, Pedersen, NL, Torén, K, Svartengren, M, Bäckstrand, B, Johnsson, T, Christiana M. Cooper-Kuhn, CM, Åberg, ND, Nilsson, M and Kuhn, HG 2009, *Cardiovascular fitness is associated with cognition in young adulthood*, in Proceedings of the National Academy of Sciences, USA, 106(49), 20906-20911, viewed 8 January 2021, <https://www.pnas.org/content/106/49/20906>

Activebabiessmartkids.com.au 2021, *Before you start our baby classes,* Active Babies Smart Kids TV, viewed 8 February 2021, <https://activebabiessmartkids.com.au/episodes/active-babies-smart-kids/?v=322b26af01d5>

Babycentre.co.uk 2023, *When can I take my baby out of the house?,* posted 7 May 2023, viewed 27 July 2025, <https://www.babycentre.co.uk/a538423/when-can-i-take-my-baby-out-of-the-house>

Belcher, BR, Berrigan, D, Papachrisotopoulou, A, Brady, SM, Bernstein, SB, Brychta, RJ, Hattenbach, JD, Tigner, IL, Courville, AB, Drinkard, BE, Smith, KP, Rosing, DR, Wolters, PL, Chen, KY and Yanovski, JA 2015, *Effects of Interrupting Children's Sedentary Behaviors With Activity on Metabolic Function: A Randomized Trial*, The Journal of Clinical Endocrinology and Metabolism, 100(10), 3735-3743, viewed 11 January 2021, <https://academic.oup.com/jcem/article/100/10/3735/2835791>

Bento, G and Dias, G 2017, *The importance of outdoor play for young children's healthy development*, Porto Biomedical Journal, 2(5), 157-160, viewed 13 December 2020, <https://www.sciencedirect.com/science/article/pii/S2444866416301234>

Borreli, L 2016, *4 Brain Benefits of Swimming: Improved Blood Flow Boosts Cognitive Function, Alleviates Depression Symptoms*, posted 25 October, 2016, viewed 16 August 2020, <https://www.medicaldaily.com/4-brain-benefits-swimming-improved-blood-flow-boosts-cognitive-function-402385>

Doman, G, Doman, D and Hagy, B 2012, *Fit Baby, Smart Baby, Your Baby!: From Birth to Age Six,* Paperback version, Square One Publishers, accessed 30 April 2023 from Amazon.com

Feigelson, M 2016, *Why Walking Is So Good for Parents, Toddlers, and the Cities Where They Live: How can making a city more walkable improve early childhood development?*, posted 24 October 2016, viewed 7 January 2021, <https://ssir.org/articles/entry/why_walking_is_so_good_for_parents_toddlers_and_the_cities_where_they_live>

Gehrman, E 2022, *A Child's Need for Sleep*, Harvard Medicine Magazine, viewed 4 November 2024, <https://magazine.hms.harvard.edu/articles/childs-need-sleep>

Goddard-Blythe, S 2005, *The Well-Balanced Child: Movement and Early Learning*, 2nd revised edn, Paperback version, Hawthorn Press Ltd., accessed 6 February 2021 from Amazon.com

Grogan, A 2023, *46 Essential Vestibular Activities and Input Ideas*, viewed 27 July 2025, <https://yourkidstable.com/vestibular-activities-and-input/>

Healthdirect.gov.au 2020, *Benefits of Physical Activity for Children*, viewed 13 December 2020, <https://www.healthdirect.gov.au/benefits-of-physical-activity-for-children>

Health.gov.au 2021, *Physical Activity and Exercise Guidelines for Infants, Toddlers and Preschoolers*, viewed 30 April 2023, <https://www.health.gov.au/topics/physical-activity-and-exercise/physical-activity-and-exercise-guidelines-for-all-australians/for-infants-toddlers-and-preschoolers-birth-to-5-years>

Health.harvard.edu 2014, *Regular exercise changes the brain to improve memory, thinking skills*, posted 9 April 2014, viewed 13 December 2020, <https://www.health.harvard.edu/blog/regular-exercise-changes-brain-improve-memory-thinking-skills-201404097110>

Health.harvard.edu 2016, *Can you grow new brain cells?* posted September 2016, viewed 13 December 2020, <https://www.health.harvard.edu/mind-and-mood/can-you-grow-new-brain-cells>

Health.harvard.edu 2017, *6 ways to help keep your baby at a healthy weight*, posted 11 April 2017, viewed 14 December 2020, <https://www.health.harvard.edu/blog/6-ways-to-help-keep-your-baby-at-a-healthy-weight-2017041111575>

Health.harvard.edu 2020, *Exercising to relax: How does exercise reduce stress? Surprising answers to this question and more*, updated 7 July 2020, viewed 11 January 2021, <https://www.health.harvard.edu/staying-healthy/exercising-to-relax>

Health.harvard.edu 2024, *Swimming lessons save lives: what parents should know*, posted 27 June 2024, viewed 5 August 2025, <http://www.health.harvard.edu/blog/swimming-lessons-save-lives-what-parents-should-know-201806151630>

Healthline.com 2019, *8 Benefits of Infant Swim Time*, posted 5 February 2019, viewed 17 December 2020, <https://www.healthline.com/health/parenting/infant-swimming>

Healthline.com 2020, *When Can a Baby Go in a Pool?*, posted 11 June 2020, viewed 17 December 2020, <https://www.healthline.com/health/baby/when-can-a-baby-go-in-a-pool#risks>

ilslearningcorner.com.au 2016, *The Vestibular System: An Internal GPS System for the Body*, Integrated Learning Strategies (ILS), posted 13 April 2016, viewed 30 April 2023, <https://ilslearningcorner.com/2016-04-vestibular-system-your-childs-internal-gps-system-for-motor-planning-and-attention/>

Jorgensen, R 2013, *Early-years swimming: Adding Capital to Young Australians*, Final Report, Griffith Institute for Educational Research, Griffith University, viewed 19 December 2020, <https://kidsalive.com.au/wp-content/uploads/2014/08/2013-EYS-Final-Report-30-July-13-JM.pdf>

Khan, NA and Hillman, CH 2014, *The Relation of Childhood Physical Activity and Aerobic Fitness to Brain Function and Cognition: A Review*, Pediatric Exercise Science, 26, 138-146, viewed 4 January 2021, <https://www.researchgate.net/publication/261604527_The_Relation_of_Childhood_Physical_Activity_and_Aerobic_Fitness_to_Brain_Function_and_Cognition_A_Review>

Lepore, M 2019, *Harvard researchers agree this is the best exercise ever*, posted 16 November 2019, viewed 13 December 2020, <https://www.theladders.com/career-advice/harvard-researchers-agree-this-is-the-best-exercise-ever>

Mann, D 2003, *Negative Ions Create Positive Vibes*, posted 6 May 2002, viewed 10 January 2021, <https://www.webmd.com/balance/features/negative-ions-create-positive-vibes#1>

Mayoclinic.org 2020, *Exercise and stress: Get moving to manage stress*, posted 18 August 2020, viewed 16 December 2020, <https://www.mayoclinic.org/healthy-lifestyle/stress-management/in-depth/exercise-and-stress/art-20044469>

Morris, JN and Hardman, AE 1997, *Walking to Health,* Sports Med 23, 306-332, published 9 October 2012, viewed 25 March 2023, <https://link.springer.com/article/10.2165/00007256-199723050-00004>

Neuroscientificallychallenged.com 2023, *Know Your Brain: Vestibular System*, viewed 30 April 2023, <https://www.neuroscientificallychallenged.com/blog/know-your-brain-vestibular-system>

Oppezzo, M and Schwartz, DL 2014, *Give Your Ideas Some Legs: The Positive Effect of Walking on Creative Thinking*, Journal of Experimental Psychology: Learning, Memory, and Cognition, 40(4), 1142-1152, viewed 8 January 2021, <https://www.apa.org/pubs/journals/releases/xlm-a0036577.pdf>

Postal, K 2009, *Exercise improves our memory*, posted 4 June 2009, viewed 14 March 2023, <https://karenpostal.com/2009-6-4-exercise-improves-our-memory-html/>

Psychologytoday.com 2020, *How Walking Enhances Cognitive Performance*, posted 23 January 2020, viewed 11 January 2021, <https://www.psychologytoday.com/us/blog/experience-engineering/202001/how-walking-enhances-cognitive-performance>

Ratey, JJ and Hagerman, E 2013, *Spark! How exercise can improve the performance of your brain*, Paperback version, reprint edn, Little, Brown Spark, accessed 30 April 2023 from Amazon.com

Rowley, S and Williams, J 2015, *Multi-sensory stimulation and infant development*, Research Review Educational Series, viewed 6 February 2021, <https://www.researchreview.com.au/getmedia/3334ba98-e03e-4183-8fb5-95e8c318487a/Educational-Series-Multisensory-Stimulation-and-infant-development.pdf.aspx?ext=.pdf>

Sandler, A and Coren, A 1981, *Vestibular Stimulation in Early Childhood: A Review*, Journal of the Division for Early Childhood, 3(1), 48-55, viewed 6 February 2021, <https://journals.sagepub.com/doi/abs/10.1177/105381518100300108>

Stetka, B 2019, *Why Rocking to Sleep is a Matchless Sedative—and Elixir*, posted 24 January 2019, viewed 6 February 2021, <https://www.scientificamerican.com/article/why-rocking-to-sleep-is-a-matchless-sedative-mdash-and-elixir1/>

Stevens-Smith, D and Murdock, J 2021, *7 Elements of Play and how they Impact Learning in the Classroom Element #3: Brachiating*, viewed 14 February 2021, <https://www.thegeniusofplay.org/genius/expert-advice/articles/7-elements-of-play-brachiating.aspx>

Swimming.org 2020, *The benefits of baby swimming*, viewed 19 December 2020, <https://www.swimming.org/learntoswim/the-benefits-of-baby-swimming/>

Tumbokon, R 2020, *The Benefits of Exercise On Your Kid's Brain*, viewed 3 January 2021, <https://www.raisesmartkid.com/3-to-6-years-old/4-articles/35-the-benefits-of-exercise-on-your-kids-brain>

Williams, J 2021, *Babies and children need to swing. Why, how, when and when not to swing*, viewed 13 February 2021, <https://activebabiessmartkids.com.au/articles/swing/?v=322b26af01d5>

Williams, J and Grigg, T 2019, *Ten Vestibular Activities to do with your Baby or Toddler*, posted 1 October 2019, viewed 6 February 2021, <https://www.whatson4kids.com.au/why-babies-need-to-rock-and-roll/>

APPENDIX 2—RESOURCES

This compilation of helpful web-based resources below is not prescriptive but is provided to enhance the teaching experiences with your child. They come in many forms and cover essential background information and knowledge, specific activity instructions and teaching aids that will facilitate the learning outcomes.

The links to the Resources will be maintained and accessible via the References and Resources page on the author's website marglarden.com. If you have any issues or questions, please do not hesitate to contact the author at marglarden@gmail.com.

CHAPTER 1

COURSES AND TALKS

- Adult Child and Baby First Aid Course—Red Cross (USA)
- Caring for Babies and Kids—St John Ambulance (Aust)
- First Aid for Babies and Children Course—Red Cross (Aust)
- First Aid for Babies and Children Webinar
- How To Multiply Your Child's Intelligence Course
- Introduction to Montessori Education
- Newborn Course
- Online Montessori Training Courses
- Paediatric First Aid Course—Red Cross (UK)
- Paediatric First Aid—St John Ambulance (UK)

INFORMATION

- A Parent's Guide to Kidsafe Homes
- American Montessori Society
- British Nutrition Foundation: Nutrition for Baby
- Childproofing Your Home
- Delvy.ai
- Feeding Your Baby
- Gentle Revolution
- Healthy Eating for Kids
- Keeping Children Safe from Poisonous Substances
- Kidsafe—Poisoning Information Sheet
- Nidirect: Healthy Eating for Children
- Nutritional Psychiatry: Your Brain on Food
- Pregnancy, Birth & Baby
- Stanford Children's Health
- The Institutes for the Achievement of Human Potential
- Up and Away Initiative
- USDA.gov

APPS

- Delvy

BOOKS FOR PARENTS

- How To Raise an Amazing Child the Montessori Way

APPENDIX 2 | RESOURCES

CHAPTER 2

ACTIVITY INSTRUCTIONS

- Early Years Wellbeing Program
- Empathy, Gratitude and Mindfulness Activities
- Finding My Calm
- Mindfulness for Little Ones
- Teaching Character Development in Early Childhood
- Teaching Self-Control
- The Kindness Curriculum—Prior to School
- What is Self-Esteem?

AIDS

- Busy Box
- Feelings Scale + Coping Skills
- Gratitude Journal
- Mindfulness Apps
- Sand Timer
- Yoga Mats for Kids
- World Map Floor Puzzle

BOOKS FOR CHILDREN

- All Are Welcome
- Be Kind
- Dinosaur Learns Empathy
- Emily's Everyday Manners
- Ferdie Makes a Friend, a Story About Caring
- Grody's Not So Golden Rules
- I Am Stronger Than Anger
- I'll Wait, Mr. Panda
- Kindness Makes Us Strong
- Llama Llama Red Pajama
- Miss Rumphius
- Rumpelstiltskin's Daughter
- The Carrot Seed
- The Quiltmaker's Gift
- The Rag Coat
- The Story of Conservation
- The Thankful Book
- Too Much Noise
- Waiting

COURSES AND TALKS

- The Resilience Project

EARLY CHILDHOOD | WHERE THE MAGIC HAPPENS

CHAPTER 3

INFORMATION	ACTIVITY INSTRUCTIONS
- The Importance of Early Bonding - The Power of Touch - What is Secure Attachment and Bonding - Young Children Develop in an Environment of Relationships	- Nursery Rhyme—1,2,3,4,5 Once I caught a fish alive

AIDS	BOOKS FOR PARENTS
- Briefcase - Cleaning Tools - Hard Hat - Kitchen Tools - Medical Kit - Rechargeable Torch/Flashlight - Toolbox - Unbreakable Mirror - Wooden Tool Set - Work Bench	- Born For Love: Why Empathy Is Essential—and Endangered - How to Teach Your Baby to Read: The Gentle Revolution - Pink Brain, Blue Brain: How Small Differences Grow into Troublesome Gaps—and What We Can Do About It - The Gendered Brain: The New Neuroscience that Shatters the Myth of the Female Brain - What's Going on in There? - Whispers Through Time

BOOKS FOR CHILDREN	
- Baby Touch and Feel Animals - Hattie and the Fox	- Time for Bed - Who Sank the Boat?

APPENDIX 2 | RESOURCES

CHAPTER 4

INFORMATION

- Aboriginal Art
- American Academy of Pediatrics, USA
- A Naturalist's Guide to the Butterflies of Australia
- A Parent's Guide To Kidsafe Homes
- A Positive Approach to Discipline: Babies and Children
- Books to Build Character and Teach Your Child Important Values
- Build a Campfire—Boy Scouts of America Handbook Hacks
- Care for a Goldfish
- CDC Developmental Milestones
- Chihuly Glass Creations
- Childproofing Your Home
- Collective Nouns for Groups of Animals
- Companion Planting for Beginners
- Constellations
- Crop Rotation
- Effective Discipline for Children
- Familiar Butterflies of North America
- FFY Developmental Milestones 1-2 Years
- FFY Developmental Milestones 2-3 Years
- FFY Development Milestones 3-5 Years
- Firstfiveyear.org.au
- First Man
- First Phase Results (GUD) Australia
- Flightless Birds
- Flowers Leaves and Other Plant Parts
- Glassmaking
- Growing Up Digital (GUD) Alberta
- Growing Up Digital (GUD) Australia
- Guide to Ladybirds of the British Isles
- Helping Kids Identify and Express Feelings
- How a Seed Becomes a Plant
- How Farmers Shear Sheep
- How to Prepare Tomato Seeds for Growing
- Immune System
- Keeping Children Safe from Poisonous Substances
- Kidsafe—Poisoning Information Sheet
- Ladybirds
- Marshmallow Roasting Safety
- National Geographic Stargazer's Atlas: The Ultimate Guide to the Night Sky
- Rainbow Facts for Kids
- Raisingchildren.net.au
- Requests and Instructions: Helping Children Cooperate
- Roasting Marshmallows
- Royal Society for the Prevention of Accidents, UK
- Second Phase Results (GUD) Australia
- Shell Fossil
- SunSmart
- Suzuki (Australia)
- Suzuki (United Kingdom)
- Suzuki (United States of America)
- The Lifecycle of the Butterfly
- The Royal Children's Hospital Melbourne, Australia
- Up and Away Initiative
- Various Articles on Discipline and Self-Discipline
- What are Magnets?
- Yamaha (Australia)
- Yamaha (United Kingdom)
- Yamaha (United States of America)

APPS

- Night Sky
- SkyView®Lite

CHAPTER 4 Continued

ACTIVITY INSTRUCTIONS

- Australian Aboriginal Art Coloring Book
- Australian Aboriginal Dot Painting for Kids
- Australian Aboriginal Crane Dance
- Australian Scouts Program Resources Library
- Backyard Bug Book for Kids
- Beginner Yoyo Tricks
- Blowing Out an Egg
- Build a Rocket Using a Cardboard Paper Roll
- Chocolate and Marshmallow Bananas in Coals
- Color the Egg Using Vegetable Dye
- Corner Page Bookmarks
- DIY Pom Poms
- Dry/Press Leaves and Make a Bookmark
- Dry Your Strawberries in the Oven
- Easy Christmas Origami
- Finger Knitting
- Fresh Pasta Recipe
- Garbage Bag Kite
- Homemade Playdough Recipes
- How To Eat with Chopsticks
- How To Hula-Hoop
- How To Juggle
- How To Make a Bookmark
- How To Make Hand Shadow Puppets
- How To Make Homemade Butter
- How to Make a Native-American Headband
- How To Make a Telephone with Cans
- How To Play Baby Shark on The Xylophone
- How to Play the Ukulele
- I Love It When It Rains
- Kite Coloring Book for Kids
- Learning About Insects
- Let's Get Gardening
- Make a Rain Gauge
- Make a Pinwheel
- Making Music with Water
- Montessori at Home: Activities for Newborn Babies
- Montessori at Home: Activities for Babies 3-6 Months
- Montessori at Home: Activities for Babies 6-9 Months
- Montessori at Home: Activities for Babies 9-12 Months
- Montessori at Home: Activities for Babies 12-15 Months
- Montessori Finger Knitting
- Nature Craft Projects for Kids
- Origami Butterflies Kit
- Paper Airplane Book
- Paper Plate Animal Masks
- Phonetic Alphabet A to Z
- Printable Placemat
- Quick and Easy Envelope Hand Puppets
- Science Alive
- Science Kinetics
- Smithsonian 10-Minute Science Experiments
- Spectacular Science Days Out in the UK
- Strawberry Santas
- Sun-Earth-Moon Model
- The Harvey Sisters Irish Dance Performance
- The Scouting Guide to Hiking
- The Scouting Guide to Survival
- Thrivebyfive.org.au
- Tie-Dye Easter Eggs
- Tummy Time
- What Makes a Magnet?
- 365 Things to Make and Do

CHAPTER 4 *Continued*

AIDS

- A Raindrop's Journey
- Animal Snap Card Game
- Art of Conversation
- Australian Cork Hat
- Baby Bird Pull Along Toy
- BabyBjorn Smart Potty
- Baby Crib Mobile
- Backyard Birds of North America
- Ball for Baby
- Basketball
- Basketball Hoop with an Adjustable Stand
- Beginner Juggling Balls
- Bird Calls
- Black And White Baby Mobile
- Bubble Blowing Toy
- Busy Book for Toddlers
- Calm Music for Babies
- Cleaning Tool Set
- Clock Face
- Cloud Chart
- Concept of Diversity
- Cookie Cutters
- Corolle Doll and Accessories
- Dance of the Sugar-Plum Fairy
- Dartboard
- Dragonflies
- Dream Doll and Accessories
- Drums
- Early Education Activity Board
- Explore my World: Honey Bees
- Explorer Compass
- Flashcards
- Four Seasons by Vivaldi
- Fruit Salad
- George Meets the Orchestra
- Glow in the Dark Stars
- Magnetic Boats
- Magnifying Glass
- Match a Pair of Birds
- Match a Leaf: A Tree Memory Game
- Milk from Cow to Carton
- Montessori Children's Knife
- Montessori Doctor's Tool Kit
- Montessori Nature Resource
- Montessori Wooden Busy Board
- Multi-Purpose Floor Mobile
- Musical Instruments for Toddlers
- My Shadow by Robert Louis Stevenson
- Papua New Guinean National Anthem
- Percussion Instruments for Toddlers (1-3)
- Plastic Ten Pin Bowling Set
- Plastic Shape Sorter
- Popsicle Molds
- Pop Up Activity Toy
- Pounding Bench
- Push Toy
- Rattle and Rock Maracas
- Rocking Chair
- Sand Timer
- Scissors
- Shapes
- Shearing Sheep
- Sippy Cups
- Soft Stacking Blocks
- Space Bingo
- Sweeping Tools
- Teach Me French
- The Days of the Week
- The First Years Stack Up Cup Toys
- The Wheels on the Bus

CHAPTER 4 Continued

AIDS Continued

- Harmonica
- Indian National Anthem
- Italian Music—Background Chill Out
- Japanese National Anthem
- Junior Learning Emotion Dominoes
- Kids Talking Point Cards
- Learning About Animals with the Wiggles
- Lily

- Traditional Didgeridoo Rhythms
- Trumpet
- Tunnel
- Ukulele
- Ukulele Tuner
- Unbreakable Mirror
- Water Balloons
- Wind on the Hill
- Windsock
- Xylophone

BOOKS FOR CHILDREN

- At the Beach with Lizzie and Luke
- Baby Animals Black and White
- Beginnings and Endings with Lifetimes in Between
- Curious George's First Day of School
- First Book About the Orchestra
- Little Kids First Big Book of Birds
- Little Kids First Big Book of Space
- My Culture and Me
- The Big Book of Bugs
- The Great Big Book of Families
- The Very Hungry Caterpillar
- This Is How We Do It
- What If We Were All The Same!
- Wind
- When We Were Very Young
- 101 Poems for Children: A Laureate's Choice

BOOKS FOR PARENTS

- Contact: The First 4 Minutes
- How Toddlers Thrive
- How to Teach Your Baby to Read: The Gentle Revolution
- Peaceful Parent, Happy Kids: How to Stop Yelling and Start Connecting
- Positive Discipline: The First Three Years

APPENDIX 2 | RESOURCES

CHAPTER 5

INFORMATION

- Brain Gym Australia
- Brain Gym UK
- The Brain Gym Program
- Music Neuroscience
- Pencils or Crayons

ACTIVITY INSTRUCTIONS

- Brain Gym
- Brain Gym: The Complete Brain Warm-Up
- Easy Christmas Origami
- Finger Knit
- Finger Strings
- Hide-and-Seek
- How to Eat with Chopsticks
- How to Hold and Use Scissors
- How to Properly Grip Pencils
- How to Use Cutlery
- Lemonade Scone Recipe
- Nursery Rhyme—1,2,3,4,5 Once I caught a fish alive
- Readingeggs.com.au
- Transition to School

AIDS

- ABC of Body Safety and Consent
- Easy-Grip Colored Pencils
- Flashcards with Big Red Words
- Connect the Dot Activities
- Connect 4
- GPS Child Tracker
- Jumbo Tweezers
- Kids Darts
- Left and Right-Handed Kids Scissors
- Marble Run Toy Sets
- Montessori Children's Knives
- Montessori Screwdriver Board
- Pick up Sticks
- Readingeggs.com.au
- Resources for General Knowledge
- Shutterstock Maps
- The New World Champion Paper Airplane Book
- Toddler-Sized Paintbrushes
- World Globe

BOOKS FOR CHILDREN

- Starting School
- The Great Big Book of Families
- The Invisible String

BOOKS FOR PARENTS

- How to Teach Your Baby to Read: The Gentle Revolution
- Smart Moves: Why Learning Is Not All in Your Head

EARLY CHILDHOOD | WHERE THE MAGIC HAPPENS

CHAPTER 6

INFORMATION

- It's Not as Simple as "Praise Effort"
- Multiple Intelligences Developmental Assessment Scales
- The Connell Multiple Intelligence Questionnaire for Children

ACTIVITY INSTRUCTIONS

- Big Life Journal Resources for 4 to 6-year-olds
- Brain-Based Strategies to Reach Every Learner
- Chess for Children
- Chess for Children Activity Book
- Hide and Seek
- How to Play the Harmonica
- How to Play the Ukulele
- Learning Activities That Connect with Multiple Intelligences
- Snap
- The Different Ways Your Child Learns

AIDS

- Beginner Harmonica in the Key of C
- Big Life Journal Resources for 4 to 6-year-olds
- Charades
- Dominoes
- Explorer Compass
- GPS Child Tracker
- Growth Mindset Conversation Cards
- Growth Mindset Poster
- Jr. Boggle
- Junior Monopoly
- Junior Scrabble
- Kid's Ukulele
- Magnetic Chess Set
- Maracas
- One Potato Two Potato
- Readingeggs.com.au
- Simon Says
- Spellie
- Ten-Pin Bowling
- The ABC Song
- The Gamesman-Children's Chess (Australia only)
- Times Tables
- Twister
- Ukulele Tuner

BOOKS FOR CHILDREN

- I Believe I Can
- Mistakes Are How I Learn
- The Girl Who Never Makes Mistakes
- The Power of Yet
- Your Fantastic Elastic Brain

BOOKS FOR PARENTS

- Frames of Mind: The Theory of Multiple Intelligences
- In Their Own Way
- Multiple Intelligences in the Classroom
- The Art of Growing Up
- The 7 Habits of Highly Effective People

APPENDIX 2 | RESOURCES

CHAPTER 7

INFORMATION

- A Child's Need for Sleep
- Australian 24-Hour Movement Guidelines for the Early Years (birth to 5 years)
- Australian Parenting Website
- Balance and Coordination
- Benefits of Exercise on your Kid's Brain
- Harvard Health: Get Your Baby Moving
- Images of Rock Art in Newfoundland
- Kids Alive
- Negative Ions Create Positive Vibes

- Pedestrian Safety and Road Safety for Kids (AUS)
- Physical Activity and Exercise Guidelines for Infants, Toddlers and Preschoolers
- Road Safety and Pedestrian Safety (USA)
- Rules for Pedestrians (UK)
- Swimming Lessons Save Lives: What Parents Should Know
- When Can a Baby Go in a Pool?
- 8 Benefits of Infant Swim Time

ACTIVITY INSTRUCTIONS

- Hickory Dickory Dock
- How to Paint Rocks
- Make a Seashell Necklace or Bracelet
- Pin the Tail on the Donkey
- Play Ideas to Encourage Movement for Babies 0-12 months
- Preparing Babies for Vestibular Activities
- Preschool Handstands
- Row, Row, Row Your Boat

- Spinning, Rolling and Swinging for the Preschooler
- Teaching Your Child to Hula Hoop
- Ten Vestibular Activities to do With Your Baby or Toddler
- The Grand Old Duke of York
- Tummy Time
- Vestibular Activities
- Yankee Doodle Went to Town

AIDS

- Armagado Brachiation Ladder
- Beanbags
- Best Kid Friendly Trails in Australia
- Best Kid Friendly Trails in England
- Best Kid Friendly Trails in the USA
- Explorer Compass
- Forever Redwood Monkey Bars

- Funky Monkey bars
- Hammock
- Images of Rock Art in Newfoundland
- Juggling Balls
- Pedometer
- Surveyor's Measuring Wheel—Imperial
- Surveyor's Measuring Wheel—Metric

BOOKS FOR PARENTS

- Fit Baby, Smart Baby, Your Baby! From Birth to Age Six

- Spark! How exercise will improve the performance of your brain

ABOUT THE AUTHOR

Margaret Larden graduated from the Nursery School Teachers' College in Sydney. Under the charismatic leadership of Joan Fry OBE, the College established a reputation as one of Australia's pioneering institutions in Early Childhood Education before amalgamating with Macquarie University.

Margaret has had a lifetime passion for helping children to flourish and reach their full potential. She was inspired by the specialized education she received on the fundamental practices of early childhood education, including the Montessori philosophy and techniques.

These practices require a thorough understanding of each stage of Child Development and curriculum areas and a keen awareness of each child's unique skills and abilities. This knowledge enables tailored teaching methods that cater to individual needs. Margaret has taught in Australia, the United States and as a volunteer teacher at an orphanage in the Philippines.

Margaret draws widely on her teaching experience and expertise to inform the methodologies expounded in this book. She is the proud mother of two adult children, who enjoy successful international careers. Her hobbies and interests include reading, gardening, the theatre, music, and photography.

INDEX

A

accidents and mishaps, dealing with, 133–136
accredited health organizations, 24
activities for baby
    0-3 months, 98–99
    3-5 months, 100–102
    5-7 months, 103
    7-9 months, 104–105
    9-12 months, 106–107
    extension activities, 108–109
activities for preschoolers, 3-5 years, 139–184
activities for toddlers, 1-3 years, 112–128
alphabet, 110, 112, 218
American Montessori Society, 23
aromatherapy. See creative learning techniques
attention
    focused, 58, 86
    span, 31, 51, 111
attitude
    parent's, 49, 86, 134
    positive, 33, 149, 227
    toward everyday life, 31
    toward learning, 67, 227

B

balance. See vestibular system
balloons, 113, 124
basic mathematics
    addition and subtraction, 197, 216, 220–222
    fractions, 164, 197–199, 214–215
bathtime, 80, 81, 87
    toys, 105
beach, day at the, 116, 171
beach safety, 171
belonging, sense of, 177, 202, 238
birthdays, 151, 168, 195–196
body safety and consent, 202
bonding, 66, 252, 254
bookmarks, 151, 177, 178

books, 98, 103, 108, 114, 128
boredom, 191, 239–241
botanical garden, visiting the, 115
brain development, 71, 90, 99, 157
    stereotyping, 72
brain gym. See creative learning techniques
bribes, avoiding, 53
bubbles, blowing, 47, 81, 105, 125
building blocks of knowledge
    incremental, 90–91, 100
busy
    boards, 127
    box, 57
butterfly farm, visiting a, 117

C

calm
    creating, 45–48, 55
    music for babies, 98
camping, activities, 182–184
camp safety, 182, 183
cards
    crafty, 153
    talking point, 176
caring, 29, 39–41
cause and effect, 104, 180
chess, benefits of, 237–238
child development
    critical years, 67–68
    intellectual (cognitive), 85, 110
    mechanistic language, 89
    physical, 85, 110, 111
    social-emotional, 85, 110
    three key areas of, 85
choices, making, 52, 57, 130, 141, 150, 187
cloud formations, 161
cognitive process, 85

colors
  mixing, 122, 156
  primary, 121
  rainbow, 155
comparisons, avoid peer, 87, 236
compass directions, 160, 184, 217, 256
construction blocks, 97, 105, 217
  Lego, 175, 200
conversation
  art of, 176
  cards, 225
  respectful, 36
coping mechanisms, 48, 52, 56, 58
counting, 102, 125, 139, 160, 175, 197
countryside, drive in the, 116
courses for parents
  first aid for babies and children, 24
  Montessori education, 23
  multiplying your child's intelligence, 23
  newborn course, 22
crafts, 114, 116, 119, 151
crawling, 67, 104, 109, 205
creative learning techniques
  aromatherapy, 206
  brain gym, 205
creativity, 180, 200, 239
curiosity
  asking questions, 48, 144
  encouraging, 88, 89, 160, 162–164

D

dancing, 77, 123
days of the week, 167
development milestones
  for baby, 97–98, 99–100, 102, 104, 105, 107
  for preschooler, 137–138
  for toddler, 110–112
dexterity, 110, 111, 125, 138
discipline, positive, 130–131, 188
distance, 113, 126, 160, 172, 257
diversity, 49, 50, 113, 128, 139, 143
  cultural, 150
Doman, Dr. Glenn, 22
Doman, Janet, 180
dressing, 200
Dweck, Prof. Carol, 223

E

eating, 48, 103, 104, 106, 144, 200
education, value-driven, 30, 60
effective discipline, 186
effective effort. See mindset
elementary school
  location and layout, 201–202
  parental involvement, 209
  preparing for, 193–207
emotions, 55, 58, 111, 131, 136, 149
empathy, 31, 41–43, 66, 134, 136
encouragement, positive, 86, 225, 235
endorphins, 123, 251
engagement, 67, 98, 100, 103, 104, 106, 108
environment
  birdlife, 118
  noisy, 70
  respect for, 37
exercise
  age-appropriate, 245–246
  benefits of, 244
  connection with nature, 243
  how to promote, 245
  injury mitigation, 257
expectations
  clarifying rules and behaviors, 35, 56
  realistic, 65, 73, 129, 188
  rewarding good behavior, 148

F

facial expressions, 77, 81, 107, 135
family interactions, 61, 137, 176, 191
farmers' market, 171
farm stay experience, 168
feelings
  acknowledging and validating, 35, 47
  expressing and managing, 149
fine motor skills, developing, 67, 110, 127, 199–201, 251
finger knitting, 151, 164, 200
finger painting, 122, 156
fire station, visiting the, 180
first aid, emergency, 24
flare-ups, 55
flashcards, 78, 103, 108, 114, 194–195, 203–204
flashlight, 81, 101
food preparation, 25, 128, 150, 200
fragrances, 102

G

games
- ball, 125
- board, 214, 220, 237
- Connect 4, 200
- Hide and Seek, 109, 213
- marbles, 200
- movement, 215
- rule-based, 57
- sharing, 190
- 'twig' races, 126
- word, 212

gardening
- crop rotation, 170
- insects and bugs, 118, 120
- organic gardens, 170
- plants, 115
- skills, 169

Gardner, Prof. Howard, 210
general hygiene, 200
general knowledge
- building the foundation, 202
- resources for, 203
- some examples, 202–203

Gentle Revolution, 23, 103
goodness, innate, 37
GPS child tracker, 207
gratitude, 31, 43–45
gratitude journal, 44
gripping and dominant hand, 199
grit, 173, 224, 227

H

hammering, 124
height, 160
holidays, 151
home
- childproofing, 26
- creating a safe learning environment, 106
- safety measures and rules, 145

household chores, 33, 128, 177, 245
hula hoop, 175

I

imagination, story-telling, 173
imaginative play, 73, 178, 180
Indigenous art, 181
individuality, 50, 173

Institutes for the Achievement of Human Potential, 22
intelligences
- encouraging interests and strengths, 235
- how to assess and measure, 211
- (IQ) tests, 210–211
- multiple, 210
- nurturing and growing, 22

interactions, balanced, 72–74
interactive toys, 77, 107
interest groups, 204

J

juggling, 175, 250

K

key takeaways, 259
kindness, 30, 37–39
kite flying, 125, 172
knowledge ready, be, 21, 112, 139

L

landmarks, identifying, 120, 201, 256
language
- good grammar, 143
- mechanistic, 89
- negative, 38
- polite, 39, 148
- using correct terminology, 90

Lawrence, Laurie
- 'Kids Alive' swim program, 253

leading and following, 147
learning
- home-based, 96
- multi-dimensional, 113
- multi-faceted, 222
- parent's attitude towards, 86, 227
- praising effort. See mindset
- styles, 210
- talk, talk, talk, 67
- three key elements, 86
- tips for positive outcomes, 223, 227
- to listen, 56

M

magnets, 123, 164
magnifying glass, 115, 117, 120, 160
manners, 35–36, 129, 176

maps, 203, 256
Marshmallow Test, 56
mindfulness, 31, 45–48
mindset, 223
    behaviors and actions, 226
    be process focused, 229
    celebrate mistakes, 226
    developing a growth mindset, 87, 223–230
    fixed v. growth, 223–224
    language, 225
    positive self-talk, 227–229
    praising effort, 230–235
mobile, 99, 101
Monopoly, 214, 220
Montessori Academy, 92
Montessori, Dr. Maria, 23
Montessori education
    basic principles, 23–24
    schools, 23
months of the year, 167, 196
museums, visit to, 163, 165, 181
music
    awareness, 158
    classical, 104
    concerts, 158
    genres, 87, 158
    magic of, 157
    neuroscience, 196
    Suzuki and Yamaha programs, 158–159
musical instruments, 108, 122, 159, 218

N

native crafts, 181
needs, development, 65
negative ions, 256
nutrition
    infant and toddler guidelines, 25–26
    making healthy choices, 25–26

O

obstacle courses, 124, 250
orchards, visit to, 170
origami creations, 117, 172, 201
outings, locating your child, 207

P

paper airplanes, 172, 201
parental tips
    for preschoolers, 185–191
    for toddlers, 128–136
parent, as role model, 30
parent-child bond, 30, 61, 66
parenting, preparing for role, 21–26
patchwork sewing, 101
patience, 50–53
pedestrian safety, 256
personal information
    address and contact details, 196–197
    age and birthday, 195–196
    name recognition, 194–195
pet care, 40, 154
phonetic pronunciation, 110, 112, 214, 220
planetarium/observatory, visiting the, 154
planets, 155
playdough, 120, 177, 200, 217
poetry, reading, 161, 164
poisonous substances, 26, 106
popsicle, making, 127
potty training, a practical approach, 92–96
practicing, 174, 221, 229
praising effort. See mindset
preschool
    as a cultural setting, 60
    parent-teacher relationship, 60
    selecting a school, 59
problem-solving, 54, 73, 141, 187, 227
public transport, riding on, 172
puppets, 178, 219
push and pull toys, 108, 123, 124, 164
puzzles, 52, 200, 201, 217

R

rainbow, colors of the, 125, 155
raindrops, 162
rattles, 101
reading
    accelerating skills, 71
    aloud, 70, 108
    Doman technique, 203–204
    early exposure, 70
    Reading Eggs program, 204
real life venues, 165
reference material and sources, 260–269
reflection, 60, 184, 211, 226
relaxation time, 58–59, 176, 239, 244
repetition, 86, 91–92, 113

Resilience Project, 31
respect, 34–37
responsibility, 32–34
road safety, 256
rock art, 256
rocking chair, 101
role-playing activities, 147, 178, 219
routine, establishing a, 34, 75–81, 130
rules, following, 186–188

S

school. See preschool and/or elementary school
science experiments and exhibitions, 165
scissors, 199
scrapbook, 119, 221
screen time, 53
    impact of, 191
self-control, 54–59
    rewarding. See Marshmallow Test
self-discipline, 186–188
    strategies for teaching, 187–188
sensory experiences
    for exploring and understanding, 67–68
    hearing, 47, 69–70, 101
    sight, 48, 69, 76
    smell, 69, 76, 79, 102, 109, 116
    taste, 48, 69, 77
    touch, 69, 81, 166, 174
separation, feelings of, 201
shapes, 108, 161, 177
sharing, 111, 129, 132–133, 142, 188–190
    practical applications of, 190
    setting realistic expectations, 188–189
    strategies for teaching, 189–190
shower, makeshift, 184
singing, 99, 123, 152, 159, 167, 183, 197
sketching, 181
sleep, 191
smiling, 66, 102
sound, 48, 68, 69–70, 114, 124, 157, 177
space travel, 155
stacking blocks, 109
star-gazing, 154, 183
story time, at the library, 86, 178, 205
strawberry farm, visiting a, 169
success, a practical view, 21, 129, 173

swimming
    benefits for babies, 252
    benefits for toddlers and preschoolers, 253
    when to learn, 252

T

table setting, 139, 175, 187
teaching
    aids and resources, 270–279
    essential life skills, 139–149
    methods, tailoring, 210–212, 222
    spaces, 87
temptation, avoiding, 58
textures, different, 81, 108, 125
thankful, being, 45
Theory of Multiple Intelligences, 210–212
    bodily-kinesthetic, 215–216
    challenges for traditional teaching, 211–212
    interpersonal, 219–220
    intrapersonal, 220–222
    logical-mathematical, 214–215
    musical-rhythmic, 218–219
    verbal-linguistic, 212–213
    visual-spatial, 217
threading activities, 181, 184, 200
time and sequencing, 146, 166
timers, 53, 146, 190
times tables, 219
tolerance, 48–50
touch, physical contact, 66
toy safety, 97
tracing, 157
treasure hunt, 184, 217, 256
trust, 65
tummy time, 99, 101, 103
tweezers, 200

V

values
    how to instill, 32–59
    informing behavior and building character, 30–31, 185
    prerequisites for child development, 30
    reinforcing, 59, 185
    teaching in the preschool years, 59–62, 185
    teaching strategies, 31–32

vestibular system, 246–249
    activities for babies or toddlers, 248–249
    activities for preschoolers, 249–250
    activities for school-aged children, 250–251
    balance, 246
    basic gymnastics, 250
    brachiation, 250–251
    role of, 246–247
    stimulation and movement, 78, 247–248
    trampolining, 250
visual aids
    photos, 195
    picture charts, 56
    sand timer, 53
    unbreakable mirror, 104
visual perception. See fine motor skills
volunteer work, 38, 60

W

walking
    benefits, 254
    how to encourage, 255–257
    make it a routine, 254
weather
    conditions, 161–162
    patterns and seasons, 152
    wind, 172
writing, practice, 195, 216, 217

Y

yet, the power of, 227
yoga, 48
yoyo tricks, 175

Z

zoo, visiting the, 112, 114

www.ingramcontent.com/pod-product-compliance
Lightning Source LLC
Chambersburg PA
CBHW042034100526
44587CB00030B/4425